FORMOSAN ODYSSEY

# Formosan Odyssey:
# Taiwan, Past and Present

Second Edition

## by John Grant Ross

A Camphor Press book

Published by Camphor Press Ltd
83 Ducie Street, Manchester, M1 2JQ
United Kingdom

www.camphorpress.com

ISBN 978-1-910736-22-7

The moral right of the author has been asserted.

Set in 10 pt Linux Libertine

# Contents

# Acknowledgements

For the original version I owe a great debt to my Taiwanese friends and former employers, Dennis and Maggie Young, for their generosity in putting me up while I wrote this book. I'm grateful to Father Weber Anton, Chris Bates, Dr. Ko Chi-sheng, Jack Geddes, Jack Butterworth, Professor Chen Mau-tai, and Lin Sheng-yi for taking the time to talk to me. And thanks to Wei Te-wen of SMC Publications for reprinting long-forgotten works on Taiwan such as *From Far Formosa* and *Pioneering in Formosa*.

For this new Camphor Press edition I would like to thank Mark Swofford for his expert copyediting and Michael Cannings for designing the cover.

# About the Author

John Grant Ross was born in New Zealand in 1968. He has spent most of the past quarter century living in and writing about Asia. His extensive travels – undertaken alone and far off the beaten track – include exploration in Papua New Guinea, dispatches from the Karen insurgency in Burma, and searches in the Gobi Desert and Altai Mountains on the trail of an ancient Mongolian myth.

Ross lives in a small town in southern Taiwan with his Taiwanese wife. In 2014 he released *You Don't Know China*, a book that debunks myths about the country with insight and wit. When not writing, reading, or lusting over maps, he can be found working on the family farm.

# A Note on Romanization

Romanization in Taiwan is a nightmare; it is not uncommon to walk down a city street and see three different renderings of the same name. Over the centuries several systems have been developed to romanize the Chinese language. Wade-Giles is the system traditionally favoured in Taiwan but is typically used incorrectly; for example, Taiwan's largest city, Taipei, should actually be written as T'ai-pei. For the second edition of *Formosan Odyssey*, most place names and some personal names have been updated to the Hanyu Pinyin romanization system, which is the international standard and, increasingly, the standard in Taiwan. Exceptions have been made for Taiwan's largest cities, the names of counties, and some historical figures. For example, Chiang Kai-shek is used rather than the Hanyu Pinyin version, Jiang Jieshi.

# Preface to the Second Edition

The original has long been out of print, so I'm delighted to finally offer readers this second edition of *Formosan Odyssey*. It's a much-improved version, with errors corrected and the writing tightened up. I've deleted a few dated references and added an afterword. The alterations, though, have not included the use of hindsight to rewrite my opinions; I've kept the tone of the original, even if at times the younger me now sounds a touch naïve.

Getting this edition ready has been fun. I hadn't reread the book since 2002. Late at night after a bottle or two I would occasionally pull a copy from a shelf and peruse a few pages, but never from beginning to end. What struck me on rereading the whole book was the exuberance. Yes, I was younger and Taiwan was newer to me, but I hope there's something more to it than that; perhaps my early years here were also an especially exuberant time for Taiwan, or perhaps it reflects the excitement of discovery of the pre-Internet world, a time when stumbling upon a rare book was like a feast for the famished, a time when what lay beyond the hill held more mystery. The Internet (which I started using tentatively only in 2001) has completely changed expat life, travel, and the writing process. But above everything, I think the exuberance comes from the story of Taiwan itself being so immensely fascinating. And as packed as *Formosan Odyssey* is with colourful facets of Taiwan's culture and history, it is merely a taster. I hope this new edition encourages you to further explore this lovely island.

FORMOSAN ODYSSEY

# 1

# The 9-21 Earthquake

As summer and months of preparation drew to a close, I spread my relief maps of Taiwan out across the floor one last time. The contour lines of the central ranges were so closely packed they merged into a single dark foreboding mass running the length of my room. This shadow marked the route of my intended journey from the northernmost point in Taiwan, along the mountainous spine, to the southernmost point. I would travel entirely on foot, a two-month solo trek that my Taiwanese friends said was "impossible."

At first glance Taiwan seems an unlikely place for outdoor adventure. It is after all a polluted, crowded little island full of factories churning out electronics and consumer goods, a country where environmental consciousness is so low that not until 1984 was the first national park established (and even that has a nuclear reactor in it). As well, the Chinese belief in eating anything that moves has ensured that most of the nation's wildlife has long since been ground up into aphrodisiac potions or stir-fried into oblivion. All depressingly true, yet Taiwan has some surprisingly majestic landscapes. Over half of the country is made up of rugged mountain ranges, with more than two hundred peaks rising above three thousand metres. Mount Jade (Yu Shan) at 3,952 metres, is higher than any peaks in Japan, Korea, eastern China, or the Philippines.

After years of living in a small town in the crowded lowlands I was eager to get away from the horrible traffic, pollution and heat, to escape the landscape of factories and concrete-box architecture, and travel alone through the parallel world of the high mountains – so close, yet so often hidden behind smog.

I had one last drinking session with my good friend Conn and went to bed contemplating my trip. At 1:47 a.m. on the twenty-first of September, central Taiwan was hit by a massive earthquake measuring 7.3 on the Richter scale. By the time the last bodies were dragged from the rubble the death toll would be well over two thousand, but when it first struck I, like many others, didn't realize the magnitude of the disaster. Woken by the rocking motion and the clang of metal windows, my initial reaction was just annoyance. "Bloody earthquake," I thought, rolled over and tried to get back to sleep. Earthquakes are common in Taiwan and I figured the shaking would pass. The summer before I had experienced what seemed like a worse one – at that time I'd been awake and sober on the seventh floor of a building with things crashing down around me and had feared for my life.

This time the shaking was violent enough but nothing was falling off desks and bookshelves, and I was only on the third floor of a four-storey building. My room was in a private cram school, and I shared the building with Miss Su, an eccentric old cleaning lady, and Conn, an English teacher from Ireland. I could hear excited voices gathering in the street outside, Miss Su bellowing, and Conn walking up the stairs, "You alright, John?"

"Yeah. Earthquake – all I need!" The aftershocks kept hitting, shaking me fully awake, and I had to give up trying to sleep through it. I usually have a hellish time getting back to sleep, so I decided to go and get some beer, drink for a while then hit the sack. I got dressed and went outside. All the neighbours were out in the street, some in bedclothes. I walked past them zombie-like to a nearby 7-Eleven. The 24-hour convenience store, amazingly still open, stank of whisky and the floor was strewn with broken glass and pools of liquid. The shell-shocked young clerk who served me was certainly earning his money that night.

Aftershocks were announced a second before they hit by an ominous metallic roar. They kept rolling in one after another, sometimes so strongly that they had the ground waving for several seconds. The realization was starting to dawn on us that this was something out of the ordinary, and as details came through on the radio – reports of mass destruction, bridges and roads torn up, high-rise apartments collapsing – our worst fears were realized. Taiwan was suffering a terrible disaster. Standing out on the street with my neighbours, as most Taiwanese were doing at that moment, there was a strange mixture of feelings, both individual and collective, of fear, shock, sorrow, and thankfulness at being safe. And increasingly, weariness, for there would be no sleep for the next two days – the ground had seemingly turned to liquid, and aftershocks were only minutes apart.

One saving grace was that the epicentre was beneath Jiji, a small town 12.5 kilometres west of Sun-Moon Lake in Nantou County, central Taiwan. If it had hit a major city like Taipei or Kaohsiung, instead of the relatively sparsely populated rural area around Jiji, the damage would have been catastrophic. Even though the quake's strength in Taipei was only four on the Richter scale, it was not spared; a twelve-storey building collapsed on itself, floor after floor driven into the basement, leaving eighty-seven dead.

The 9-21 earthquake (as it became known) was the island's strongest of the century, and one of the world's biggest of the 1990s. It left 2,444 dead, over 11,000 injured, and more than 100,000 homeless. Considering Taiwan's history of quakes, the authorities were not particularly well prepared but the immediate response was quick.

The rescue teams, soldiers, medical teams, and volunteers who rushed into the area worked around the clock looking for trapped survivors and pulling out dead bodies in the face of great danger from "the endless aftershocks. There were hundreds of aftershocks every day, some of them over six on the Richter scale.

Meanwhile the country watched the drama on television. The disaster brought a sense of warmth and unity to communities across the nation. Almost everyone had been woken by it, could imagine the worst, were thankful to be alive, and many people knew someone affected. People pulled together – there was no chaos, no looting, little panic – and throughout the island neighbours and strangers alike were out in the streets talking to each other in a way they had never done before.

Even during Taiwan's darkest hour, China could not refrain from playing politics. As news of the earthquake broke, condolences and offers of assistance poured in from world leaders, among them President Clinton. Foreign rescue teams were dispatched, but there were several notable exceptions. The United Nations could not send any immediate assistance because it considers Taiwan a province of China and needed the Beijing government to request help on behalf of Taiwan. In fact, Beijing insisted that foreign countries seek its permission before sending emergency relief supplies. The United Nations eventually sent an embarrassingly small six-man team. That was in stark contrast to Taiwan's generous donation of US$300 million to the organization, made just months previously, for humanitarian work in Kosovo.

Chinese President Jiang Zemin sent condolences and offers of assistance. This opportunity for a thawing of relations was spoiled by political bigotry: the statements of sympathy were soured by nationalist slogans reasserting the fiction of Taiwan being part of China and constant references to bonds between the two, reminders that "blood is thicker than water," and that the people across the Taiwan Strait were "as closely linked as flesh and blood." China's state television fabricated news reports to suggest that Chinese rescue workers and supplies were on their way.

For the Communist leaders the quake was a good opportunity to push their "One China" policy – the idea that Taiwan is an inseparable part of Chinese territory rather than a sovereign nation – but in trying to make political capital of the disaster they went too far. In the words of an old proverb that was much on people's lips, China was "stealing from a house on fire."

In a statement that caused great offence, U.N. Secretary General Kofi Annan sent his sympathies to the people of the "Taiwan Province of China." A province? Even worse, the Chinese Foreign Minister, speaking at the United Nations as if he could speak on behalf of the Taiwanese, thanked the international community for its assistance.

Although a little disorganized and uncoordinated, Taiwan's rescue and relief effort generally earned high praise, making up for a lack of professionalism with human effort. The public joined in with a flood of donated money, supplies, and helping hands. So many blood donors came forward there weren't enough places to store blood. And amid the tragic stream of news stories there were heart-warming scenes of rescues, such as when a six-year-old boy was pulled from a wrecked apartment building where he and his family had been buried for eighty-eight hours. Once he had been located, Korean and Japanese rescue workers had toiled for six hours to reach the boy.

For a country that is so often politically isolated and has few diplomatic friends, the international help – over 750 foreigners from twenty-one countries from as far afield as Mexico, Austria, Spain, Israel, and the Czech Republic – made a deep impression on the Taiwanese. And made China look all the worse. While the earthquakes in Turkey and Greece in 1999 allowed an improvement in relations between those two ancient foes, the 9-21 quake widened the rift, leaving people in Taiwan angry, hurt, and evermore distrustful. It strengthened the Taiwanese sense of identity and unity, and highlighted the chasm between democratic island and authoritarian state.

China was not the only villain of the drama. As the pattern of damage emerged and crews worked their way through buildings, it became obvious that countless lives had been lost because of shoddy construction. In the small city of Douliu, just eight kilometres from where I lived, three new apartment buildings, all built by the same company, had collapsed. In the debris, cooking-oil cans were found in the structural supports. Elsewhere similar cost-saving shortcuts in construction such as watered-down cement and sub-standard materials were uncovered.

One of the most shocking things about the damage was the proportionally high rate of damage suffered by public buildings. They are, in theory anyway, subject to a stricter building code than private buildings and so should have been the last to collapse. Much the reverse – 120 schools were destroyed or severely damaged in the earthquake and another 700 suffered slight damage. The engineers' verdict was that the blame lay with basic flaws in the standard school design and the unsupervised contract system, which led to cost-cutting, corruption and shoddy work. A lot of parents and teachers were wondering what would have happened if the earthquake had struck during school hours.

Modern buildings, especially high ones, are supposed to be built to strict Japanese standards but the regulations are not strictly followed or policed, so once again, the pattern of damage one would have expected – old buildings collapsing whereas newer, safer ones stood – didn't occur.

The ruins and buried corpses were a ghastly monument to the ugly side of Taiwanese society: carelessness (best expressed in a common expression, *chabuduo*, meaning "close enough"), corruption, and greed. But in the mood emerging after the initial shock and anger there was optimism for the future, people re-evaluating life's priorities and expressing hopes of rebuilding a better society from the rubble. Materialism and consumerism had gone wild. What had seemed important before the quake, such as collecting Hello Kitty dolls (a Japanese cartoon character) and having the latest-model cell phone, now seemed trivial, almost grotesque.

My hiking trip, of course, was over before it had begun. The central ranges had been ripped apart, whole mountains disappearing, rivers blocked and lakes formed. In an instant my maps had become historical documents. Rock falls and landslides had obliterated trails. Bridges were destroyed and roads made impassable. The greater part of my intended route lay in an emergency zone – unreachable by land and officially closed.

Seismologists had been warning that Taiwan was overdue for a big earthquake for years because of a build-up of pressure along the tectonic plates that converge under the island, but had been unable, however, to give any specific warning of the 9-21 quake. The bad news was that they were unsure whether it was in fact "the big one," and weren't ruling out another massive jolt.

Rumours of impending disaster – quakes even stronger than the first – spread around the island by word-of-mouth, radio phone-ins, and internet bulletin boards. Sometimes the rumours gave exact places, dates and times. The source of many of these rumours and apocalyptic predictions were temples. There was a story circulating, which many people believed, that a temple had actually warned of the earthquake. The omen supposedly took place at the Taoist Taichi Kung temple in Taoyuan on the night of June 23. The temple worshippers were using divining blocks, small wooden boards shaped like crescent moons. After asking a question, these boards are dropped on the floor three times, the answer determined by whether they land with the flat or rounded side up.

But that night in Taoyuan the laws of physics took a time out – the boards stood on end, balancing on their tips, (and remained like that for two months until two young girls picked them up). The surprised worshippers consulted the heavens. The answer, channelled through one of the worshippers, was the usual vague stuff of prophesies – stop sinning or face destruction. God gave another, more specific, message in August: "You do not fulfil your obligations to lead a virtuous life. This is not allowed. This earthquake is just a small sample of the bad luck to come. You must listen to me. Because of God's will Formosa will suffer many disasters this year." The story was obviously the work of opportunists trying to get a little publicity for their temple, and with it money, but Taiwanese people are very superstitious and many believed it.

Considering the thousands of fortune-tellers there are throughout Taiwan, their pre-quake silence was rather poor. Now with the benefit of hindsight, people started uncovering all sorts of strange omens that had passed unnoticed; from the story of a giant white fish – a warning of disaster – said to have been caught off the southwestern coast just days before the quake, to the story of a winning lottery ticket with the numbers 94445421 (in Chinese the numbers sound like "9-death-death-death-definitely-death-2-1").

Temples rushed to make predictions of further calamity. It was a low-risk gamble; if the predictions didn't come true no one would bother, or remember, but if something happened then it would mean an immense boost to the temple's reputation and, with that, donations. Police brought charges against the Taoyuan temple for inciting public disorder when it started handing out thousands of fliers warning people that another huge quake would hit on October 4.

# 2

# The Tooth-Pulling Preacher

A WEEK after the earthquake I packed my bags and headed north to begin my trip through Taiwan. At least I wouldn't have to worry about crowds, and I was actually safer up north than down in central Taiwan. From Taipei's outer suburbs I took a bus along the northern coast. An hour later I was on a beach, walking along a lovely stretch of sand as a fresh breeze rolled in with large breakers off a blue-green sea. Clear sky shone overhead while cumulus clouds in the north kept time to a lone container ship skimming the horizon. Behind me green mountains squeezed rain from dark clouds rubbing against their upper slopes. The beach was deserted and quiet save for the sound of breaking waves. But being Taiwan it was the beauty of a despoiled nature; the area was littered with garbage, there were abandoned bunkers at the crest of the beach, and in the distance stood blocks of the concrete-box architecture that mars much of the island's landscape.

The beach led me to a rocky headland where a stubby black and white lighthouse marks the northernmost point in Taiwan. There was a real sense of being at land's end: wild sea-lashed vegetation, the smell of salt in the air, the creak of stunted trees swaying and flax bushes rustling in the wind – a good place to spend a few melancholy moments contemplating the trip that might have been. Even here the earthquake cast a pall, a Taiwanese flag flapping at half-mast as part of an official period of mourning for the earthquake victims.

A military compound, bristling with antennas and other intelligence-gathering equipment, blocked my intended path around the headland. I retraced my steps and took the long way around to the other side of the headland where there was a tiny fishing port. Don't imagine some quaint little place; it was just your standard Taiwanese fishing port, in other words, ugly, which really takes some doing for something that is by nature so picturesque. It was all concrete and rows of cheap seafood restaurants. When I say "cheap," I mean the buildings, not the seafood, which is very often surprisingly expensive. For Taiwanese the aesthetics of a restaurant aren't very important and buildings are put up with the skill and cost you might normally expect employed on a farm shed. These restaurants were in that mould: corrugated iron top, back and sides, the front either large glass windows or left open. The classier places had a bit of painted plywood thrown in. Architectural beauty may not rate but freshness is important, and the seafood on display was very fresh indeed, still alive in plastic containers arranged in various levels from the restaurant fronts down to the roadside.

I decided to walk along the coastal highway to Danshui, thirty kilometres away. The quake had forced me to abandon my plan to walk from here to Kending in the extreme south of Taiwan, but I just wanted some exercise after the inertia of a week of riding out aftershocks. The road was not even close to scenic, the ocean unseen for all but a few stretches, yet I still enjoyed it. Walking is a very meditative activity, and some of my best ideas have come to me when I've been on a long march (ideas such as stopping and having a drink!). Walking makes you look at things differently and it hones your powers of reflection. My first observation was, "Shit, it's hot!" It was mid-day and scorching, 33 degrees in the shade but much hotter out on the road.

While I was walking, several cars and a motorcycle stopped and asked me whether I wanted a ride, and each time saying no was harder, especially with the last one, a sexy young woman in a BMW. Luckily, I remembered my mother's warning about taking rides from strangers, politely declined, and went on my way unharmed. There were some other female distractions along the road: scantily clad girls in glass-fronted boxes, the large windows designed to give the best view and entice customers to stop and buy their betel nut. I stopped at one of these betel nut girls who had a well-stocked fridge and bought some cold drinks.

Locals sometimes refer to betel nut as "Taiwanese chewing gum" but it is actually common throughout Southeast Asia. What is uniquely Taiwanese, however, are these "betel nut beauties" selling it by the roadside. The very first time I saw them was at night and I didn't know what to make of it – little shops raised on blocks at the side of the road, encased in flashing neon, and through the glass windows in the brightly lit interior were women in tiny skirts, bikini tops, and slinky, tight-fitting dresses. Cars would pull up and the girls would come sauntering down the few steps on impossibly high heels and bend over to talk to the drivers. Prostitution? The truth was a little disappointing; all this glamour and sleaze was just for selling the revolting substance of betel nut to passing motorists.

Betel nut is the seed of the tall palm of the same name (also called an areca palm or *Areca catechu*) and it is sold with a lime paste and wrapped in a leaf. It's very much an acquired taste but once acquired the chewer can become addicted to the mild high the nut gives. Two-and-a-half million Taiwanese can't be wrong! Together they spend a whopping NT$3.45 billion on betel nut each year, making it the fourth most important farm product behind pigs, rice, and chickens. Betel nut causes excessive salivation, which means the chewers are constantly spitting and staining the roads with blood-red splotches. Chewing it also blackens teeth and greatly increases the likelihood of oral cancer. Betel-nut plantations – often planted illegally on high mountain slopes – are an environmental scourge because of the increased soil erosion that results from their shallow root systems.

The walk along the northern coast was long and hot but cooling rehydration was never far away. One of the great pleasures of living in Taiwan is ease with which you can buy beer and the freedom to drink it in public.

I took a short break in a roadside restaurant. Well, everything in Taiwan is "roadside" because the high population density means there's simply not enough space to waste on the luxury of a gap between the road and shops or houses. I ordered a meal and sank a couple of ice-cold Taiwan Beers. Two young children stared at me until they got bored and then resumed the conversation my meal had interrupted, whining on like a scratched record, "Mum, you lied to me. You said we were going to McDonald's." A rainbow and curtains of grey hung on the mountains of Yangming Shan, promising rain – but none came.

Five hours after setting off I reached the outskirts of Danshui, an old port town at the mouth of the Danshui River, twenty kilometres northwest of Taipei. The place has a long and colourful history – it was once the haunt of Chinese and Japanese pirates, occupied by both the Spanish and Dutch in the 1600s, and was for a long time Taiwan's major port. Competition with the port of Keelung saw it decline to little more than a fishing village. Today, there's little maritime flavour left, and it's basically a suburb of Taipei that is a popular weekend destination known for its seafood sunsets. Sadly, most of the history has been buried under an avalanche of development.

The streets were busy with schoolchildren going home. It was September 28, Teacher's Day, a holiday that celebrates the great teacher and sage Confucius, but this year hadn't been designated a public holiday. Anyway, with so many schools destroyed, and classrooms with the empty desks of dead and injured students, nobody was in the mood for celebration. People around the island were participating in a special day of religious mourning – worshippers praying and burning ghost money (wads of printed money-like paper for the spirits), while monks led mournful chants from the night through to the dawn. According to traditional beliefs the dead return on the seventh day after their death expecting to see ceremonies that will take them into a better next life. A ceremony is held every seven days for a total of seven times, and the funeral takes place at the end of this forty-nine-day period.

Rush-hour traffic was starting to clog the streets, and I found myself stuck in a solid stream of cars and scooters that were belching out so much noise and fumes that my head was starting to swim. The pollution was so thick the sun looked like a pink moon. As an early dusk settled over Danshui the city was even more crowded than normal and peculiarly gloomy. Power rationing was in effect throughout northern Taiwan because of earthquake damage to transmission lines, and people were spilling out of their homes and shops onto the sidewalks and street sides. Walking was an obstacle course and I was continually having to detour around shop merchandise and illegally parked scooters. One moment I'd be stepping between mechanics repairing scooters, the next over noisy electric generators, or squeezing around children at desks doing their homework, all the time ducking and weaving through the shuffling crowd, and when brought to a standstill, I would step out onto the road and walk along with the crawling scooters weaving their way around gridlocked cars.

I found a cheap hotel in a small side street called the "Enjoying Good Time Hotel." The owner-receptionist looked surprised, either at the idea of someone wanting to stay at his hotel, or at seeing a foreigner, perhaps both. He pulled himself up out of a cane chair, took a couple of steps toward the street gutter, spat out some betel nut. With red juice still dribbling down his chin, he asked, "Rest (*xiuxi*) or night?" The two rates were written in Chinese on a board. *Xiuxi* literally means to rest or take a nap, but for hotels is a euphemism for checking in for a quick bout of fornication.

The power rationing meant trudging upstairs to the sixth floor with candles for lighting. I walked past a couple of sleazy-looking men dressed in clothes straight out of 1970s Las Vegas. Behind them followed two women, who to give the benefit of the doubt I'll call "hostesses." From their high heels to their fur handbags to their layers of makeup, the hostesses were the living embodiment of the phrase, "mutton dressed as lamb." Even candlelight couldn't hide the fact they'd clocked up enough mileage for frequent flier points for first-class seats to Mars and back. There was a time when I would have thought them too unattractive to be in the trade, but years of observing the comings and goings of a brothel masquerading as a barber's shop just a couple of doors from where I lived had taught me otherwise. (Though having said that, the brothel did later close down due to a lack of customers.)

My hotel room was on the sixth floor – a "Chinese" sixth floor. Because the words for "death" and "four" sound alike, the number is considered unlucky and the floors were numbered 1, 2, 3, and then jumped to 5 and 6. "Six," although an improvement on "death," isn't that lucky a number either; in Taiwanese it sounds like "to lose something."

When the power came on I had a quick look around the walls of my room for suspicious holes, and checked the light fittings and other equipment for "unusual" apparatus. *Xiuxi* hotels and motels are not infrequently fitted out with Peeping Tom cameras. All I needed was some gorgeous nymphomaniac banging on my door at midnight, begging me to give her a good ravaging, and a week later I'd be making a guest appearance in a porn video, peddled out the back of a van in some sleazy night market. There have been a few funny cases of couples buying these "candid camera" porn videos and seeing themselves featured, one such case involving a guy who bought a video and saw his wife having sex with someone else in a hotel room.

I was up early the next morning to avoid the heat. The city was stirring to life in the narrow street below my window. While listening to the radio for the latest earthquake news – the on-going search for fifteen Taipei climbers who'd been on a hiking trip when the quake struck – I watched the street transform into a food market. Householders rolled up the metal doors of their four-storey shop-houses and started setting up small tables out front. A few street vendors wheeled their mobile food stands into position. Little blue Isuzu trucks parked alongside and started selling produce from the back of their vehicles.

One of these was a butcher's complete with geese – feet in the air and necks hanging limp over the side – and a pig's head proudly displayed.

Apart from the market activity there wasn't much to look at. The view was one of ugly concrete block architecture and, rising up in the mid-distance, writhing multi-coloured dragons on the roof of a Taoist temple. As if to compensate for the drabness of the surrounding buildings it was overly decorative – all the ornamentation and colour of an entire block piled into a single building, a single roof.

I had an easy morning looking around the Danshui waterfront. There wasn't much happening: a row of coffee shops and restaurants not yet open for business, and the single little ferry boat that shuttles passengers across the river lying at anchor. A few women were strolling with parasols, and clusters of senior citizens were sitting on tree-shaded benches. It was a beautiful day and the view across the wide river mouth to the opposite shore was lovely, the skyline dominated by a huge pyramid-shaped landmark, the 616-metre Guanyin (Goddess of Mercy) Mountain.

Danshui means "fresh water," which is rather funny considering the state of the water. I was reminded of a publicity stunt carried out by the Taipei Mayor Ma Ying-jeou that went badly wrong. He was out on the Danshui River with TV cameras and photographers to sing the praises of a clean-up campaign, holding up a glass of river water to show how clean it was, when a dead body floated by.

\* \* \*

If you had been down by the river on March 9, 1872, you would have heard the distant whistle of a small steamship announcing its arrival outside the dangerous bar at the confluence of river and sea. It was high tide and a fine day so the steamship passed safely and came chugging into port. Fishermen looked up from their baskets and nets. Townsfolk and villagers, who had come in from the neighbouring countryside to sell their produce, gathered around. The first steamship had visited about a decade before, but these fire-breathing ships were still rare and exciting enough to draw a crowd. This small ship, the *Hailoong* (the Sea Dragon), was one of the first steamships in Taiwan's waters, and had started a fortnightly run between Taiwan and the mainland the year before. Standing at the railings was a young man of small build, bearded, and with an intense stare that scanned the beautiful setting of river, hills and mountains. There was a fiery look in his eyes as he heard a reassuring inner-voice, "This is the land." The man was

George MacKay, a zealous twenty-seven-year-old missionary from Canada, and the first missionary to preach in northern Taiwan since the brief colonial period of the Dutch and Spanish centuries before. He was undaunted by the challenge and actually thankful for "the glorious privilege to lay the foundation of Christ's church in unbroken heathenism!" He would spend the rest of his life in Danshui, and today lies buried in a shady cemetery on a hill overlooking the town.

MacKay was a first-generation Canadian of Scottish blood and had inherited the tough stubborn character and the stern Calvinist morality of his ancestral homeland. Though he had come to Taiwan as a colonizer of souls he had no love of imperialism. His parents had been forced from the land during the "clearances" – a time when tenant farmers were moved off the land to make way for sheep – and had sailed to Canada to start a new life. From an early age MacKay had felt the calling to be a missionary. He studied in Toronto and Princeton, was ordained, and sent by the Canadian Presbyterian Church to China. In 1871 MacKay set sail from San Francisco not knowing if he would ever see his home or loved ones again. A snow-clad Mount Fuji was a welcome sight after a rough twenty-six day voyage across the Pacific to Yokohama. From Japan he went to Hong Kong, then to Amoy (Xiamen) and finally, on what proved to be the worst part of the entire journey, took passage on a schooner across the channel to Kaohsiung.

For the previous seven years the English Presbyterians had been working in the southern area around Tainan, at that time both the island's capital and largest city, but MacKay chose to head into the unknown rather than follow their advice to work in a tamer area. He settled in Danshui and stayed there for thirty years, using it as his base from which to spread the gospel throughout the north.

The early days must have been hard. He was alone in a place that was hostile to foreigners, he couldn't speak the language, and he didn't have an interpreter. His first task was to learn Taiwanese and the Chinese written script. He overcame the handicaps of not having a teacher or any suitable books by hard work and persistence. First he had his servant teach him the basics and then he went wandering out into the countryside to meet and converse with farmers. In the evening he would come back and practise with his reluctant servant. Teaching the crazy foreigner quickly proved too stressful and MacKay later recalled how, "After a few weeks in my service he collapsed, and left me to march up and down the room reciting and rehearsing by myself. I never saw him again."

On one of his walks MacKay saw a dozen boys herding buffaloes. As the missionary approached them they yelled, "Foreign devil, foreign devil!" and hid behind some boulders. The next day he came again, but this time the boys looked at him in silence, and although scared did not run away. On the third day MacKay spoke to them, curiosity overcame fear, and the boys gathered around to feel his skin, clothes, and beard. "The herdboys and I became friends that day, and ever after they would wait my coming with eager interest." He spent four or five hours every day with the boys, talking, listening, and writing down new words and expressions. This was how MacKay learnt most of his Taiwanese, and made the first of many lasting friendships. Several of the boys later converted and one became a preacher.

MacKay kept away from the few foreign trading agents and English-speaking Chinese in town, and was able to preach his first sermon after just five months. He went on to study Chinese culture, philosophy, religion, and the classics of literature in order to be able to debate religion with the local literati.

He preached all over northern Taiwan, as far afield as the East Coast – not yet under Chinese control – and among headhunting tribes in the mountains. He possessed an explorer's passion for places untrodden, felt the tiring marches over rough trails were more than compensated for by "scenery of extraordinary beauty," and relished the challenge of missionary work. He was untroubled by any doubts about the inferiority of the local religions in Taiwan, which he thought were "of the same kind and quality as the heathenism of China. It is the same poisonous mixture, the same dark, damning nightmare."

In the nineteenth century Taiwan was still very much a wild frontier area with weak state control and notoriously corrupt, lazy, and incompetent officials. This state of unrest was encapsulated in a common saying: "A minor revolt every three years and a major one every five years." Violence was endemic, not only between the Aborigines and Chinese, but between the different Aboriginal tribes, Chinese of different provinces, different towns, and different clans. Banditry was rife, and the justice system was often little better than legalized robbery.

MacKay looked upon most Chinese officials with contempt. They were mercenary and the common people tried to have as few dealings with them as possible. Government consisted of a pyramid of people squeezing those under them, and never more so than in matters of justice. In the courthouse – "the scene of unmitigated lying, scheming, and oppression" – the mandarin (high official) had supreme power, and the justice he meted out was often determined by the bribes he received. Trials were shams where often the "witness whose evidence is not pleasing to the mandarin is immediately beaten."

Fines and strokes of the bamboo were the most common punishments for minor offenses. Then there was the "cangue," a heavy wooden collar worn in public. Prisons were filthy death traps where money was extorted from relatives by torture of the inmates. Criminals found guilty of serious crimes such as murder, treason, or even lesser ones like theft and arson, were beheaded. The swiftness of the executioner's sword blow was subject to bribery. MacKay personally witnessed the execution of four soldiers condemned for burglary.

> One was on his knees, and in an instant the work was done. Three blows were required for the second. The third was slowly sawed off with a long knife. The fourth was taken a quarter of a mile farther, and amid shouts and screams and many protestations of innocence he was subjected to torture and finally beheaded. The difference in the bribe made the difference in the execution.

MacKay describes a bizarre system of punishing criminals by proxy. "If the guilty party cannot be found, or if he can bribe the magistrate, some careless fellow can easily be procured to suffer the punishment." Once the missionary was called to the courthouse and told that the thief who had stolen from one of the chapels had been captured. When MacKay explained that this was not the right man the mandarin "confessed that it was a case of proxy, but argued that by punishing this man the real culprit would be so afraid that the moral influence would be quite as salutary."

Although it's often tempting when you're stuck in a traffic jam and choking on pollution to think of pre-industrialized Taiwan as some kind of agrarian paradise, the reality was that there was no "Golden Age" and the country was a dangerous and unhealthy place: a malarial hell that took a very heavy toll on native Taiwanese, and even more so on foreigners. MacKay, who almost died from malaria, called it "the blackest foe that hangs longest over our beautiful island," and that it was not an uncommon thing to find half the inhabitants of a town prostrated by malarial fever at once. The menace that this disease posed cannot be overestimated. I've had four bouts of malaria myself in Burma, and if it wasn't for modern medicine I'd almost certainly be dead.

At that time Europeans had yet to discover the mosquito's part in the spread of malaria and thought it came from the poisonous vapours of decaying vegetation. Chinese explanations were a little more colourful. They thought malaria was caused by stepping on mock-money put in the street or on the roadside by a priest or sorcerer. Another view held that two devils, one hot and one cold, were responsible. Treatment was equally eccentric. Taoist charms were made from peach-leaves, green bamboo, and yellow paper, or more simply just seven hairs plucked from a black dog, then tied around the patient's hand. Buddhist priests had various medicines, or failing those the sufferer was sent to a temple and kept under the idol's altar table for protection. Another method was to construct a man out of rice-straw, invite the evil spirits to enter it, then take the scarecrow away from the house and make food offerings to the spirit.

Once MacKay had established a church in Danshui and had some followers, he made regular trips further afield, setting up chapels and congregations elsewhere. Touring followed a familiar pattern; in places where he had already established congregations he would first visit the sick, find an open place to dispense medicine and extract teeth, discuss business matters concerning the running of the chapel, and then do some Bible study, singing, preaching, and baptism. In "heathen" places he often chose the steps of a temple, began by singing a hymn or two, set to extracting teeth, then followed up by preaching.

MacKay was sure that dentistry was the quickest way to a man's soul. Recovery from an illness could be attributed to the gods as readily as medicine, "but the relief from toothache is too unmistakable, and because of this tooth-extracting has done more than anything else in breaking down prejudice and opposition." Anyone who has suffered the torment of bad toothache will be able to appreciate his reasoning.

People's teeth were generally in terrible condition because of so much betel-nut chewing. Local dentistry was "crude and cruel," and something as simple as having a couple of teeth pulled could maim or kill you: "jaw-breaking, excessive hemorrhage, fainting, and even death frequently result from the barbarous treatment." The missionary's dentistry wasn't too sophisticated either and, as he admitted, his first dental instruments were "very rude, having been hammered out by a native blacksmith" according to his instructions. And the "Doctor" in the name Dr MacKay was for Doctor of Theology, not for medicine or dentistry.

It must have been a strange sight: a foreign devil in a white suit and pith helmet outside a temple, and a hundred or so sufferers waiting in line. Teeth were extracted at a frightening pace – better than one a minute – so quickly in fact that there was no time for the patients to sit down, and teeth were pulled while they stood. MacKay calculated he had more than twenty-one thousand extractions to his credit.

*Dr. MacKay and students pulling teeth*

\* \* \*

One of the Canadian's longer trips, as usual on foot and in the company of some of his students, took him over the rugged mountain ranges south of Keelung to the Yilan Plain where he hoped to convert the local "civilized" aborigines. MacKay and his party crossed paths with a Chinese man who was escaping from "savages" who had speared and beheaded four of his companions. Further on, the missionary party had to dodge spears thrown by three aborigines. Unscathed they continued until, lost and overtaken by night, they were forced to sleep under the stars. When the weary travellers finally reached a village they were greeted with shouts of "barbarian" and "foreign devil," and "wolfish-looking dogs" were set upon them. Up and down the plain they received the same hostile response: curses, closed doors, and dogs, until some sympathetic men from a fishing village invited them to their home. The villagers were so impressed that they built a chapel. MacKay stayed on for nearly two months, converted many of the inhabitants, and then repeated that success in neighbouring villages.

As the first missionary in northern Taiwan, MacKay met with considerable curiosity and opposition, and some of his earliest Christian converts paid for their new-found faith with their lives. In a village near Bang-kah, the present-day Taipei neighbourhood of Wanhua, the missionary's success drew the hostility of local leaders. Eight converts were framed and falsely accused of trying to assassinate a mandarin. (The perpetrators admitted years later that the charges had been fabricated and the Christians entirely innocent.) They were kept in stocks in a dungeon, tortured before, during and after mock trials, and then taken down to Tainan and imprisoned. Two converts, a teacher and his father, were dragged out and beheaded, the father forced to see his son's head hacked off. The two heads were put in buckets, labelled "Heads of the Christians" and carried back to Bang-kah. Along the way villagers were summoned to see the fate of those who followed the "barbarian." Once returned to Bang-kah the heads were put on the city gates. The remaining six men were imprisoned, where two died from torture and starvation.

Some of the darkest days for the first Christians occurred during a short war between France and China in 1884–1885. Although the conflict was over a territorial dispute in Indochina, the French decided to exert pressure on Peking by blockading and attacking ports around Taiwan. Into Danshui alone, upward of a thousand shells were fired, and with little accuracy. Every European house was hit, and a shell fragment weighing thirty pounds came crashing through MacKay's roof and into a hall. Always ready with a bit of appropriate scripture he shot back with words of encouragement for his household: "Thou shall not be afraid for the terror by night, not for the arrow that flieth by day."

One of the tragedies of the bombardment was that as many Chinese were killed by tampering with the unexploded shells found on shore as were killed by the French shelling itself. Not far from MacKay's house "one poor heathen" sat astride a shell and proceeded to attack it with a hammer and chisel to get to the gunpowder. His researches were answered with an explosion that carried his limbs into the tree above him, and, "for that last moment, with half his body blown away, his mind was still on the treasures of earth. Seeing the contents of his pocket on the ground, he said with his last breath, 'Pick up that dollar.' Poor, dark, hopeless heathenism."

Not surprisingly the French blockade stirred anti-foreigner sentiment among the locals that spilled over into violence; seven chapels were destroyed, Chinese converts were assaulted and several murdered.

It would be unfair, however, to paint too black a picture of religious intolerance in those early times. MacKay and his followers were not entirely blameless; they would sing hymns and preach outside temples and burn the idols of the newly converted. Imagine the situation reversed, as the zealous MacKay failed to do. What kind of welcome would have awaited a "heathen Chinaman" in any Western country in the nineteenth century if he had stood outside a church, barefoot and wearing Buddhist robes, chanting mantras and preaching the true word?

Today Taiwan enjoys religious freedom that is second to none. There is no discrimination, overt or otherwise, and unlike in many Western countries religion is not an obstacle to high office or a source of conflict. Although the former President, Lee Teng-hui, was a devout Presbyterian, and liked to think of himself as a Moses-like figure leading his people to democracy, his faith was never an issue, and he became the first president of a Chinese nation to be popularly elected. His landslide win certainly wasn't on the back of Christian voters, since they account for only 3 percent of the population.

Most Taoists and Buddhists feel comfortable going to Christian hospitals and many send their children to Christian schools. Foreign missionaries – of which there are more than a thousand – are free to spread their gospel, and many of the old hands have received awards from the government for their service to the community.

# 3
# To the Mountains

AFTER a couple of days exploring Danshui it was time to give my camping equipment a final road test, and have a couple of days off the grog. The clock had struck twelve before I heaved my pack on my back and left the "Enjoying Good Time Hotel." By the time I got off a bus at Yangming Shan National Park, it was already mid-afternoon and I was starting to regret staying up late to watch the World Cup rugby the night before. "No matter," I told myself as I sweated my way up to the top of Seven-Star Mountain, "You've cleverly avoided the mid-day heat."

The auspiciously named Seven-Star Mountain (Qixing Shan) is, when it's not raining, a dominant feature of the skyline in the Taipei area, and at 1,120 metres is the highest peak north of the city. It's a very popular day trip from Taipei; but people were still a bit jumpy about hiking so soon after the quake and I'd chosen a weekday, so it was nice and quiet.

The trail was a never-ending series of steps through thick forest. Half an hour up I met a cloud coming the opposite way, a dense white soup slowly rolling its way down the mountainside and robbing me of my hard-earned view. The path became increasingly steep, practically a stairway, and moved from forest into coarse waist-height grass. The wind picked up and the cloud condensed into rain. It was almost dark when I reached the wind-blown summit, from where I'm told, on a good day, you can see a beautiful 360-degree view that takes in all the park, other peaks, Taipei, and in the distance, the sea. I could see no further than twenty metres. Rather than press on down the other side of the mountain I decided to camp, though finding a place to do so wasn't easy; the summit was too windy, the mountainside too steep, and the vegetation too thick, so I had to settle for a tiny space skirting the stone path leeward of a huge boulder.

Just as I was putting up my small tent there was a strong aftershock. Worse still was the sensation that the ground I was standing on was unstable, and it seemed to be constantly moving. The smell of sulphur in the air was an unwelcome reminder that the mountain was a volcano, dormant but not dead, and it struck me that earthquake activity and a volcanic mountain were not the best combination.

It may have been raining lightly outside my tent but this was my first "dry" night for many months, and I lay there wide-eyed sober wondering whether the earth really was moving or it was just my imagination, perhaps withdrawal symptoms – a bad case of the shakes. Getting to sleep wasn't made any easier by the fact that my campsite was underneath the flight path of airplanes flying into the airport.

I was woken abruptly at about five the next morning by voices and footsteps walking past my tent, and because the path was so narrow their steps were just a foot or so from me lying there in my sleeping bag – literally close enough to hear them breathing. It sounded like a group of elderly men and women. Talk about keen; they had walked up in the dark. Still in my sleeping bag, I unzipped the tent door and poked my head out. An old man, straggling behind his friends, rose into view. I greeted him with a rather embarrassed, *Zao'an* (Good morning). His mouth dropped, and he looked like he'd just seen a ghost. His mouth moved as a reflex action but no sound came out. He drew a double lungful of air and hurried on without looking back.

I quickly broke camp, packed, and climbed the short distance to the top. The cloud hadn't lifted and the visibility was still atrocious. I found the hiking fanatics, half a dozen men and women in their fifties and sixties, at the small clearing on the summit. Two were catching their breath, and the others were engaged in bizarre looking exercises: one man bobbing up and down on his knees with his arms hanging lose at his side, another swinging his arms around like a windmill, and a woman playing an invisible accordion. I could have thought of more convenient places and times to do some *taiji*, but for practitioners it doesn't get any better than a mist-shrouded mountaintop at dawn.

Taoists believe that mountains are rich in *qi* and it's interesting to note that the Chinese character for "immortal" is a combination of the characters for "man" and "mountain." Mists and clouds are supposed to contain a large amount of cosmic vital essence and early in the morning (around five o'clock) is considered the best time for harnessing *qi* because trees are said to give off "original energy" and by doing breathing exercises the energy can be absorbed.

I waited a while but the cloud showed no signs of thinning – a pity not just for the obscured view, but also for the lost chance to go looking for a "pyramid" recently discovered by a rogue amateur archaeologist, Lin Sheng-yi. The fifty-eight-year-old shoe store owner, propelled by his mother's last words and the desire to unearth a noble history for his dying tribe, which has all but been assimilated, has spent a decade hunting for ancient remains of the lowland aborigines called Ketagalan. He made his greatest discovery in a basin between two peaks at the top of Seven-Star Mountain: a small pyramid he claims was built by his ancestors twelve thousand years ago. And at the base of the mountains, in front, and behind, he found two "dinosaur sculptures" in what he says were areas of worship. When Mr. Lin later showed me his photographs I had trouble making out the dinosaurs – they were simply big rocks. I asked how his ancestors could have known what dinosaurs looked like, seeing as they were over sixty million years too late to have seen them. He answered with one of his favourite words, "Intuition ... at that time my ancestors had special mental powers we no longer have. We can't imagine how wonderful they were, how developed their minds were."

I started the steep descent down the other side of the mountain through a volcanic area where sulphurous steam spewed forth from gashes in the earth. I was reminded of an account written by a low-ranking official about 160 years ago that had been in the newspaper a few days before: "One day an earthquake shook the island. A woodsman was walking in front of me. The earth cracked and he fell into it. The fissure closed up."

Once back in Taipei it was hard to stop thinking about seismic activity, thanks to my hotel. The Paradise Hotel is an old favourite, well, old anyway, and a favourite in a sentimental way as it was where I spent my very first night in Taiwan. It's run-down, yes, but you can't complain at US$22 for a central location and all of life's necessities except a fridge. The problem with my room was that it was right next to the lift; and every time the lift moved up or down I would hear a rattle and feel a shudder pass through the floor – a perfect imitation of an earthquake that had me bracing for the big one.

Taipei was due for a shock. Parts of it spent much of the eighteenth century underwater thanks to a massive quake that struck in 1694 and turned the Taipei basin into a large saltwater lake. More recently, a week before Christmas in 1867, an earthquake destroyed the nearby town of Keelung. When the quake struck, the water drained out of the harbour so quickly it left boats sitting and fish flapping helplessly on the dry bottom of the bay. Some of the townsfolk rushed out to collect the fish. The last thing they ever saw was a huge returning wave that swept them away, tore the ships to pieces, and ran through the town.

On my second night in Taipei I took a Sunday evening stroll around the old neighbourhood of Wanhua, a place that has a hard time living up to its name, "ten thousand glories." It does at least have one glorious building. After living next to a very active Matsu temple for years I have trouble getting enthusiastic about temples, but Wanhua's Longshan ("Dragon Mountain") Temple is impressive – easily the most atmospheric temple I've visited in Taiwan. Incense hung heavy in the air as warm shafts of light cut through smoke to bring exquisitely carved dragons and figures flickering to life. Originally built in 1738, the temple has gone through trials of fire and earthquakes that have required extensive rebuilding. Its greatest claim to fame is a wooden statue of Guanyin, the Buddhist goddess of mercy, which is highly venerated on account of its miraculous survival from an American bombing raid in 1945 that destroyed the hall housing it. The popularity of the temple is evident in the surrounding area, which is packed with little shops selling fruit offerings, ghost money, and other religious paraphernalia.

Back in MacKay's time Wanhua was the largest city in the north and was known by the Taiwanese name of Bang-kah. In the Protestant missionary's eyes it was the "Gibraltar of heathenism," and although he was no stranger to hostile receptions – being followed down streets by angry mobs shouting "Foreign devil! Black-bearded barbarian," and the like – he thought Wanhua was in a league of its own. In a journal entry of 1875 from a visit he made with A Hoa, his first convert and faithful follower, he gives full vent to his indignation:

"At every visit, when passing through their streets, we were maligned, jeered at, and abused. Hundreds of children run ahead, yelling with derisive shouts; others follow, pelting us with orange-peel, mud, and rotten eggs. For hatred to foreigners, for pride, swaggering ignorance, and conceit, for superstitious, sensual, haughty, double-faced wickedness, Bang-kah takes the palm. But remember, O haughty city, even these eyes will see you humble in the dust. Thou art mighty now, proud, and full of malice; but thy power shall fall, and thou shall be brought low. Thy filthy streets are indicative of thy moral rottenness; thy low houses show thy baseness in the face of heaven. Repent, O Bang-kah, thou wicked city, or the trumpet shall blow and thy tears be in vain."

In spite of violence, threatened and actual, MacKay managed to establish a mission there. In time the locals softened in their opposition. So much so, in fact, that just before he departed for Canada in 1893 for some well-earned leave, the townspeople gave him a tremendous send-off. He was in Bang-kah on the eve of his departure from Danshui and the town laid on a procession that included eight music bands, men and boys with flags and streamers, officials, Mackay in a silk-lined sedan chair, and three hundred footmen.

Bang-kah still retains some of its dirty "Chinatown" feel and it doesn't take much effort to find "Thy low houses." Prostitution is (with a few exceptions) officially illegal, and in recent years the Taipei City Government has actually been trying to enforce the law. The brothels, which include a few officially licensed ones, are clustered around a tourist market called "Snake Alley," which is a unique synthesis of the traditional and the modern. The problem is that it somehow manages to combine the worst of the old and the worst of the new, and it has all the ambience of a supermarket and the sophisticated charm of a bookstore selling second-hand porno mags. Under the glare of fluorescent strip lighting, vendors selling fake designer clothes and cheap plastic goods rub shoulders with sleazy shops selling electrical sex aids, and restaurants offering freshly killed turtles and snakes. Cooks stand juggling cobras in their hands as they work the crowd, ready to disembowel the serpent for any willing customer. A sign warns, "No taking pictures." Little wonder that with so-called tourist attractions like Snake Alley, Taiwan has the reputation of being a conservation black hole.

From downtown Taipei I caught a bus for Wulai, an aboriginal village up in the mountains, thirty kilometres south of Taipei. The driver and some of the passengers were aborigines of the Atayal tribe, which is the most numerous and widespread aboriginal group in the north, and were speaking their native tongue. Taiwan's indigenous peoples are distinguishable from Taiwanese of Chinese ancestry by their appearance; they are a little shorter and have light brown skin without a yellow tinge, and their eyes are larger and have a double eyelid fold (the crease in the upper eyelid).

When MacKay came this way late in the nineteenth century it was still the abode of headhunters and he was offered raw bear meat. Today Wulai is a tacky tourist spot for weekend day-trippers; but I arrived on a Monday and it was almost deserted – more ghost town than tourist town – and the dozing taxi driver I woke looked both surprised and happy to get a customer. From Wulai we drove eighteen kilometres up a winding road through a river-worn gorge. Because I was going into an aboriginal area I had to stop and register at a police checkpoint where the policeman did his best to dissuade me from going hiking. Further on, work crews were clearing away landslides, and in one place we needed to get out and move the rocks by hand. Clouds thickened overhead and the air cooled.

The driver was worried about me; he was a friendly man but I think most of his concern stemmed from the fact that because my Chinese is pretty bad he obviously thought I was an idiot. I had nuanced answers to his many questions but they couldn't make it past my tongue. After I told him I was going hiking and wanted to be dropped off at a trailhead, he screwed up his face.

"Have you been there before?

"No."

"Are you going with someone else, or a guide?"

"No."

"Do you have a map?" he asked, growing more wide-eyed with each question.

"Um, yes, but not, er not really," I mumbled.

"Where are you going to sleep tonight?"

"The forest."

He shook his head and gave a nervous giggle, "You should stay the night in the village – it's two-thirty already, it looks like rain, and you don't know where to camp. The trail is narrow and steep and you might not find a place in time."

I stretched my lousy Chinese to breaking point trying to assure him I'd be fine. Anyway, it seemed to work, a bit of Tarzan talk just the trick for a jungle trip, and changing the topic, he now began cross-examining me as to whether I knew all the foreign passengers he'd ever had in his taxi.

"Two Americans, husband and wife, last summer?"

"I don't think I know them."

"The man was very fat, the woman had blonde hair."

"Er, no, sorry."

And so he continued for a while oblivious to the fact there are thousands of foreigners living in Taipei, and I was actually from Dounan, a small town four hours south of the big city. Dounan and the small neighbouring towns are the kind of places where you can get in a taxi, and although the driver may never have seen you before he has heard about you and actually knows where you want to go before you tell him. For about half of the time I've lived in Dounan I've been the only Westerner, but for the past couple of years the number has doubled to two, thanks to the arrival of my housemate, Conn. The two of us took some pleasure in having our own little Guinness Book of Records; Conn, the "Tallest Man in Dounan," and me, the "Heaviest Man in Dounan," but with the hiking training I'd been forced to relinquish that title and make do with being the "Hairiest Man in Dounan."

Forty minutes and as many questions after leaving Wulai we arrived at a swing bridge marking the trailhead; the taxi driver shook my hand and wished me luck. A narrow forest trail took me up and along the side of a gorge. The gloomy silence of the forest interior was a little foreboding but at least I didn't have to worry about headhunters, as did MacKay, who came this way in 1873.

Just one year after arriving in Danshui, MacKay made a long trip into the interior with Captain Donham Bax, commander of the unfortunately named British gunboat, HMS Dwarf. The forest was in places so strangled by creepers and vegetation that they had to cut their way through with long knives. On the fourth evening MacKay's escort of "tame" aborigines delivered them to their wild cousins. Relations got off to a bad start the next morning. The missionary was furious at the chief's plan to use his visitors as decoys to draw some Chinese settlers out from safety in order to remove their heads. And at the end of that day the two Europeans came close to having their own heads become decoration for some aboriginal house. MacKay and the sea captain were interested in the architecture of the aborigines' huts and had taken out notebooks and pencils and begun sketching. It caused a storm – angry braves rushed off into their huts and returned with long spears. "They were mad with rage," and couldn't be convinced of the harmlessness of the sketches. In the same way that many cultures believe photographs steal the soul, the aborigines thought the sketches could extract the essence of a thing and then be used for black magic.

MacKay and Captain Bax determined to climb Mount Sylvia (now called Snow Mountain in English and Xue Shan in Mandarin), probably the most beautiful mountain on the island, and at 3,884 metres, the highest peak in northern Taiwan. A chief and a dozen braves were hired for the trek. Although two men went ahead and cut a way through the thorny creepers, by the end of the first day the two Europeans' clothes and hands were still badly torn. They spent three more days of hard walking through forests festooned with ferns and orchids, taking them deeper and higher than any foreigner had ever ventured until finally the snow-capped summit of Mt. Sylvia lay within reach.

MacKay went to bed in good spirits, almost drunk with what he had seen, "Standing there on that jutting crag, gazing on that marvelous scene above, around, below, listening to the music of a torrent tumbling from a chasm high overhead, far to the west the waters of the Formosa Channel gleaming like a long line of blue light, and, between, the mountain-ranges, looking as though the dark-green sea stood still, 'with all its rounded billows fixed and motionless forever,' the effect of it all was overwhelming."

Ecstasy turned to despair. The morning brought unwelcome news – they had to turn back because the chief had been out conversing with the birds and they had warned ill. These birds were seen as messengers from the spirit world, and in the notes and flight of a bird were the guidance of some ancestor. Back down they trod, dejected but making good time to the village where they had slept the night before last. The village was wild with celebration for a head had just been taken!

Headhunting was the great passion of the Atayal aborigines, and although not absolutely essential for marriage a man was still expected to take a head. The headhunter was not restricted by any sense of fair play – the ends justified the means. Raids were well-planned, and the target people and area were scouted out in advance. The warriors travelled light and relied on ambush rather than open combat. The basic headhunter kit consisted of a long bamboo spear tipped with an iron arrow-shaped head, a long knife, and a bag to carry the head home. This kit was sometimes beefed up with the addition of bows and arrows, and occasionally a matchlock. Night was the preferred time of attack; a group would surround a house, set the thatch roof on fire, wait for the unfortunate occupants to be smoked out, spear them, hack off their heads and then hurry home to a hero's welcome. Celebrations of drinking and dancing lasted days. The flesh on the head was left to rot away from the skull and then hung up as a trophy, usually under the eaves but sometimes on the walls inside.

According to James Davidson, American consul in Taiwan and author of the definitive work *The Island of Formosa, Past and Present* (1903), the Atayal skull shelves were well stocked. Some villages had several hundred, and that "the average at present for a recognized brave is about ten."

For all their bloodthirstiness, MacKay recognized the civil morality of tribal culture:

> These savages are singularly free from many moral and social vices common alike among civilized and uncivilized peoples. Gambling and opium smoking are very rare; murder, theft, incendiarism, polygamy, and social impurity are almost unknown, except where the baneful influence of Chinese traders and border-men has corrupted the simplicity of the savage. Tribes are continually at war with one another, and all agree in regarding raids on the Chinese as both legitimate and praiseworthy; but among themselves crime is rare.

As it turned out the taxi driver was right. I was an idiot, the rain did come pelting down and, as he had predicted, I had started out too late to get to a suitable camping site before nightfall. The fact that I could walk for hours without finding even a half-decent tent-sized piece of land gives some idea of the very steep and thickly forested terrain. The rain and the long deep shadows of forest and mountains brought on an early night and I felt very alone. There weren't even any footprints for company because nobody had come this way for two weeks, and that made for some very hungry leeches.

I pitched camp in a tiny clearing high up in the mountains in the darkness. It rained solidly through the night. Raindrops that fall from the tree canopy are much larger than those falling freely from the sky – larger and louder. My tent was hit by both kinds; smaller raindrops making a background hiss and the larger ones rolling a rapid drum beat. And every so often gusts of wind would sweep over the forest, heard before they were felt as a loud hissing roar in the distance like surf breaking on a beach. A moment later came the rustle of trees, and then the loud pelting of rain.

And so I found myself stuck inside my tent waiting for the rain to ease off, just me and a bottle of grog, slipping sip by sip into the warm embrace of reminiscences, and the dangerous territory of inspiration. There was something strikingly familiar about this situation. It was during such a time of forced confinement under canvas with nothing to do but drink homemade wine that I'd first come up with, and decided upon, the idea of teaching English in Taiwan. That was back in New Zealand in the autumn of 1992, when I was trying to earn enough money to go to Mongolia to do some private research on the country's wildlife and traditional folklore.

And so I found myself gold prospecting alone in the rugged mountain ranges of the South Island's West Coast. I had located a creek that looked worth working, carted in about sixty kilos of equipment and supplies, and set up a small camp. Next came the hard work: damming part of the creek and diverting the flow in order to expose the river bottom and digging down through the gravel to the hard bedrock. It's on this bedrock which alluvial gold is most likely to be found. After two backbreaking days of moving rocks and shovelling gravel the skies opened up and didn't stop for another three days. The creek flooded, washing away the small dam I'd built, and stranding me on a small clearing beneath a cliff.

There was nothing to do but drink the four litres of homebrewed grapefruit and apple wine and wait for the water level to drop. It was out of the ensuing alcoholic haze that the idea of working in Taiwan materialized, perhaps a couple of long-forgotten conversations with teachers who had been to the island had bubbled to the surface – I still don't know why. The idea had never occurred to me before, yet I made my mind up that very instant. The following year I did some teacher training and taught for eight months in Auckland before starting work in Taiwan in 1994.

Thankfully this time I didn't have enough grog to come up with any bright ideas and I soon fell asleep. Come morning it was still hosing down. The sky was liquid grey, and the ground a sodden mess studded with tea-coloured pools of water.

While listening to ICRT, Taiwan's only English-language radio station, I killed the bloated leeches that had gorged on me during the night and were now escaping the scene of the crime. Crackling over the radio was the ominous news of a typhoon rolling in off the Philippine Sea. The weather service had issued a storm warning for mountain areas and because this was the first heavy rain since the earthquake they were warning of landslides. There was some very sad news, too; fourteen members of the Flying Eagles (a Taipei climbing club) and a driver had been found dead in a mini-bus. They had been on their way to climb some peaks when an earthquake-triggered rockfall had buried them alive. The recent rain had washed away some of the debris, allowing rescue teams to spot the bus.

I accepted defeat and decided to turn back. The rain was pelting down, and in many places the trail had become a flowing stream, the mountainside a solid sheet of moving water. As anyone who has ever lived in Taipei or nearby can testify, northern Taiwan can really lay on the rain. The Atayal tribe had a rain dance with a twist – it was designed to get rid of rain rather than bring it. And in keeping with the courageous nature of the tribe, the rain dance didn't involve offerings or grovelling but priestesses chanting and dancing with headhunting swords, cursing the rain god, and working themselves up bit by bit into a frenzy until they collapsed. This was a signal that the rain devil had been cut to pieces or at least wounded and forced to flee.

It was early afternoon before I got down to the aboriginal village of Fushan. The village looked pretty much like any small rural one in Taiwan – no savages in loin clothes or bare-breasted maidens – and the only differences were a few signs in the Atayal language, aboriginal artwork, and a lack of Chinese religious objects such as temples and altars. Of Taiwan's 380,000 aborigines, just over half are mountain dwellers, and most have been assimilated into Taiwanese culture. Two of their main distinguishing characteristics of the population from Taiwanese are the high number of alcoholics and Christians (not that I'm suggesting any connection).

I was asking about getting transportation down to civilization when two local men pulled up alongside in a car: "Are you going down to Wulai? We're going there now, jump in!" We sped off down the road. The driving conditions were atrocious: pouring rain, the asphalt submerged under huge puddles and streams of moving water, and an extremely narrow and winding road with a sheer fall to the side. What did the situation call for? Yes, some beer. The young man on the passenger side took a large bottle of Taiwan Beer from the car floor, skilfully opened it with the flick of a lighter, and passed it back to me. Ah, heaven sent. And then he opened a beer for the driver and one for himself. The driver turned the steering wheel with his left hand and held the bottle with his right, while his friend, whilst holding a baby in his arms, drank with the beer in his right hand, and changed gear with his free left hand. I should have been very worried but I wasn't – too thirsty I guess, and I'd gone thirty hours without beer! Well, perhaps a little worried that I wasn't worried.

Anyway, both the beer and the car went down nice and smoothly, and it looked as though these guys were used to driving like this. A good job too because the road was an obstacle course of blind corners, rocks, and vertical drops where a single mistake would have sent us plunging down the ravine to a watery grave. Then just when I was getting used to it they decided to make things more interesting by having a smoke, and in another piece of amazing teamwork, pulled out a pack of Marlboros and lit a couple of cigarettes. One close miss later they dropped me off at Wulai bus station.

"Leeches, take your boots off and wash them off," instructed the sharp-eyed aboriginal bus driver pointing at my socks. I looked at my watch – the bus was due to leave in two minutes.

"No time," I said.

"Don't worry. I'll wait for you."

I took off my wet boots and socks. Bloated leeches spilled out – a few remained fastened to my skin. The passengers in the bus looked on aghast at my blood-streaked ankles with faces that seemed to ask, "Was that a hike or a blood transfusion?"

"Here, they're afraid of cigarettes," the bus driver said as he came forward and burnt off a couple of leeches. A middle-aged lady got off the bus and gave me some tiger balm to apply to the three-dozen odd wounds around my ankles. "Keep the container," she said, "it's almost finished anyway." I changed into dry socks and shoes, and got on the waiting bus. Seeing that I didn't have the exact change for the bus fare, a passenger came forward and gave me some coins. This was Taiwan at its best – friendly, generous, and laid-back – and as the bus wound its way down to Taipei I felt very proud to call Taiwan my second home. Like most foreign residents my feelings about the country are rather mixed. It's a love-hate relationship, and you sometimes ask yourself what the hell you're doing here, are often six months away from leaving, and leaving for good, but the wonderful people make up for the country's other shortcomings.

* * *

MacKay wrote a book about the first twenty-one years of his mission work in Taiwan called *From Far Formosa*, and it is one of the most fascinating works ever written about Taiwan. Although some of the pleasure of reading *From Far Formosa* comes from it being so politically incorrect, and while there is no question that he was overzealous, it would be too harsh to judge him a racist simply on the basis of the language he used. MacKay loved the people of Taiwan and he makes this clear on the first page of the first chapter: "To serve them in the gospel I would gladly, a thousand times over, give up my life." He wrote the book while on leave in Canada and his thoughts were still very much with his "beloved home beyond the sea. There I hope to spend what remains of my life, and when my day of service is over I should like to find a resting-place within the sound of its surf and under the shade of its waving bamboo."

Every year on Tomb Sweeping Day, which falls on the fifth of April, families all across Taiwan travel to cemeteries to clean their departed relatives' graves and worship their ancestors. At this time of the year an old white-bearded missionary can be seen under the gnarled old trees of the foreigners' cemetery in Danshui, tending to the time-worn graves which include that of the Rev. George MacKay. The man is Jack Geddes, a retired Canadian Presbyterian missionary and university lecturer who has been out in Taiwan with his wife Betty since 1959, and like MacKay is a Canadian of Scottish ancestry.

Hoping that Jack Geddes would be able to tell me something about MacKay's family, I met up with him one Friday morning at his home in the Taipei suburb of Shipai where he was busy babysitting his grandson. With his good-natured face, glasses, and full white head of hair and beard he looked like a thin Santa Claus.

One of the intriguing things about MacKay's book is a beautiful family portrait at the front which shows MacKay with a Taiwanese wife, two girls, and a boy in a kilt. In the book he only makes the most incidental references to having a wife and children, and I was both amused and curious. Most single men who spend any time out here, regardless of whether they arrived thinking Taiwanese women are attractive or not, will sooner or later come down with "yellow fever," which is a taste, either a temporary bout or a lifelong affliction, for Asian women. The majority of Western men get a local girlfriend and not a few end up taking a wife. It seemed even MacKay had succumbed and in doing so had been breaking down cultural barriers long before marrying a non-white became acceptable. For the times his marriage was scandalous behaviour indeed.

Jack rummaged through his library, pulled out a handful of books, and worked his way through the MacKay family tree with a series of old photographs.

"And what can you tell me about his wife?" I asked.

"She came from a village on the other side of the Danshui River, at one of the first places he'd established a chapel, but nothing is known about the courtship. The marriage was something of a shock. He announced in a letter to the Foreign Mission Committee back in Canada that he'd been married though he had never mentioned anything beforehand. And he was the only missionary out here at the time so nobody else knew anything about it."

Mr Geddes flipped through a couple of books and found the extract from MacKay's letter in Duncan MacLeod's *The Island Beautiful*; "In May I was married to a Chinese lady by the British Consul at Tamsui [Danshui] and at once returned to the country to visit the stations with her."

"Not much of a honeymoon!"

"I suspect that he got married mainly to make preaching easier, to access the women."

How much the marriage was one of love or convenience we'll never know, but the MacKays had two girls and a boy, and all of them stayed on in Taiwan and lie buried in the cemetery near their parents. Their descendants live in North America and Taiwan.

*Canadian missionary Dr. MacKay and family*

At the time of MacKay's death from throat cancer in 1901 there were sixty Presbyterian chapels in the north, and in keeping with his emphasis on a native ministry all of them were run by local preachers. On top of his missionary work and dentistry he set up a hospital, established Oxford College (the first modern school in Taiwan), and followed that up with the first girls' school.

MacKay had an artist's appreciation of nature coupled with a scientist's curiosity, and on his travels he always collected plant and rock specimens. From his travels he turned his living room into a museum, which for a generation was the first stop for any visiting scientist. It was a vast collection of everything from shells and corals, insects, to agricultural implements, weapons to musical instruments, "idols enough to stock a temple," and artefacts from aboriginal villages. Today the collection from his museum is split between Taiwan and the Royal Ontario Museum in Toronto.

MacKay was described by his counterpart in southern Taiwan, the Rev. William Campbell, as "a little man, firm and active, of few words, unflinching courage, and one whose sound common sense is equalled only by his earnest devotion to the Master." A later missionary who worked in the north, Duncan MacLeod, had a more accurate assessment of the missionary; he thought that MacKay was "a soldier by nature," a reserved man with a fiery temperament who did not easily find close companionship with those around him, and that "he created, perhaps, more awe than affection, more admiration than appreciation...."

# 4

# Taipei

AFTER years of hit-and-run visits to Taipei I decided to stay and spend some time looking around. The city has improved a lot since I first visited it back in December 1993. In fact, I hated it so much that after just four days, I scrapped my plans to live and work on the island, and took the next plane out. It wasn't culture shock because I'd lived and travelled in Asia – perhaps more a case of toxic shock. Stepping straight from a New Zealand summer into a concrete jungle choking on a cold, grey, acid-rain winter, made me think that I'd just walked into the science-fiction movie *Bladerunner*. It was a claustrophobic nightmare of noise, pollution, traffic jams, piles of trash, construction sites and sheer ugliness. It wasn't all bad though – the people were friendly, especially considering the rat-race environment they had to live in.

Part of the claustrophobic feel came from the lack of personal space, and it's something I'm still getting used to it. That there's no personal space is hardly surprising because there's little space of any kind; from a lack of space for parking (even illegally), to the absence of sidewalks, to clothes shops' changing rooms which are so small that getting changed inside them is like some Harry Houdini escape act.

With an average of 607 people per square kilometre Taiwan's population density is second only to Bangladesh. It is almost twice as crowded as Japan and if the island were a province of China then it would be the most densely populated one. Taiwan has the world's highest vehicle density, factory density, and energy consumption density. And because most of the 22.5 million inhabitants are restricted to the lowlands, these densities are in reality much higher than the numbers indicates. On top of population pressures, rapid economic growth has increased the environmental burden to the point where pollution and environmental degradation have reached dangerous levels. Taiwan's economic miracle has truly given the sub-tropical island a high GNP – high Garbage, Noise, and Pollution!

For me, what best exemplifies the lack of space and the resulting loss of privacy is the dentist. I can still clearly recall my first Taiwanese dental experience. My wisdom teeth had been pushing through my gums for a while when pain finally overcame fear and I had to pay the local dentist a visit. The clinic consisted of just one room with patients having to wait on a couple of benches that were facing the dental chairs: no magazines to distract, no tropical fish or soothing music to calm the nerves. Instead, I got to watch the dentist drilling away in a woman's mouth, and hear the full whine of the drill cutting into her teeth. By coincidence the patient before my turn was also having a wisdom tooth extracted. It was a long wait but at least the bill was painless.

Taipei is Taiwan's largest city and many of the city's problems stem from its size and rapid expansion. It exploded from about 326,000 residents in 1947 to two million by 1974, and then grew more slowly to 2.6 million people in 2000 (with most of the recent population growth occurring in the surrounding greater Taipei area). Thankfully the rate of urbanization has eased, and Taipei's rising wealth and education levels have been accompanied by an increasing concern for the quality of life. A new public transit system has made getting around the city much easier. The streets are cleaner and improvements to the waste-sewage system have taken some of the stench out of summer.

During the Japanese occupation, 1895–1945, things were rather more orderly. Owen Rutter, a British administrator in Borneo who visited the island in 1921, was so impressed by Taipei he thought it "a model of what a colonial city should be." Although Rutter thought Taiwan's towns were "for the most part, anything but beautiful and their modern buildings hideous," he had high praise for how the Japanese had transformed Taipei from "little more than a dirty Chinese village" to a thriving city "with wide streets, spacious parks, and public buildings which would not disgrace any capital in the world."

* * *

Walking around any city centre in Taiwan is a lesson in KMT politics. The main road is invariably named Zhongshan after the founder of the KMT and the ROC (Republic of China), Sun Yat-sen. It comes from Sun Zhongshan, the name by which he is more commonly known in Chinese. Nearby you are certain to find a Zhongzheng Road. This is from a preferred given name for Chiang Kai-shek, the man who put the Republic of China in Taiwan. And there will also be three other roads named after Sun Yat-sen's Three Principles of the People doctrine: *minzu* (nationalism), *minquan* (democracy), and *minsheng* (livelihood or economic well-being).

Chiang Kai-shek has fallen from grace, his smiling portrait on the NT$1,000 banknote replaced, but the reputation of the man on the NT$100 bill, the other KMT titan, Dr. Sun Yat-sen, remains largely intact. The Republic of China's founding father was a strange figure: idealistic, charming, an inspirational orator, but also naïve and egotistical. Sun had the knack of survival matched with incredible persistence. He seems to have blundered his way through where more able people perished, and one of his greatest achievements was simply to survive at a time when political opponents had a very short life expectancy.

Sun was born into a rural peasant family in a coastal village in southeastern China. When he was twelve he joined his elder brother who was working in Hawaii, attended an Anglican school, and went on to college. He developed an interest in politics and Christianity – too much of an interest for his elder brother, who, fearful that he would become a Christian, sent him home. Unable to fit back into traditional village life, Sun started keeping bad company, learnt martial arts, and joined the local branch of a triad. He was forced to flee from the village after he and a friend desecrated the idol of the village deity. Sun went to Hong Kong, was baptized, resumed his studies and graduated from Hong Kong medical college in 1892. Part of his decision to pursue politics instead of medicine sprung from the frustration that his qualifications didn't come up to British standards and he couldn't practise medicine in Hong Kong.

Two years later in Hawaii, Sun formed a small secret society sworn to the overthrow of the Qing dynasty rulers called the *Revive China Society*. With this group – and help from triads and local mercenaries – he sought to seize power in Canton. Before the badly organized revolt was launched, the plan was uncovered and ringleaders caught and executed. Sun fled to the Portuguese enclave of Macau disguised as a woman. He was now a fugitive with a price on his head, but at least he had some revolutionary credentials. The next sixteen years were spent in exile on the run, travelling from country to country, seeking support and finance from the overseas Chinese community.

Sun's narrowest escape from the executioner's sword occurred in London. On visits to a friend and former dean of his college he would walk past the Chinese Consulate. One day his overconfidence got the better of him, and he couldn't resist the temptation to walk into the consulate, have a casual chat, then stroll out. The following day the Chinese, now alerted to his real identity, were waiting for him. As

Sun walked by he saw the translator he had spoken to the day before standing at the legation entrance and stopped for a few words. Sun was manhandled inside, locked up, and arrangements were made to smuggle him out of the country and back to China where he would have faced death. He finally managed to persuade the man guarding him, the legation's English porter, to deliver a message to his friend. News of his kidnapping hit the front pages of the papers and a crowd of journalists gathered outside the legation. The authorities demanded his release and Sun Yat-sen emerged triumphant although he had to lie about the circumstances of his capture. By a wonderful turn of luck his act of supreme stupidity had turned him into a celebrity.

During his sixteen-year exile Sun and his followers launched nine unsuccessful uprisings. Ironically it was the Wuchang Uprising, a rebellion in which Sun played no direct part, that snowballed into a revolution that toppled the Qing dynasty in 1911. At the time of the Wuchang Uprising, Sun Yat-sen was on a fund-raising trip in the United States and the first he heard of it was from a newspaper in Denver.

Sun Yat-sen returned to China, serving as the first provisional president for just six weeks before being pushed aside by Yuan Shikai, a powerful northern warlord. As China sank into the chaos of the warlord era, Sun was shunted into the political wilderness, a famous name without the muscle to put it to use.

During this time Sun had a romance with and proposed to Soong Ching-ling, a girl less than half his age, and the daughter of his best friend. To further complicate matters he had yet to divorce his first wife. When Ching-ling's family, one of the richest and most powerful in China, refused permission, she ran away and they were wed in Japan. Chiang Kai-shek later married Ching-ling's younger sister, Soong May-ling.

In 1919 Sun Yat-sen reorganized his party into the present-day Kuomintang (KMT) and established a fragile military government in Canton. Tenacious and forever the optimist, he set about implementing his grand plans of saving China, but with a pitiful military force of only five hundred soldiers he obviously needed help. He wanted to turn China into a modern democratic nation modelled after the West, but the countries he asked for help were uninterested. A divided and weak China made it easier for them to extract favourable trading concessions. He found a willing ally in the Soviet Union.

In the heady days after the 1917 Russian Revolution, Lenin set out to fulfil his dream of world revolution, starting with the capitalist West.

When insurrections in Europe failed to materialize he turned his gaze toward Asia. "The East will help us conquer the West," he proclaimed, but was too busy fighting a bloody civil war against the Russian White Army to put his plan into action before his death in 1924. The mission fell to his successor, Joseph Stalin.

The Soviets found that the fledgling Chinese Communist Party (CCP) was much too small and weak to liberate a country the size of China and began looking around for a stronger ally. Sun Yat-sen was a popular figure and his Kuomintang party in need of support. According to Stalin, the Kuomintang were to be "squeezed out like a lemon, and then thrown away." The man for the job was Mikhail Borodin, the Soviet's top international secret agent and a master of disguises who has been described as a "Bolshevik T.E. Lawrence." Borodin, by all accounts an immensely capable and likeable man, was a Russian Jew from Latvia, and had carried out secret assignments in Mexico, the United States, and Europe. He slipped into China in late 1923 and negotiated an alliance between the CCP and the KMT. With his small staff of Soviet experts – men hardened by years of fierce battle on various fronts – he reorganized the KMT and rebuilt its army into a credible modern fighting force.

A new military academy was established in 1924 and Chiang Kai-shek was chosen to head it. Supplies of Soviet weaponry flowed in. Chinese Communists slowly began to infiltrate the KMT, while other radicals were sent for revolutionary training at the University for the Toilers of the East in Russia

Sun Yat-sen died of liver cancer in 1925. His deathbed wishes were that the KMT maintain their alliance with the Soviets; but he had named no heir and a struggle ensued. Chiang Kai-shek won, swung the KMT to the right, and it would be the Communists who were to be squeezed like a lemon and a few years later thrown away. First, Chiang launched a three-year military campaign known as the Northern Expedition, defeating several warlords, and bringing most of the nation under his control. In 1927 the time was right to jettison his allies, and the slaughter of Communists began in Shanghai.

* * *

Taiwan's urban areas, from the smallest towns to the largest cities, are the kinds of places that would make any self-respecting architects or town-planners think seriously about stringing themselves up. Taipei is slightly better and would probably just turn an architect to the bottle. As the largest and richest city, and as the capital receiving a disproportionately large slice of the tax pie, it has some very nice buildings. One of the most imposing is the Chiang Kai-shek Memorial Hall – a large blue and white temple-shaped building of beautiful simplicity set in spacious grounds. The epic scale and wide-open spaces that let the building breathe are in stark contrast to the cram-packed chaos outside through which I had walked to reach it. On the road that runs along the southern side there was a long row of wedding shops strategically located for a quick photo shoot in the grounds. The shop windows were full of incredibly ornate gowns, and behind them staff burying the brides under make-up. One of them, a pale, ghost-like figure floated out of the shop in a fire death-trap of a dress, followed by her beau, some assistants and photographers. They piled into a van and sped off, no doubt to some local romantic backdrop. The wedding industry in Taiwan is huge and outdoor wedding photo shoots are a common sight, especially in parks and at tourist spots.

I entered the grounds of the Chiang Kai-shek Memorial Hall through the "Gate of Great Piety" and climbed the steps up to a huge inner chamber where a statue of a seated Chiang Kai-shek looked out over soldiers performing a slow synchronized drill as they changed guard.

Stairs led down to exhibition rooms full of propaganda that was unintentionally funny and instructive. Wall after wall of photographs showed Chiang Kai-shek as a heroic warrior and sage ruler. Beneath large portraits of the dictator, a couple of old men sat talking on a bench, their sharper features and northern Chinese accents marking them out as old KMT soldiers who had come over in 1949. Elsewhere a family with noisy children looked like they were setting up house; perhaps the post-earthquake power rationing had robbed them of air-conditioning and they were escaping from the heat.

From the exhibits you would have thought that the Chinese Civil War had never ended and that Taiwan was still devoted heart and soul to retaking the mainland. The memorial was a time capsule of KMT military rule and their Cold War rhetoric that kept up the fallacy that they would liberate China. Right up until 1991, the same year the Soviet Union disintegrated, the KMT continued to claim sovereignty over all of China and insisted that the Communist government in Beijing was illegal.

As distant as Chiang Kai-shek's era now seems, an understanding of modern Taiwan is impossible without some knowledge of the man.

A proper assessment of Chiang has yet to be undertaken in Taiwan because it is a divisive issue that many prefer to let be. Although most Taiwanese have an unfavourable opinion of him, for an aging minority, mostly mainlanders, he was a Chinese patriot who saved Taiwan from the Communists, and the guardian of Chinese culture.

*Chiang Kai-shek Memorial Hall, Taipei*

Chiang Kai-shek was born to the third wife of a salt merchant in 1887, and was a sickly child with a moody disposition. While at school he came across a book that changed his life – the classic *The Art of War* written by Sun Tzu in the fourth century BC during a time of chaos known as the Warring States Period. Chiang's time was also one of turmoil. From the fall of the Manchu Qing dynasty in 1911 to the Communist victory in 1949, the country was torn apart by revolution, warlords and gangsters, corruption, civil war between the KMT and Communists, war with Japan, and then resumption of the civil war. *The Art of War* stressed brains over brawn, the use of spies, diplomacy, deception, and treachery rather than military muscle. The aim of Sun Tzu's war strategy was to win without wasting any effort and money on actual fighting. "Use espionage and mystification in every enterprise. All life is based on deception."

Chiang studied at a military school in Japan for several years, and it was among the overseas Chinese community there that he became involved with revolutionaries and their gangster connections. The two have always been very closely connected – in fact, the origin of the criminal groups was as secret societies with intent of overthrowing the Manchu dynasty and restoring the Ming, the stuff of countless Hong Kong kung fu movies. On his return to China, Chiang became deeply involved in both politics and the Shanghai underworld. Support from the notorious Green Gang was instrumental in his climb up the political ladder to leadership of the KMT.

In 1927 Chiang married (for the third time) into one of China's richest and most powerful families, the Soongs. His wife, Soong Mei-ling, an American-educated Christian, encouraged Chiang to convert, and used her considerable charm to seduce America. In what must rank as one of the biggest public relations con-jobs in history, they were for decades the darlings of the American media. The duo was on the cover of the January 1938 edition of *Time* magazine as "Man and Wife of the Year." With his Western veneer of Christian and progressive ideals coupled with vehemently anti-communist views, he received enormous support from the United States, which helped bankroll his corrupt regime, earning himself the nickname "General Cash My-Check." The Americans poured billions of dollars into China to help him battle the Japanese and the Communists.

The straight-talking American General Stilwell – sent to China as Allied chief of staff to Chiang Kai-shek – considered him "a vacillating, tricky, undependable old scoundrel who never keeps his word," and felt that there were a lot of parallels between America's ally, the KMT, and the Nazi enemy, "a one-party government, supported by a Gestapo and headed by an unbalanced man with little education."

If Chiang's regime hadn't been so deeply mired in corruption, and if he had followed Sun Tzu as well as Mao Zedong did, he probably wouldn't have lost China. Still, he can't have been too stupid, because he's a clear exception to the saying that those that live by the sword die by the sword. Not too many dictators die peacefully at eighty-seven, still in power after fifty years at the helm.

In 1949 Chiang retreated to Taiwan (it had been handed over to the KMT following the Japanese surrender), where he remained president right up until his death in 1975. During those last decades he lived a simple life on the outskirts of Taipei surrounded by beautiful gardens and green hills.

The grounds of his former estate had been recently opened to the public and I took a walk around them on my way to the National Palace Museum. A light rain was falling from a melancholy grey sky, adding a fresh lustre to the foliage and bringing out an earthy smell. The two-storey wooden house, the small private chapel and other buildings, were nice but seemed rather modest for one of the twentieth century's most important dictators. He was the self-styled ruler of China, and had brought considerable wealth over from the mainland. But then again, building himself a huge palace would have been an admission that he was never going to retake China.

I walked on to Taipei's number-one tourist attraction, the National Palace Museum, home to the world's largest collection of Chinese artefacts. I'd visited the museum before but because the exhibits are constantly rotated there is always something new to see. There are about 700,000 items in total so at any one time you can only see a tiny fraction of them. Even if you could view them all at once, would you want to, or have the time? Allowing one minute per piece, and working forty-hour weeks, it would take almost six years to look at everything.

To most Taiwanese having such an internationally acclaimed storehouse of Chinese culture is a source of national pride, but for China it represents first and foremost the richest haul of stolen artworks in history, works that were produced there, belong there, and must be returned. Taiwanese officials argue that they have taken far better care of the collection than the Chinese would have, and there is always the hypothetical question: What would have happened to the art treasures during the terrible days of the Cultural Revolution?

The nucleus of the museum is the royal collection of the eighteenth-century emperor Qianlong, who adorned the Forbidden Palace in Peking with the finest art, past and present. Although the year 1911 saw the end of dynastic rule in China, the last emperor, Puyi, stayed on behind the walls of the palace until 1924. The following year the palace was turned into the National Palace Museum, but it stayed open for only eight years. The Japanese occupied Manchuria in 1931 and, using the former emperor Puyi as a figurehead, established a puppet country called Manchingkuo. As the threat of further Japanese advance grew, the KMT decided to remove the collection to safety. In 1933 nearly twenty thousand boxes of exquisite porcelain, jade, bronzes, paintings and calligraphy were packed and carried south to safety. Thus began a 12,000-kilometre, sixteen-year trek from Peking to Taiwan that saw the treasure trove carried back and forth across China to keep it out of the hands of the Japanese and the Communists. Across rivers and over mountains it went, surviving bombing raids along the way, and incredibly, not a single piece was broken. Well, perhaps not broken but some works were "lost," and given the chaos of the times it's impossible not to imagine that a good few pieces were stolen.

Because the KMT saw Taiwan as a base from which to retake the mainland rather than as a new home, the artworks were put into storage inside mountain caves, and that is where they stayed for another sixteen years. The National Palace Museum was finally opened in Taipei in 1965 on the hundredth anniversary of the birth of Dr. Sun Yat-sen, the founding father of the Republic of China. Despite the delay it was pretty good timing because events in China were to provide a nice contrast in how the two nations preserved their national heritage. With the launch of the Cultural Revolution in 1966, Mao Zedong called for the destruction of the "four olds:" old customs, old habits, old culture, and old thinking. Schools and universities were closed, and the students mobilized into revolutionary bands of "Red Guards." They were encouraged to demolish old buildings and temples, destroy art objects and books, and attack their elders.

As impressive as the museum's individual works are and as fascinating as the background story of how they got there is, I found it disappointing. The building is too small and the interior looks a little shabby, the displays are often poor, and the exhibits lack variety. The artefacts, mostly pottery, porcelain, calligraphy, bronze and jade pieces, don't give a full range of China's history. How much better it would be to have exhibit rooms made up in replicas of, say, a scholar's study, a wine-house, an imperial bedroom, rather than rows of vases after rows of pots after rows of pot-sized, pot-like artefacts, set behind glass cabinets in staid poorly-lit displays.

Some guidebooks rank the National Palace Museum as one of the four best in the world, comparable to the British Museum, the Louvre, and New York's Metropolitan Museum of Art, but I overheard a more telling description from a young boy visiting with his parents: "Let's go. It's so boring!"

48

Foot-sore and dizzy from looking down at too many exhibits, I decided to take a break in a traditional-style teahouse on the fourth-floor. It was a little too crowded, however, and I took the boy's advice and left the museum. Besides, I'd seen enough teapots.

I do like antiques, grew up in a house full of them as my mother collects pottery, but I don't count myself amongst the ranks of the fanatical. When is the last time I, or the vast majority of visitors to the museum, went to the library and got a book out on Chinese porcelain? Never. Or sat around with your friends talking about Chinese jade late into the night? Never. People don't like to admit that a lot of the stuff on show is a little on the boring side. There's an element of guilt in confessing a lack of interest and making an early exit, some shame in not showing an appreciation for the finer things in life, and perhaps the fear of being mistaken for an Australian.

The museum is definitely worth a look, but just don't expect too much, don't feel obliged to look at everything in it, don't take children, and don't take a girl there for a first date (some personal advice – try a zoo, it worked for my parents).

There are some things in life, however, that have the power to make even pots seem fascinating, and I found one of them across from the National Palace Museum. Walking a little up the road, I went past the entrance to a small commercial "fishing pool." Two men, wearing yellow rain-capes and holding umbrellas to fend off the rain, were fishing in a grungy little concrete pool the size of a living room. The small plot of land had all the appeal of a junkyard – it was wall-to-wall corrugated iron, concrete, and plastic, surrounded by buildings on three sides, and a busy road on the other. How bored would you need to be to go there? These two hardy anglers had actually paid for the privilege of sitting out in the rain in those ugly surroundings. What does that say about recreational opportunities in Taipei, or the sanity of fishermen? You can find these DIY fishing farms all over Taiwan, often just a pool next to a commercial fish farm, but with its urban setting and the rain this one seemed especially bleak. I later asked one of my friends how it worked: "You can pay for the time, and after you catch the fish you have the chance to buy it. And if you catch a lot of fish you can win money." Now I understand the attraction: the activity combines the twin loves of eating and gambling.

The day before I had visited the small but excellent Chang Foundation Museum, a private museum quietly tucked away in the basement of a high-rise building in central Taipei. What wonderful timing – there was an exhibition about a Ming dynasty explorer called Zheng He. I had seen a single model of one of his giant ships in Danshui's Maritime Museum, but here there were model boats aplenty, navigation instruments, and a wide assortment of artefacts from the period that would have been used on the boats, or carried as trade goods or tribute. There were textiles, lacquerware, metalwork, silks, Buddhist images, cloisonné, money, and even porcelain (but not too much). In sharp contrast to the exhibits at the National Palace Museum, the whole was greater than the sum of the parts. They told a story, and it was a story well worth telling.

In the autumn of 1405, the greatest armada the world had ever seen – 317 ships and over 27,000 men – set sail from Nanjing under the command of Admiral Zheng He. The pride of the fleet were gigantic "treasure ships" used to carry the most precious of the cargoes. Scholars argue about the great dimensions reported for these ships, but even estimates at the lower end suggest an astonishing length of sixty metres.

There were grain ships and water tankers to supply this floating city, troop and cavalry transports to provide firepower, and smaller oared vessels used as tugs and for transporting men and material between ships. There were also warships clad with iron armour, and armed with rockets, guns, giant crossbows, and flamethrowers, and equipped with giant claws to hold enemy ships at a distance from which they could be set alight

Between 1405 and 1433 seven great voyages were made to Southeast Asia, India and Sri Lanka, the Arabian Gulf, and East Africa. These expeditions were a means of projecting Chinese power beyond its borders, increasing the lucrative state monopoly of overseas trade, and boosting the emperor's prestige by having foreign nations send tribute and ambassadors to his court.

To lead these great voyages Yongle picked one of his most trusted high officials, a thirty-five-year-old Muslim eunuch called Ma Sanbao. His name meant "Ma of the three jewels," a Chinese play on words, the three jewels being the Buddhist trinity of Buddha, doctrines, and believers, but in vulgar terms referring to the testicles and penis. Ma was the second son of a Hui family who lived near Kunming in Yunnan Province. The Hui were a Muslim people of Mongol-Turkic blood whom the Mongol rulers had incorporated into their armies. The young boy grew up speaking both Arabic and Chinese, and listening to tales of travels far to the west from his father and grandfather, who had made an overland pilgrimage to Mecca.

During a military campaign to push the Mongols from the southwest of China, Ma, just ten years old at the time, was captured. When questioned by a Ming general about the whereabouts of a Mongol ruler, the boy answered defiantly: "He jumped in a pond." Impressed by the boy's boldness the general had him taken prisoner and made a eunuch. It was standard practice for the boys of rebel peoples to be castrated. The castration was brutal and total (all the sex organs) and death from blood loss or resulting infections was common. Ma survived and was put to work in the household of (then Prince) Yongle. By the time he was twenty-five his great intelligence, ability, and luck had seen him rise through the ranks to the head of the Imperial Household Agency. He was given command of the several thousand eunuchs in the emperor's service, and also the new name of Zheng He.

Zheng He took command of the first great fleet aged just thirty-five. By the time of his death in 1433 at the age of sixty-two – on the last and perhaps greatest of the seven voyages – he had probably travelled more widely than any other person in history. Fittingly he was buried at sea. There can be no higher praise for the man's competence than to note that the trips were largely free from adventure (blunder and misfortune by another name), and over the course of three decades of exploration there were very few military engagements. The striking thing, when comparing the Chinese explorers with the Portuguese and Spanish who set sail a generation or two later, is the relatively peaceful nature of the visits. Zheng He came bearing gifts, trade, and submission (a loose acceptance of Chinese dominance and some tribute rather than colonization) and overawed by the show of force rather than its use. The European age of discovery was an absolute bloodbath. It was a search for spices, gold, and plunder that unleashed the worst instincts for greed, coupled with the mad Crusader mentality of putting heathens to the sword.

If you compare what Europe and the Orient had to offer, it becomes obvious why the Europeans were more interested in plunder than trade. When the Portuguese explorer Vasco da Gama first visited the Indian port of Calicut in 1498 and presented the gifts he had brought – wash-basins, sugar, oil, honey, and cloth – the king laughed at them.

The Chinese treasure fleets were full of sumptuous porcelain and silks, gold, silver, and spices, which were traded for luxuries such as rubies, sapphires, gems, pearls, and carpets. Among the tribute that flowed back was an incredible assortment of wildlife: lions, leopards, zebras, ostriches, and on the fourth trip a giraffe. When the giraffe arrived in Nanjing it caused a sensation because it was thought to be a *qilin*, a mythical animal that was an auspicious omen of peace and prosperity, and thus a heavenly stamp of approval for the emperor.

Zheng He also visited Taiwan, although unintentionally. While returning from a trip to Thailand in 1430 he was driven by a storm and shipwrecked on Taiwan's southwest coast. He made friendly contact with the aborigines from whom he acquired supplies and medicinal plants.

During the time of the treasure fleet voyages, China stood at the crossroads of world history. Here was an opportunity for the largest, most powerful, most technically advanced nation in the world, to become a global power. But suddenly the voyages stopped and the country turned in on itself. Why didn't Chinese ships sail across the Pacific and colonize the Americas? Why didn't Chinese ships sail around southern Africa to Europe? There were many cultural and economic factors at play, but the immediate causes were political.

Emperor Yongle's successors were not interested in further maritime adventures, and at the imperial court the voyages became a victim of the age-old struggle between the Confucian bureaucrats and the imperial eunuchs. The latter, so often the villains of Chinese history, were the driving force behind the maritime policy and most of the fleet's generals were, like Zheng He, eunuchs.

To the more sober-minded Confucian bureaucrats these huge fleets of treasure ships represented an extravagant waste of state funds that could be better spent at home. With the relocation of the capital from Nanjing to Beijing in 1420 and the re-emergence of the Mongolian threat, imperial attention and energies were focused on the north, in particular the building of defensive walls. (The Great Wall of China as we know it is essentially a Ming-era construction.)

The Confucianists thought the Middle Kingdom needed little from the barbarian lands beyond; in their eyes, the luxury goods and tribute that flowed back only corrupted the court, and gave their rivals, the eunuchs, greater wealth and influence. The bureaucrats' opposition to Chinese internationalism was so strong that most of the archived records of Zheng He's expeditions were destroyed, and the building of large ocean-going ships was made a capital offence.

# 5

# The Shoe Man

CHINA's comparative failure to capitalize on its long superiority in science and technology is a great puzzle of world history that has not been adequately explained. I came across part of the answer in a doctor's private collection of "golden lotus" shoes in a small suburban hospital in Taipei.

Foot-binding is something of Chinese civilization's dirty little secret, and like a mad relative the family pretends doesn't exist, it's seen as something shameful and to be forgotten. Most books on Chinese culture and history make no, or only passing, reference to it.

For many Westerners, their introduction to the cruel process came from reading Jung Chang's *Wild Swans – Three Daughters of China*. The book tells the story of China's tumultuous twentieth century through the lives of three generations of women in her family. The author's grandmother had her feet bound by her mother when she was two years old. This involved bending and crushing the feet and then she "passed out repeatedly from the pain."

The binding process lasted for several years during which time she was unable to walk. Jung Chang says: "For years my grandmother lived in relentless, excruciating pain. When she pleaded with her mother to untie the bindings, her mother would weep and tell her that unbound feet would ruin her entire life, and that she was doing it for her own future happiness."

The ugly truth was that if a mother did listen to the pleas and remove the bindings the daughter would face a life of contempt, be an outcast, and in later years blame rather than thank her mother.

What kind of culture would compel mothers to cripple and torture their daughters, perpetuate the pain that they could remember so well themselves? And through a thousand years of torture where were all the great scholars and philosophers, the outrage? Where was the criticism, the resistance? There was almost nothing but complete silence until missionaries and Western ideas came into China. One remarkable exception was the novel *Flowers in the Mirror* (1828), the first ever to detail the procedure of foot-binding and show it for what it was. The author, Li Ruzhen, was a scholar who questioned the basic tenets of his Confucian education. In one episode of the novel a merchant named Lin travels to a strange world far away from China where the sex roles are reversed. Not only do the men there do the work of women but they also have to take on a feminine appearance, and so it is the men who suffer the humiliation and pain of foot-binding.

Merchant Lin is chosen by the female ruler of the country to be a "court lady" and his nightmare begins: "In due course, his feet lost much of their original shape. Blood and flesh were squeezed into a pulp and then little remained of his feet but dry bones and skin, shrunk, indeed, to a dainty size."

Before visiting Dr. Ko Chi-sheng and his collection I scoured my small private library for information on foot-binding. According to tradition, the custom began during the reign of Li Yu (961–975), the last ruler of the Southern Tang. Li was one of China's great romantic poets, but being more interested in wine, women, and song than matters of state, didn't stay too long upon the throne. He supposedly had one of his favourite consorts bandage her feet to make them pointed in order for her to dance more beautifully. This caused great excitement in the court and others followed suit. Whether the story is true or not, the practice of foot-binding definitely took hold at this time, and gradually spread from the court to the upper class to the majority of the population.

Over time small feet became synonymous with beauty, so much so that it was difficult for a woman with large feet to find a husband. The perfect foot was, according to a well-known seven-word expression, one that was: "thin, small, pointed, crooked, perfumed, soft, and symmetrical."

Bound feet also had strong sexual connotations, something that Western anti-binding campaigners were not always aware of. My favourite anecdote comes from the late nineteenth century. A missionary called Alicia Archibald, despite being a leading campaigner was ignorant of the sexual aspects and made some rather embarrassing blunders. During a lecture to five hundred college students in Hong Kong she showed them slides of bare bound feet and was perplexed as to why the boys laughed and snickered all through her presentation. At that time a man would not see a woman's naked feet until after marriage and only during sex, so the missionary's lecture was equivalent to a hall packed with Western schoolboys being shown photos of naked women.

* * *

Small feet have been a lifetime's passion for Dr. Ko, a boyish-looking forty-six-year-old surgeon and something of a Taiwanese renaissance man. He is the owner and head of Tucheng Hospital, a district chief of the Democratic Progressive Party, and a respected expert on foot-binding. On a wet afternoon he showed me into one of three rooms that house his collection; the far wall was lined with a glass cabinet holding hundreds of pairs of tiny shoes which the Chinese called "three inch golden lotuses," another wall was covered in books, and the other two by large drawers holding various items related to foot-binding.

"This will help you understand the physical process," the doctor handed me a plastic model of a foot – small, pointed, and not too unattractive – until I turned it around to see the underside, the toes bent around and embedded in the flesh of the sole. It seemed inconceivable that this could have been done to all but a few women. He quickly corrected me.

"During its peak in the Qing dynasty, it was over ninety percent. The Qing rulers, the Manchu, forbade their women to bind their feet but they accounted for no more than two percent of the population. The Manchus actually tried to stamp it out when they took power but failed, and some Manchu women even risked severe punishment to do it. The custom was so strong! Jews living in China took up the practice. Bound feet were a mark of Han Chinese, the mark of civilized people, those without were barbarians.

"It is the longest lasting and most widespread fetish custom in history. It lasted for a thousand years, and I've calculated that over that time it was done to three billion women." The doctor leaned forward toward me and repeated these last words slowly and deliberately, "Three billion women! That's exactly half the world's current population – in other words, the number of women who have had their feet bound is equal to the number of every woman on earth today, every single woman on Earth!"

Binding usually began when the girl was four and took about five years to complete. If started too late the feet would be too large and not supple enough to bend, but starting too soon carried the danger that the girl would be crippled for life and unable to walk.

Dr. Ko handed me a pot shaped like a huge donut without the hole on the bottom, "A bed pot for urinating – during this time their feet were often too painful for them to walk, even to the toilet."

And why did so many parents inflict so much pain on three billion daughters? "This is why," he answered pulling out a large plastic drawer and placing it on his lap. Inside were little human figurines about half the size of Barbie and Ken dolls but considerably naughtier – they were naked and joined together in a bizarre variety of sexual positions. "This is why," he repeated, taking out a copulating pair and holding it in front of me. The woman was using her feet in an inventive way on a man who was obviously in a state of high arousal. "This is why!" He pulled out some more dolls, this time a threesome, an equally excited man with one of the woman's tiny feet in the man's mouth.

"There were sexual reasons behind binding – fetishism and other...."

As he searched for the right word I tried to guess his thoughts. "I've heard that the vaginal muscles became more developed."

"Yes. After binding the feet, the lower legs atrophied, so when they walked," he jumped to his feet and demonstrated an exaggerated hip-swaying motion, "they used their hip muscles to move, like this, with resulting hypertrophy [enlargement] of the hip muscles," then hitting his buttocks added, "and also the perineum muscle." (The perineum is the small area between the anus and vagina.)

"When the Japanese took control of Taiwan in 1895 they outlawed foot-binding but studied it. Japanese doctors took X-rays of women with bound feet and compared them with those with normal feet. They found the skeletal structure was identical. The difference was in the muscles. Binding increased the shrinkage power of the vagina."

The price to pay for increased "shrinkage power" seemed pretty damned high. Apart from the obvious pain there were the physical limitations imposed on the women, and a corresponding increased workload for men, as the doctor went on to explain.

"The maximum distance they could walk was about three or five miles, so it shrunk their world, made them conservative, they needed care and support, needed large families. It also had an important influence on architecture – Chinese houses have a single floor, two at most, because women couldn't climb up stairs. Everything was small, villages, narrow lanes, and so on because women needed support to walk, a man's help, a rail, or a wall, or they carried umbrellas to use as walking sticks.

"The women couldn't travel. So while the West was able to explore the world, to colonize the world and send settlers out to America, Canada, South America, New Zealand and Australia, the Chinese were restricted by the both the physical and mental consequences of foot-binding. They couldn't take their women. The Chinese stayed in China. The Chinatowns you see in America, the overseas Chinese were all from Guangdong in southern China, because they generally didn't practise binding." Indeed, the Hakkas, some of the earliest settlers in Taiwan, and notable for not binding, were likewise from Guangdong.

Doctor Ko's argument had a brilliant simplicity to it – how Chinese history and culture had been restricted by bound feet. It was blindingly obvious yet I'd never heard it before. History is, of course, too complicated to attribute single causes too great a significance, yet could you have nearly half the population severely disabled, enduring years of intense pain followed with a lifetime of great discomfort, and not have that adversely affect the culture? The doctor argued his case with passion and logic. He was right – foot-binding was a central fact, not some obscure exotica, not some missionary hammer with which to slam Chinese society as sick and degenerate.

"Foot-binding was a way of controlling women. A rich man had several wives in his household, and keeping an eye on them was difficult. Binding restricted their movements, stopped them escaping and having romantic interests outside."

The doctor paused for breath and brushed his moppish hair, thick and black, away from his glasses. He was becoming increasingly intense and expressive.

"How to control two or more wives, the problem of jealousy between them?" he asked as he reached once more for the drawer with the fornicating dolls and took out a threesome so intricately interwoven I had trouble making out whose limbs were whose.

"For us, for modern people, we cannot imagine having sex with more than one woman – too incredible. But for them it was completely normal." According to his argument, small feet helped prevent jealousy, moved sex to another plane – away from the emotional and the personal and onto something physical, a rather abstract type of love.

"It was different from Western romantic love. The man's mentality was 'I don't love you, I love your feet.' The woman may not have had a beautiful body, or a pretty face, but she had small feet, and he was

57

in love with her small feet. The woman could think, 'It's not that you love me, or the other wives, you love our feet, you're playing with us.'"

I had trouble keeping up with his line of thought, and it didn't help that at the same time several people were walking past the open door and glancing in. I felt rather self-conscious of how the two of us must have looked; we were sitting half an arm's length from each other, face to face and leaning forward in a conspiratorial fashion, one holding a sexual orgy in his hands, and the other studiously taking notes.

The subject turned to the shoes themselves. These ranged in size from two to five inches, and had wooden soles and silk uppers that were embroidered in an infinite variety of designs.

"Unlike other items of clothing, you could tell where a woman came from just by looking at her shoes – they made the shoes themselves and styles varied not just between areas, but between districts within a city."

"I want to tell you a story," the doctor announced as he took a shoe from a shelf, placed a small cup inside, and cradling it in his hands, held it up before his face, "Chinese men of leisure, gentlemen, would drink together with a group of friends at a wine house. There would be hostesses, some prostitutes, to pour the drinks, chat and so on. The men played drinking games, and the loser would have to drink the cup of wine, but look –." He raised the shoe and cup to his smiling lips, half-closed his eyes in a perfect imitation of a moment's drunken bliss. "As you drink you can fondle the shoe, press it against your face, smell the shoe, mmm." He ran his fingers along the curve of the fabric and inhaled a long deep breath, "the shoes were perfumed, you could smell them, wonderful!"

"It was good to lose."

"Yes, it was very good to lose!" the doctor guffawed.

"That must have been quite exciting for a Chinese man – in today's terms something like feeling a breast," I said as I placed my right hand on my chest.

"No, no. Much better!" came his rebuke. "Women's feet were considered the most intimate part of her body, and her shoes were also very precious and intimate."

The doctor pulled out a large book of old colour erotic prints, placed it on his lap and turned the pages. "You see here, completely naked except for the feet, and here again." Copulating couple after copulating couple flashed before me in a variety of positions and places, and there were some very graphic details of private parts, but the women were always wearing their little shoes, or at least socks.

*Dr. Ko Shi-cheng, world-renowned expert on foot-binding, with a pair of "golden lotus" shoes*

"From the thousands and thousands of pictures I've looked at, I've only seen a few pictures of naked feet." He reverted to another book, an album of photos he'd taken of elderly women's naked bound feet. "Even today they feel that feet are very private and it took a lot of persuasion to get them to take off their shoes and bindings."

He opened another drawer and took out a wine cup, a tobacco holder, and a spoon, all of which were shaped like a golden lotus shoe. "See how strongly the feet imprinted upon people's minds?"

With such strong sexual connotations these items must have been rather risqué and I asked whether they would have been acceptable in public places or strictly for private use.

"This I don't know," he admitted, throwing his hands out to the sides and smiling. "Maybe they were kept secretly by a boy, and hidden from his father," he added with a hearty laugh, no doubt recalling his own secretive youth.

Dr. Ko's interest in foot-binding had sprung from a voracious appetite for reading beginning at the age of ten, and was very much a case of the sweet taste of forbidden fruit. "When I was a boy there were two things that couldn't be talked about – politics and erotic material. I was drawn towards them, had a very strong desire to learn about them. That they were prohibited subjects only increased my desire. It wasn't easy at that time, Chiang Kai-shek was in power, and Taiwan was very –" he pressed his palms down imitating a crushing weight, "very strict, repressed. The material I wanted couldn't be published or sold, and the books and magazines that I wanted were illegal. I had to use many methods to find and keep them. I had a total of three thousand books, magazines, pictures and other items. My family had no idea. The more I read the more I was drawn to foot-binding because it was such a taboo subject, and when I was eighteen I bought my first pair of shoes. Now I have one thousand pairs of shoes, and another three thousand related items."

What had started out as a few porno mags hidden under the bed had developed into what he said was the world's greatest collection of golden lotus shoes, and the curious schoolboy was now an authority, the author of three books on the subject. According to the doctor, amassing the collection hadn't required much effort or wealth. "They're not too expensive. Taiwanese don't want them – no status such as with a painting or porcelain." Despite his modesty Dr Ko has indeed gone to great lengths to build a wide-ranging collection. For example, when he found the formula for a medicine that was given to girls to make their bones softer and easier to bind, he had it formulated at a traditional Chinese pharmacy. He has also commissioned researchers to track down shoes in China.

"Many people with small private collections leave their shoes to me when they die because they know I'll take good care of them." He showed me a few examples of donated shoes, and then somehow affected by these emotional memories straightened up his back, pursed his lips, and nodded with serious intent, for a brief moment stared half-squinting to an invisible horizon before turning back to me. "I have a duty to keep them and show the world. If I don't nobody will, and it will remain hidden. Chinese people think it's something shameful and want to ignore it. And yet, it is completely compatible with Chinese culture."

I scanned the rows of shoes, and tried to elicit an anecdote or two, "There must be some interesting stories behind some of them."

"A story of tears, perhaps," he answered after a long pause. I tried again, and asked if he had any favourites.

"I'm not a collector, I'm a philosopher!" he bellowed. "I want to share my incredible ideas with the world. My ambition is to enter the women's world, the erotic world, to get into their minds. There is no description of this from history. We have history, 'his story,' but I want to tell 'her story.' I want to get into their minds. The Chinese women's world was kept in the shoe. Oh, I'm so rich. I can get into another world, a wonderful new world where no one has ever gone before. To understand China you have to get inside the shoe. The sexual life is hidden in the shoe, Chinese philosophy – kept in the shoe."

The doctor didn't agree with the established interpretation of historical male-female roles: "The idea that women were being badly treated by men is wrong. They were useless for working in the fields, and had less work to do. The women are staying at home, the men are going out to provide for them."

"The women aren't slaves then?" The doctor misheard me and thought I was calling the men slaves.

"Slaves. Yes, the men are slaves."

* * *

After two hours of talking I still hadn't heard him condemn foot-binding for the evil it was, and I pushed him for an opinion.

"Good or bad is nonsense!" he half-shouted as a flicker of anger passed across his face. "I only want to understand it, not to judge," he explained, his friendly countenance quickly restored.

Dr. Ko had been getting more and more worked up all afternoon, and now his enthusiasm and passion were threatening to boil over. He was like a fiery Southern Baptist minister, but with none of the rehearsed performance, and no concern for society's sensibilities. After decades of silence, his passion, intelligence, and pride, so long hidden, could be set free. The doctor admitted as much himself. He had kept his interest in fetishes and the sexual aspects of foot-binding a secret. "The first person I told was my wife, but only after we got married," he laughed. He had been cautious about discussing these aspects in public but no longer cared what people thought.

"I used to worry that something was wrong with me – why I was so strange – but I found that there are many other people with similar ideas," he pulled a magazine called *Body Talk* from his bookshelf and flicked through the pages, arty black and white photos of S&M; women tied to beds, wrapped in ropes and hanging from the ceiling by their feet, and then showed me another, a Japanese magazine with the oriental equivalent. "These I can't find in Chinese, have to get them from Japan and England. When I realized that people all over the world were interested I felt much better."

"A part of human nature," I conceded, rather at a loss for words.

"Yes, human nature!"

He pointed to the books of ancient erotic prints. "It's a very rich society, a sophisticated culture, that has enough time to devote so much time to leisure, to explore the possibilities of sex. There are different ways to eat, and to feel full, a simple meal, or you could have a huge banquet, with incredible dishes, wine, friends, music, violins playing. Likewise with sex, it can be just," he thrust his pelvis forward a couple of times and screwed his face into a dismissive wince of disgust, "or it can be something wonderful," he whispered with a feverish look and a flourish of his hand toward his mating dolls.

The interview had run well into overtime; I thanked the doctor for being so generous with his time, took a few photographs, and begged my leave. He gave me one of his books and accompanied me out onto the street still in a state of excitement.

I left with a new appreciation of the importance of foot-binding. It had started off as a personal fetish, had become a fad, but rather than dying out had spread and developed into a mainstream cultural phenomenon that endured for a thousand years. Many Chinese consider the Tang dynasty (618–906), and also the Song dynasty (960–1279) that followed it, to constitute a Golden Age, a time of cultural brilliance and *joie de vivre* that was never again matched. As I walked through the streets I recalled the words of French historian René Grousset, who blamed Genghis Khan's Mongol invasion in the thirteenth century: "[I]t was as if during the Mongol domination a spring had been broken in the Chinese soul ... the Chinese organism had suffered such an intense shock, had been so fatigued that as soon as the storm was over, it recoiled tightly and timorously within itself." I think Grousset would have been more accurate if he had been talking about foot-binding.

# 6
# The Dutch

A T the beginning of the seventeenth century Taiwan lay in sleepy
obscurity off China's southeastern coast, an inhospitable wilderness of forest and mountain inhabited by aborigines. It was not part
of the Chinese empire, and was neglected by China's merchants, generals, and politicians alike. China was at that time the world's largest,
richest, and most sophisticated nation. These were the last days of the
late Ming, a politically corrupt but culturally rich period of wealth and
splendour when classic works such as *The Journey to the West* and *The
Golden Lotus* were written and exquisite porcelain was produced that
became synonymous with the dynastic name Ming.

The early European explorers and merchants ignored Taiwan, too.
Although the Portuguese gave it the name *Ilha Formosa*, meaning Beautiful Island, they never actually settled there and had merely named it
while sailing past the western shores on their way to Japan.

Taiwan's isolation was very shortly to come to a dramatic end. Two
epic struggles were underway – the overthrow of the Ming dynasty in
China, and the European struggle for supremacy of the Eastern seas –
and they were to collide in Taiwan and thrust the island into the mainstream of world history.

The Ming imperial court was beset by political weakness. Internal
rebellions, famines and epidemics brought great turmoil to the nation,
and on top of the centuries-old problem of Mongol raids from the north
there was a new menace. The Manchus – fierce nomadic tribesmen
who had settled down in the northeastern frontier area of Manchuria and emerged as a powerful, unified force – began moving into the
Middle Kingdom. Of course, to conquer, and then rule, a country as
vast as China required a lot of Chinese support; and when Beijing fell
it was not to barbarians but to Chinese rebels. Most Chinese bowed to
the new Manchu dynasty (which was given the name Qing) because
it promised order out of chaos and a continuation of traditional culture. The new rulers adopted many more Chinese customs than they
imparted from Manchu culture but were strict on several points. An

edict was passed that every Chinese male was to shave his forehead and start growing a queue (a pigtail) in the Manchu fashion within ten days or face execution.

Diehard Chinese loyalists chose to fight on in hope of restoring the house of Ming. The last Ming emperor had hanged himself when Beijing fell, but there were still plenty of princes willing to take his place; it took the Manchus nearly two decades to track down and kill all the claimants to the throne. There was, however, one man who still resisted, a remarkable figure called Koxinga, who devoted his entire life to saving China from the Manchu invaders. Koxinga's mother was Japanese and his father a famous Chinese merchant-pirate who had risen from humble origins to promotion as commander in chief by the increasingly desperate Ming emperor. His son, born Zheng Chenggong, was of unusual intelligence and energy, becoming a commander at the age of twenty-two. He was given the family name of the Ming dynasty, Zhu, but this being too sacred to be spoken aloud, was called Guoxingye (meaning "Lord of the Imperial Surname"). Koxinga is a Westernized form of Guoxingye.

Although Koxinga's father went over to the enemy two years later and implored his son to do the same, Koxinga never wavered. He took charge of his father's forces and fought on against the Manchu with great success until he marched on Nanjing with an army of one hundred thousand men and was badly defeated. Koxinga was forced to retire to the southern coastal area of Fujian, from where he offered continued resistance.

Koxinga needed a new base where he could rebuild his forces. He had long had his eye on Taiwan, then under the control of the Dutch East India Company. In 1624, the same year in which Koxinga was born, the Dutch East India Company had, in the name of Holland, established a colony in southwest Taiwan. It was actually their third choice. After repeated failures to take Macau from the Portuguese, the Dutch settled on the Pescadores (Penghu Islands) in the Taiwan Strait. The islands proved to be a good vantage point from which to trade and attack rival ships. European trade in the Far East was then a three-way tussle between the Dutch, Spanish, and Portuguese, and piracy and commerce were often one and the same. Following threats from China, the Dutch decamped to southwestern Taiwan.

They founded a colony in what is now the city of Tainan, built two forts, developed agriculture and trade, and tried to convert the local aborigines to Christianity. It was a profitable colony for the Dutch East India Company. Trade consisted of exports of venison, sugar, and rattan to China, and sugar and deerskins (around fifty thousand a year) to Japan. Porcelain was shipped from China through Taiwan on to Europe. The Spanish, who were based in the Philippines, decided to get some of the action and established short-lived colonies in northern Taiwan. They built forts near Keelung and Danshui but were driven out by the Dutch.

The first Dutch missionary, the Reverend Georgius Candidius, who arrived in 1627 at the age of thirty, wrote a fascinating book entitled *A Short Account of the Island of Formosa*. It describes the life and customs of the Siraya lowland aborigines before their age-old ways were forever changed by outside influences and the tribe pushed deep into the mountains.

Siraya society, while being egalitarian to the extent that there were "no words for master and servant in their language," still fell somewhat short of being a socialist Garden of Eden. They made up for their shortage of class terminology with an over-developed headhunting vocabulary. According to Candidius, young men put little effort into anything but hunting and fighting, the latter consisting mostly of head-gathering raids. Cunning and stealth were preferred to open combat, and even carving up an old man who might be sleeping out in his fields was considered fair game. A head was a great cause for celebration and was paraded around the village by the victorious warriors as they sang "hymns and songs in honour of their gods and idols" and drank offerings of alcohol. Then the head would be taken to the "idol house," and boiled in a pot until the flesh fell off. Pigs were slaughtered and thus began feasts and celebrations that usually lasted "a whole fortnight without any interruption."

Despite being "heathens" and having a fondness for removing heads, the missionary could recognize the aborigines' virtues: "On the whole, the people of Formosa are very friendly, faithful and good-natured." He also thought they were hospitable to foreigners, respectful toward the elderly, not treacherous except in war, intelligent, and courteous.

During the time of the Dutch, the Siraya practised bizarre marriage customs. Husbands and wives lived separately and kept separate property, with the children remaining with the mother. Women were not allowed to bear children till they were over thirty-five, and any pregnancies before that were terminated. Abortion was "a practice as common here as the christening of children is amongst ourselves."

A man only moved in with his wife around the age of fifty – which probably goes a long way toward explaining Candidius' assertion that men, although only taking one wife, were "great whoremongers" who neglected "no opportunity of committing adultery." The reason behind these customs was the belief that a pregnant woman brought back luck to a man when he was hunting for animals or on a raid. Only after the man stopped being a warrior (around the age of forty), could a couple start having children.

Another missionary, Robertus Junius, who preached on the island from 1629 to 1643, relates in a letter written in 1644 how these age-old customs had changed. "We now daily see young men there not only marrying according to Christian rites, but going together into the fields, and, not only bringing children into the world, but even living together; while formerly they would rather have died than lived thus." There is no record of the old customs coming back.

Reverend Junius founded the island's first Western-style school in 1636. Reading, writing, and religious instruction were taught using both Dutch and the local tongue. Using the Roman alphabet, the missionaries developed a written script for the Siraya language.

In correspondence to the Dutch governor, Candidius expressed the need for priests to be sent out to Formosa and recommended that they should be married in order to "resist the snares of Satan" and, rather liberally for the time, thought it would be even better if the priests took local wives.

And from the sounds of it Satan had apparently set quite a few snares. "At certain times of the year the natives go about for three months in a state of perfect nudity. They declare that, if they did not go about without any covering whatever, their gods would not send them any rain, and consequently there would be no rice harvest. If any councillor [an elected village leader] meets a man transgressing this law, he has the power to take away whatever clothing the culprit may have on, and also to inflict a fine of two small garments, or two deerskins. For this reason, these councillors go and sit by the side of the roads in the morning and at night, when the people are either going to or returning from their fields, in order to see who among them may be wearing any clothing, in which case they take away the garment and fine the offender."

Candidius had personal experience of this one day when he was walking alongside some villagers returning from their fields. One man, wearing clothes and thus in breach of the clothing law, spotted a councillor. He took off his clothes and asked Candidius to carry them. The councillor tried to get the Dutchman to say whose garments they were, but the priest refused.

The Siraya as described by Candidius certainly sound like a people who knew how to enjoy themselves: "drunkenness is not considered to be a sin; for they are very fond of drinking, women as well as men; looking upon drunkenness as being but harmless joviality. Nor do they regard fornication and adultery as sins, if committed in secret; for they are a very lewd and licentious people."

Foreigners living in Taiwan today seem to be doing a pretty good job of reviving those ancient ways, and if they travelled back in time would have much more in common with the aborigines than the Dutch missionaries of yesteryear. And yet, I wonder if the good priest wasn't rather fond of the drink himself. While the local food, with the lone exception of rice, was "excessively filthy and stinking" he waxes lyrical about the local rice wine, declaring it an "exceedingly strong and deliciously flavoured beverage," and he does not seem the slightest bit put off by the fact that human spit was one of the ingredients. The greater part of the rice harvest was used to make the wine which was a staple of the local diet. It provided both food and drink; the sediment at the bottom of the jar was eaten and the clear liquid at the top drunk to "strengthen and cheer them."

I doubt if many of the Dutch lived up to the church's high standards. They established schools to evangelize the aborigines but had trouble finding decent school teachers, having to make do for the most part with ex-soldiers. In a letter to their headquarters, the authorities complained that most of the teachers "were guilty of drunkenness, fornication, and adultery; in fact, led most scandalous lives; so much so that hardly a fourth of them came up to our expectations."

Candidius said that there were no priests among the locals, only priestesses. He witnessed ceremonies where the priestesses offered sacrifices to the gods, and went into trances during which they lay like corpses upon the ground, and could not be raised from it, even by five or six people. The ceremonies culminated with a rather amazing climax: "the prophetesses climb on the roof of the temple, stand each on a corner, and again make long speeches or orations to their gods. At last they take off their garments, and appear to their gods in their nakedness, strike their entire bodies, now perfectly naked, in presence of all the people; but the greater part of the bystanders are women; who, however, are so intoxicated that they can hardly stand."

It was a rather hard act for the zealous missionary to compete against, and he admitted that the locals were not impressed by his limited powers. He was unable to perform any miracles, to make rain, or to tell the future, as could their local priestesses.

Apart from a small area around Tainan, the direct impact of the Dutch on the natives was rather small because the number of Dutch living on the island was never more than two thousand, and about half of that number were soldiers. Indirectly though, they caused major change by opening Taiwan up to the outside world and bringing in Chinese settlers (mostly males) to work the land. On arrival the settlers were given seeds, farm implements, oxen and other assistance. By the end of Dutch rule there were between forty and fifty thousand Chinese in Taiwan.

Dutch rule was both harsh and exploitative. They sought to use force and religion to subdue and civilize the aborigines, and to use them as allies. There were heavy taxes on almost everything: taxes on growing rice, trading, fishing, butchering pigs, and even hunting deer. The Chinese settlers, who transformed the plains into rice and sugarcane fields, resented not being able to own their own farms, as all land belonged to the company in the name of the Dutch crown.

A poll tax provided the catalyst for an uprising in 1652, the first Chinese anti-Western uprising in modern history. Over a period of two weeks Dutch troops and two thousand aboriginal allies slaughtered nearly six thousand poorly armed peasants. One of the leaders of the revolt was "roasted alive before a fire ... dragged behind a horse through the town, and his head was then stuck on a pole. Two of his chieftains ... were broken upon the wheel and quartered."

The following year the Dutch saw fit to beef up their defences with a second smaller fort, Fort Provintia, a short distance from the existing Fort Zeelandia. You can visit these forts today in Anping, a small port town that has been absorbed by urban sprawl into the city of Tainan. Unfortunately, it requires a vivid imagination to come away from the forts with anything but disappointment. Fort Zeelandia must have once been impressive; it was built atop raised earthen mounds on a sand spit that formed a small island, and possessed a commanding view of the ocean and coast. Rapid silting of the harbour has moved the coastline several kilometres westward, and with it the coastal view. The nearest maritime flavour is found in seafood stalls selling oyster fritters.

Sadly, the truth is that one of the most important historical sites in Taiwan is a non-event. The only parts of the original structure that remain are small sections of the wall that were built with bricks from the Dutch colony of Java, cemented in place with a mortar made from sugar, rice, and crushed oyster shell. The fort itself was devastated by typhoons, earthquakes and the ravages of time. What you see today is a modern reconstruction from the 1970s that is topped with a hideous observation tower.

If you had been at the fort on the morning of 30 April 1661, you would have had a nasty surprise. From out of the fog materialized a massive fleet of Chinese war junks and transport ships carrying about 25,000 men. It was the Ming loyalist, Koxinga. He landed his troops a little to the north, and was welcomed by the Chinese inhabitants as a liberator. The Dutch, trying to prevent the invaders from grabbing a strong foothold, threw a force of 240 men against an advance party of 4,000 Chinese troops. The Europeans soon found out they had underestimated Koxinga's men. They weren't fighting unarmed farmers this time. Musket fire was answered with a rain of arrows and such a ferocious attack that the Dutch fled in terror, some flinging their weapons aside in haste to escape. Only half the force made it back to the fort.

Koxinga gave the Dutch an ultimatum – leave now with all their goods or stay and perish. The situation for the Dutch was hopeless; there were only about 1,200 men, two vessels, and limited ammunition. Nonetheless, the answer came back in the form of a blood-red flag – the flag of war – hoisted above the castle. They would stay and fight to the end.

The Dutch abandoned Fort Provintia and concentrated all their forces in Fort Zeelandia. The Chinese attacked several times but were driven back with heavy loss of life. Koxinga, deciding to give priority to housing and feeding his troops and followers, chose to lay siege to the stronghold and wait.

A terrible fate befell the Dutch who were caught outside the fort and in the countryside. Charged with inciting the locals to revolt, the men were killed, some crucified or impaled, and the women killed, divided among the commanders, or sold off.

The Dutch held out in Fort Zeelandia for a staggering nine months before a traitor gave away valuable information, which, combined with new attacks, made their position untenable. The stubborn defenders, now reduced to just four hundred, had earned the grudging respect of Koxinga and he let them surrender on very generous terms; they could leave on their ships, and take some of their cash and possessions with them. Furthermore, they were given the honour of being allowed to leave their fort marching out fully armed, bearing banners, and with drums beating.

As Koxinga was settling into Taiwan, the Manchus, in an effort to cut him off from supplies, support, and trade on the mainland, ordered all people living within fifteen kilometres of the southern Chinese coast to move inland; this incredibly cruel policy, enforced from 1662 to 1681, reduced the population to poverty. Millions of Chinese were forced to abandon their fertile coastal fields and fishing grounds; some headed inland into the wild forests and rugged hills, while others fled across the Taiwan Strait.

The Chinese immigrants who came with Koxinga and those who followed were not just peasants and soldiers but also included artists, scholars, monks, and other learned men. As Chiang Kai-shek would do three centuries later, Koxinga implemented a wholesale transfer of Chinese culture, established martial law, and yoked the nation's inhabitants to the task of retaking the mainland.

After securing a foothold in Taiwan, Koxinga's thoughts turned to first creating a maritime empire in the region. He sent a Spanish friar as his envoy to the Philippines to demand submission and a yearly tribute from the Spanish. The response was sharp and swift: the large local Chinese population was either expelled or killed. Koxinga was preparing a military expedition to teach the Spanish a lesson and kick them out of the Philippines when he became ill and died, probably from cerebral malaria, at the age of thirty-eight. Rule passed to his son, who governed for twenty years, then to his grandson, who surrendered to the Manchus after just one year.

By 1875 the Manchu court in Beijing had sufficiently forgiven Koxinga, or rather were so desperate to propagate an example of loyalty to the emperor because they were facing imminent demise, that they ordered a shrine to be built for him in Tainan. The shrine, which is set in a garden compound with shady old trees, houses a statue of Koxinga flanked by two of his generals. It is still visited by devotees today.

\* \* \*

The thirty-eight-year period of Dutch rule, like other countries' early colonial adventures in the East, was to have beneficial consequences for Europe far beyond the simple profits of trade.

The idea that East and West are irreconcilably different, that "never the twain shall meet," is nonsense and always has been – the two met long ago and the world in which we live is a child of that union. One underplayed aspect of Western history is how much the modern industrialized world owes to Chinese science. Renowned Sinologist Joseph Needham (1900–1995) estimated that more than half of the basic inventions and discoveries upon which the modern world rested had come from China. Although this estimate is considered an overstatement reflecting Needham's own personal biases, the basic claim of the West's great debt to Chinese science is valid.

Most people know that fireworks, the compass, paper and printing were invented in China, but the list goes on and on – from mundane things one takes for granted such as wheelbarrows, matches, and playing cards, to inventions that changed the course of history like the iron plough, stirrup, and rudder. So often things thought to be quintessentially European are found to be imports, or at least local variations of something from the East. The bells that ring from church towers, for example, originated in China.

The great age of European discovery would never have taken place without Chinese nautical technology, and without the ensuing colonial empires there would not have been the flood of newfound crops, discoveries, and goods that fuelled the agricultural and industrial revolutions that transformed Europe into the powerhouse of world history.

Shipping is not usually an area of expertise associated with China, yet for all but the last few centuries its nautical technology was far superior to the West's. European ships were crude one-masted vessels without rudders, leeboards, or watertight compartments, and were fitted with ineffectual square sails. Chinese masts and sails allowed ships, by tacking, to sail into the wind. European ones couldn't. The adoption of Chinese technology, much of it via Arab sailors, particularly the development of three-masted ships, enabled the great voyages of da Gama, Magellan, and Columbus (who, partly inspired by Marco Polo's *Travels*, was actually looking for China when he accidentally found the Americas).

\* \* \*

The fascinating stories behind the transmission of the individual technologies reveal how closely humanity is bound into the same rich tapestry, and show that we have always been more of a global village than is supposed. One of the greatest gifts China gave the world was a good plough. And the transfer most likely took place in Taiwan, down near Tainan in the 1600s when the Dutch East India Company was developing the island's first intensive agriculture. Chinese immigrants, brought over for the purpose, quickly turned the fertile plains between Tainan and Chiayi into productive farmland. The Dutch introduced many fruits and vegetables – peppers, tomatoes, tobacco, lemons, mangoes, and watermelons – though these didn't become common until much later, and most land was devoted to rice and sugarcane cultivation. The Dutch must have looked on with amazement when they saw the Chinese plough slicing through the ground with ease. The plough was taken back to Holland, introduced into England by Dutch workers hired to drain an area of marshland, then spread through Europe and was carried across the Atlantic to America. The introduction of the new plough has been described as "the single most important element in the European agricultural revolution."

Hindsight has a way of diminishing the great strides in human history. We look back at things such as a good plough that now seem so obvious, but which at the time were colossal breakthroughs, and we underestimate their importance.

Before the eighteenth century European farmers laboured behind stubborn clumsy ploughs. On the other side of the world their Chinese counterparts had been using efficient iron ploughs for two thousand years. These superior ploughs had a cast-iron share (the blade that cuts through the soil) and a moldboard (a curved plate of iron, attached above the share, that turns the soil to the side and thereby greatly reduces friction on the plough). Chinese ploughs were sturdy and allowed the ploughing depth to be adjusted. European ploughs had a crude share attached to a piece of wood, couldn't be adjusted for depth, and had no moldboard. The difference in muscle power required to work the two types is staggering: Chinese farmers could plough with a single ox whereas Europeans needed a large team of oxen.

At the same time as the Chinese plough arrived in the West, several other agricultural implements and techniques were also introduced And once again, they were things that seem so simple that you would just have assumed that they had been developed as a matter of course; these included growing crops in rows and weeding them, and using a multi-tube seed drill rather than scattering seed by hand.

Another example of Chinese technological superiority that defies belief was the harnessing of horses. In fact, China was the only ancient civilization to use efficient horse harnesses. The harness employed by the ancient Greeks and Romans went around the horse's throat, thus partially choking the animal and making it impossible to pull any heavy load. The Chinese harness rested lower down the horse so the pressure was on the chest rather than the throat. It wasn't until the late seventh century that the Chinese harness found its way across the steppes of Central Asia into Europe.

The European age of chivalry, with its heavily armoured knights on horseback, would not have been possible without another Chinese invention: the stirrup, which reached Europe in the early Middle Ages (about one thousand years after it was first used in China). And it was also Chinese military inventions, namely gunpowder and guns, which brought this age to an end.

Time and time again Western history was affected by the arrival of technology that had originated in China. The late thirteenth century saw the first great wave of technology transfer, as the Middle Kingdom came under the rule of the pro-trade Mongols. Europe obtained gunpowder, guns, cast iron, printing, and descriptions of clocks.

# 7

# Amazons and Trojan Horses

URING the first century under Qing rule, Taiwan was a lawless
frontier area with weak state control, endemic violence, corrupt
officials, and a lot of lonely men. Before 1790 the Chinese authorities
prohibited women from migrating to Taiwan, and although a few broke
the rule there was still an incredible imbalance between the sexes, a
fact expressed in a saying popular at the time; "Having a wife is better
than having a god." An official visiting Dapu in Chiayi County in 1721
observed that out of 257 residents there was just one woman. Many
of the bachelors ended up marrying aboriginal women, while others
hoped to make their fortunes and then return to China to get a wife.

Because the authorities were unwilling or unable to provide protection in Taiwan's wild frontier areas, citizens usually took matters into
their own hands. Finding safety and economic advantage in numbers,
they formed religious associations, commercial guilds, or volunteer
defence corps, and groups based on a common surname, ancestral village, or dialect.

The two main types of groups were sworn brotherhoods and secret
societies – both illegal but commonplace despite government efforts
to stamp them out. Sworn brotherhoods usually involved an initiation
ceremony where oaths were pledged to help one another. They were a
natural focus for gambling and banditry (to pay for the losses). Their
code of honour, whereby any wrong inflicted on a fellow member had
to be avenged, led to frequent feuds. Secret societies were much larger
and more structured groups where membership was kept secret and
total obedience demanded. The strongest such organization was the
Heaven and Earth Society. Although its stated goal was to restore the
Ming dynasty, the society was in reality non-political and the revolts it
initiated were in reaction to government crackdowns.

Given the superstitious nature of most Chinese settlers and the
ancient concept of a leader's right to rule coming from the Mandate
of Heaven, most rebellions took place after a reassuring heavenly sign
appearing in the form of a natural disaster or some mysterious omen.

And if the gods did not comply with the necessary stamp of approval, a few could be engineered. Such was the case with one of the first serious rebellions. A man called Liu gathered a small band around him. In a ceremony that was sealed with the drinking of blood, his followers swore allegiance to his banner against the imperial government. As the preparations for war dragged on, his followers started getting cold feet and the rebellion-to-be was in serious danger of fizzling out before it had even begun.

Then, inexplicably, a bright flame appeared one night over the rebel leader's house. This continued for many nights, drawing large crowds from the village and surrounding area, while Liu, who had been nursing the fire with healthy amounts of camphor, played his part well and modestly rebuked suggestions that the phenomenon had any significance. One evening, as a large group of local elders approached Liu's house to tell him that they'd come to the conclusion that the fire was a sign that he should lead them, a flame burst out from an seemingly empty incense dish, guiding them to where more supernatural omens awaited. From a dark hole in the backyard swords and spears spewed forth, the work of Liu's friends installed at the bottom of the pit with the band's arsenal. The people flocked to Liu's banner and marched forth with the heaven-made weapons. After a brief reign of murder and pillage, the rebels were routed and Liu captured and sent to Tainan, where he was beheaded.

A major rebellion in 1721 was preceded by a large earthquake. Its leader, Zhu Yigui (Chu I-kuei), had come from Fujian as a servant of a government official. Starting with a brotherhood of fifty-two men, his army grew into the thousands; and he was able to capture the capital city of Tainan, declare himself "Emperor of Taiwan," and hold it for fifty days until an expeditionary force from the mainland regained control. The rebellion was to have serious consequences for China because the soldiers brought over to crush it took back a new method of taking opium. Previously it had been eaten or drunk. In Taiwan they found it common practice to smoke tobacco mixed with opium. The habit, which had quickly taken hold on the island, now spread to China.

* * *

From the time of the Dutch surrender at Fort Zeelandia to the opening of treaty ports in the early 1860s only a few Europeans visited Taiwan. In 1714 the Jesuit Father De Mailla, in the service of the Chinese imperial authorities, travelled extensively around the western part of the island with two Jesuit colleagues making maps, and wrote a fascinating account of his trip.

The Jesuits, an ascetic order of Catholics, had been in China since the late Ming dynasty. They were learned men, some of the best brains of Europe, who sought to convert the Confucian elite rather than start at grass-root levels. They occupied high positions: they were in charge of the Imperial Bureau of Astronomy, worked as mathematicians, painters, and advisers in engineering and cartography. One of the priests had such a close relationship with China's ruler that the emperor called him "grandpa."

Religious dogma, however, got in the way of Jesuit successes. The Pope was unhappy with the missionaries tolerating converts' continual worship of ancestors and Confucius. These ceremonies were, according to the Vatican, religious rather than civil. The Pope dispatched a representative, who had heated and fruitless discussions with Emperor Kangxi. Some Jesuits bowed to their superiors and were forced to leave, but the majority agreed to follow the Emperor's line and stayed on in China, for which they were expelled from the church.

During his trip, Father De Mailla was repelled by the aborigines semi-naked appearance, their tattooed bodies and faces, and their savage habits such as eating half-raw meat, but, was a good enough man to see that they were: "nearer to the true philosophy than a great number of the most celebrated Chinese sages. One never sees among them, even upon Chinese testimony, either cheating or quarrelling, or robbery or litigation.... Their dealings are equitable, and they are attached to each other; a man will never dare to touch anything you give him, without those who had joined in the labour partaking also of the fruits, a fact of which I have had frequent proof myself."

The aborigines were in a constant state of warfare with the encroaching Chinese, and Father De Mailla had an escort of two hundred soldiers the whole time he was surveying in the south. The priest learnt that the state of fierce enmity between the two was the result of an act of Chinese treachery that had occurred twenty years before his visit. Shortly after taking control of the western part of the island, the Chinese began searching for gold. Failure in the west prompted a party of Chinese adventurers to fit out a small boat and set sail for the wild east coast where it was said treasure abounded. The aborigines gave them a warm welcome, food, and shelter.

A week passed and the Chinese had still not found the gold and silver mines that the aborigines were reported to possess. Then by chance they saw a few gold ingots in the huts, apparently little valued by the owners. The Chinese prepared their boat for departure, invited the aborigines to a farewell feast in gratitude for the hospitality that had been shown them. They "caused these poor men to drink until they were thoroughly inebriated; and then, after massacring them to a man, they seized upon the treasures, and set sail. The chief of this atrocious expedition is still living in Formosa, without the Chinese having even dreamt of punishing his crime." News of the outrage spread amongst the tribes, and many innocent men, women, and children paid with their lives.

Father De Mailla searched for traces of Christianity and found several aborigines who could speak and read Dutch, and remnants of Christian belief and practice. There was some uncertainty due to the interpreter not knowing the language well enough, but it seemed that they didn't worship idols, instead acknowledging a God – creator of heaven and earth – and that the first man was called Adam and the first woman Eve. Before departing the priest tried as best he could to teach them all that had been forgotten over the last half century, such as how to perform the baptism ritual. He left Taiwan with a heavy heart. Here were fertile fields for missionary work but, with the island off limits to Europeans, he could do nothing more than pray for those aborigines with fading memories, and he wrote in his account that not a day passed without him "remembering these unhappy people before the altar."

\* \* \*

One of the most remarkable Taiwan travel accounts concerns the visit of a young Hungarian nobleman, Count de Benyowsky, in the late eighteenth century. His adventure started in Poland, where he had gone to fight against the Russians. He was captured and banished to the frozen wastes of Siberia. The dashing twenty-six-year-old used his charm and powers of persuasion to befriend the daughter of the governor, and was able to gain considerable freedom of movement within the prison settlement. He stormed a fort with his fellow prisoners then forced the Cossack guards to surrender their weapons by taking their families hostage. The escapees – nearly a hundred men under Benyowsky's command – seized a ship on a nearby river and set sail for home. Not being seamen they travelled into uncharted waters, suffering badly in terrible storms, and it took over three months for the ship to reach

Taiwan. Benyowsky spent three eventful weeks on the island, which he later described in his *Memoirs and Travels in Siberia, Kamtschatka, Japan, the Liukiu Islands and Formosa* (published posthumously in 1790). Benyowsky anchored off the east coast of Taiwan on August 26, 1771. His shore party ran into trouble. The ensuing armed engagement left nearly two hundred aborigines dead. Trying another bay, they got a friendly reception and came upon a Spaniard called Don Hieronimo, who had lived among the locals for about seven years. The Spaniard claimed he had fled from the Philippines after killing his wife and her lover in a fit of jealous rage. Don Hieronimo acted as interpreter for Benyowsky throughout his stay.

A small party that was sent inland to collect fresh water was attacked and three of the men were killed. Another skirmish followed. The Europeans, backed up with the ship's cannons, and the friendly tribe, who felt indebted to the foreigners for earlier killing so many of their enemies, went to extract some revenge. By the time Count de Benyowsky called a halt to the slaughter over one thousand of the enemy lay dead. He was surprised to find that among the slain and prisoners "there were a great number of women armed in the same manner as the men."

The Spaniard introduced Benyowsky to a powerful aboriginal chief called Huapo, who said his prophets had spoken of a stranger who would come to deliver them from the Chinese yoke. Huapo, with the Spaniard acting as an interpreter, made an offer: Drive the Chinese from Formosa and the chief would give him large estates and allow him to found a colony and carry out trade.

Benyowsky explained he and his men were in a hurry to return to Europe but promised to come back. He and the chief came to an agreement on the details of establishing a colony, and swore an oath. As a parting act of goodwill the European exiles helped the chief on a military campaign. Then they set sail, rounded northern Taiwan, and made for the Portuguese enclave of Macao.

Count de Benyowsky's schemes for colonizing the island came to nothing, and his energies turned to adventures in Madagascar. In 1774 he was appointed governor of Madagascar by King Louis XV of France, and two years later was promoted to the rank of general. While living in Paris, the count became a close friend of Benjamin Franklin, and in 1779 travelled to America to fight in the Revolutionary War. He returned to Madagascar, where he was killed in 1786 whilst fighting to set up his own private settlement.

Most of the Hungarian adventurer's account of Taiwan doesn't ring true. Especially suspicious are references to troops mounted on horses. According to the Jesuit Father De Mailla horses were a rarity, to the extent that the Chinese settlers rode oxen instead, which were fitted out with harnesses, bridles, and saddles in the fashion of horses; and he was much amused that the Chinese "were just as proud, when riding on these animals, as if they were mounted upon the finest horses of Europe." It's hard to imagine then, that just fifty-six years later the Count could say his Formosan ally had 250 horsemen and that "cattle, sheep, goats, and poultry, are very abundant." De Mailla had also written that not only were horses very rare, but so too were sheep and goats. Nor is there any historical evidence for female warriors.

It's likely that Benyowsky only made a brief, uneventful stopover in Taiwan. Upon reaching Macau and relating the details of his trip from Siberia to the Portuguese authorities, he made no mention of his Formosan adventures.

Perhaps the fabrications and embellishments were designed to make the place more appealing to any potential investors. There certainly wouldn't have been many back in Europe who could have called his bluff. It was an age that offered considerable opportunity for fake accounts and bogus foreign investments. With a few false descriptions of fertile lands it was possible to raise a shipload of paying colonists for some far-flung corner of the world that would turn out to be a tropical hellhole.

*　*　*

As fantastical as it is, Benyowsky's account is not the most remarkable false account of the island to make it into print. The honour of the most outlandish fake description of Taiwan ever perpetrated belongs to a young man called George Psalmanazar.

In the early years of the eighteenth century Psalmanazar was the talk of London society. Claiming to be a native of the island of Formosa, he wrote a book in Latin called *An Historical and Geographical Description of Formosa, an Island Subject to the Emperor of Japan*. It was published in 1704 to wide acclaim. Students were enrolled in his classes to learn the "Formosan" language, and large audiences turned out to his lectures to hear of the wonders of Formosa – from the horrors of human sacrifices and cannibalism, to the splendid riches of an island where; "Utensils and Dishes, are usually made of Gold and China Earth:

Their Temples and Houses are often cover'd with Gold, both in cities and Villages...."

George Psalmanazar became a minor celebrity, spoke before the Royal Geographical Society, and mixed with some of the leading men of the time. Among his many supporters was the Bishop of London, and in his latter life he counted the great English literary figure Dr. Samuel Johnson as a friend.

The perpetrator of this hoax was indeed from overseas, but rather closer than he claimed. He was, in fact, most likely from France. Most of what is known about the impostor's background comes from his autobiography (published posthumously, in keeping with his wishes). The autobiography, however, still leaves many questions unanswered, including what his real name was.

The son of French parents, Psalmanazar was born in about 1679. After attending a Jesuit school he began a theological course at university. The teenage boy had a great aptitude for learning languages, especially Latin, but found theological lessons too dull for his active mind and soon dropped out. He became a tutor to a rich family's children, until, refusing amorous advances from the lady of the house, he lost his job and decided to hit the road as a pilgrim. Psalmanazar's first assumed identity was as an Irish pilgrim on his way to Rome. He later travelled on to Germany, Holland, and Belgium, this time passing himself off as a Japanese converted to Christianity. He soon realized, though, that exotica paid better and changed to being a Japanese heathen. Psalmanazar endured terrible hardships on the road, was reduced to rags and covered with vermin, and was at various times driven from hunger to enlist in several armies.

The Frenchman's knowledge of Japan was limited to a few incomplete accounts he had heard from his Jesuit teachers. Still, he went to the trouble of forging a Japanese passport and, to bolster his disguise, made a little "bible" filled with figures of the sun, moon, and stars, and verses in a language of his own invention that he would chant to the rising and setting sun.

In 1702 Psalmanazar had a fateful encounter with William Innes, chaplain to a Scottish regiment then stationed in Holland. It was perhaps a case of requiring one con artist to recognize another; the chaplain smelt a rat and invited the "Japanese pagan" to his house. Innes asked Psalmanazar to write a passage of his language, then pretending to have lost the piece had him rewrite it. The Scotsman presented his guest with the two different copies, thereby forcing Psalmanazar to admit he was an impostor. Rather than condemn the fraud, Innes saw a chance of fame and money, and decided instead to elaborate the hoax; he had Psalmanazar baptized publicly as a Christian, named him George, and changed his supposed origin from Japan to Formosa as little was then known about the island. Henceforth Psalmanazar's story was that he had been abducted from Formosa by Jesuits and carried off to France, and although he had been threatened with the tortures of the Inquisition, he had bravely refused to become a Roman Catholic.

Innes took Psalmanazar to England, where he was warmly received, although people were surprised to see an oriental with such a fair appearance. This, he explained, was because Formosans went to such great lengths to avoid the sun. He later wrote in his *History of Formosa*:

> Altho' the Country be very hot, yet the Men in all *Formosa* are very fair, at least those who can live upon their Means.... The Men of Estates, but especially the women, are very fair; for they during the hot season, live under ground in places that are very cold; They have also Gardens and Groves in them so thick set with Trees, that the Sun cannot penetrate thro' them; ... And hence it comes to pass, that altho the *Formosans* live in a hotter Country than the English, yet they cannot so well endure heat.

Two months after arriving in London, Psalmanazar was persuaded to translate some religious texts into the supposed Formosan language. These translations were so well received that Innes prompted him to write a complete history of Formosa. The resulting work is an amazing hodgepodge of oriental exoticism, wild imagination, and religious philosophy, with a touch of Homer and a few borrowed tales from books, sailors, and priests thrown in.

The Taiwan of Psalmanazar's invention is a rich land of good government, prosperous towns, and a magnificent capital city called Xternetsa, all built upon the wealth of fertile soils and mines of gold and silver. He described a novel form of transport; rather than using coaches drawn by horses the inhabitants had "another kind of Carriage which is much more convenient, for they are carried by two Elephants or Camels, or Horses, in a thing like a Litter, called by the aborigines

*llustrations from George Psalmanazar's*
An Historical and Geographical Description of Formosa

*Norimonnos*, into which thirty or forty Men may enter." Illustrations were supplied. The book also relates how the Japanese emperor used a Trojan Horse stratagem – litters full of soldiers instead of offerings of oxen and sheep – to conquer Formosa.

After the issue of the first edition, Psalmanazar was sent to Oxford by the Bishop of London in the hope that some men could learn the language (said by Oxford dons to be grammatically logical) then travel to Formosa to convert the inhabitants.

A few people came forward to challenge Psalmanazar – especially after French and German editions were published – but their critiques were ignored. Social London wanted to lionize Psalmanazar. The impostor certainly played his part well, and gained plausibility from his moral lifestyle and apparent dislike of fame and wealth. He also benefited enormously by being such a champion of the Protestant church. Indeed, nearly half his book was taken up with attacks against the Jesuits and descriptions of his conversion to Protestantism.

When Psalmanazar returned from Oxford to London, he was surprised to find that Innes had gone to Portugal as chaplain-general to the English forces. Without the support of his co-conspirator the impostor began to lose heart as attacks against his authenticity increased. He retired from public life to spend a decade "in a course of the most shameful idleness, vanity, and extravagance." The latter included an addiction to opium, causing Psalmanazar to run up large debts, and made all the worse by various unsuccessful business ventures. After working for a time as a clerk in an army regiment, some clergymen raised money for him to return to the study of theology. He learnt Hebrew, and spent the rest of his working life writing and translating.

Long an atheist, Psalmanazar saw the light in his middle age. During an illness in 1728 he read a religious text and was converted. Thereafter he lived a pious life, and became known for his sanctity. George Psalmanazar died in 1763, aged about eighty-four, apparently carrying a sense of shame for his lies with him to the grave. He had written in his will that, "I am to this day, and shall be as long as I live, heartily sorry for, and ashamed."

# 8

# The Mariner's Graveyard

WITH the central part of Taiwan still a disaster area, the mountains off limits, and aftershocks still a daily occurrence, I decided to get as far away as I could and headed south to the beach resort of Kending, which lies at the very end of a scenic peninsula jutting into the Philippine Sea.

The southern tip of Taiwan was once a wild, inhospitable area greatly feared by sailors, as indeed was much of the island. As the European powers pried open Chinese ports to foreign trade in the mid-nineteenth century, shipping boomed and with it the notoriety of Formosa as a mariner's graveyard. The dangers at sea were formidable enough: inhospitable, uncharted, and unlit coasts with few safe anchorages; and the many typhoons and pirates. But the dangers on land were no less, and the likely reception for any shipwrecked crew was pitiful indeed: robbery, and often murder or slavery.

Between 1850 and 1869 nearly 150 foreign vessels were wrecked and lost (and that was just in the Chinese-controlled areas, which didn't include the east coast). American mariners, sailing beautiful clipper ships between China and California in those golden decades before steam, suffered heavier losses than any other nation. The situation was so bad that the U.S. government seriously considered occupying part of the island. Reports were undertaken and a proposal put to Washington to purchase land from the aborigines in order to establish a naval base. Fate intervened in the shape of the American Civil War and the idea was shelved.

Still, something had to be done, and Western governments pressured the Chinese into building a lighthouse at the southern tip of the island. The project was a joint effort between Chinese officials and the Imperial Maritime Customs (a body set up to control the treaty ports, paid for and in service to the Chinese government but staffed mostly by Britons and other Europeans).

In 1875 assistant engineer Michael Beazeley was sent to Kending to help select a site for the lighthouse and buy the land from the aborigines. The sea route from Kaohsiung, the nearest port, was considered too dangerous so he travelled overland. The survey party totalled forty-one and included Beazeley and two senior colleagues from Customs, a Mandarin, a translator, a cook, Beazeley's "boy," twenty-two chair coolies, and eight porters. The Europeans and Chinese officials were carried in sedan chairs but had to get out and walk in the more difficult stretches.

Beazeley made his trip in June, a difficult and unhealthy time of the year in which to travel because of the summer heat, drenching rain, and disease. The route took him over dirt tracks and ox-cart roads, across rivers, along beaches, through farmland and forest. It was a region in transition, a wild frontier area being absorbed into the emperor's fold, and when Beazeley made his trip Chinese soldiers had been fighting the aborigines for the past six months at a cost of nearly a thousand troops lost to cholera and typhus. Unlike most European observers, Beazeley expressed no sorrow at the passing of age-old aboriginal ways. Years later he wrote that he was happy to see that: "the blessings of Chinese civilization have supplanted the sway of the savage, who however picturesque and interesting a being he may be, is at best but a cruel and treacherous creature."

The Englishman had been out East only six months but seems to have already been suffering from a touch of "yellow fever" because there are quite a few irrelevant references to "savage women," who he described as "handsome creatures" in his otherwise rather dry stiff upper-lip account of the trip.

The survey party spent a night at a military camp with seven thousand troops, where, on the very day he arrived, "100 savages had come in during the forenoon to have their heads shaved." A shaven forehead and a queue (pigtail) were signs of submission to the Chinese emperor and all subjects were forced – on threat of death – to follow this ancient Manchu custom.

As the survey party neared the cape, aborigines, fearful that the outsiders would bring in smallpox, told them to leave. The travellers explained that they were on a mission for the emperor and pushed on regardless. The armed aborigines followed them and a standoff ensued; the survey team were surrounded by warriors with bows and arrows and some with matchlocks, but the interlopers held their nerve, called the aborigines' bluff and pressed on.

On June 24, after a week's hard slog, they reached Eluanbi, the southernmost point of Taiwan. The locals agreed to a third of their original asking price and sold the land for one hundred dollars. As the outsiders were handing out some cloth and a few beads as a sign of goodwill, the proceedings were interrupted by the arrival of warriors from a rival tribe who, having heard that money was being paid out, came looking for compensation for cattle stolen a few months previously. With the papers already signed Beazeley and the others quietly took leave, and had gone only a short distance before they heard gunfire coming from the two tribes.

* * *

I travelled to Kending with a little less style, aboard a rattling old wreck of a bus that was sucking in exhaust fumes as if it had been geared up for a mass suicide. Taiwanese music blasted out of the radio in competition with the noise of vibrating metal. At least the bus wasn't crowded – there were only eight people on board and none of them holidaymakers.

I hate travelling at peak times and avoid it like the plague, but as I looked around at my fellow passengers it struck me that there was one small downside to picking the quiet times: you don't get to meet a normal cross section of people. Because the vast majority of the population study and work such long hours and have very short holidays, there's not much chance of seeing them during weekdays. That leaves mothers with young children, old men and women, a decided lack of single young women, and the 2 percent of the population who are unemployed – which includes criminals just released from prison, drunks, and the mentally challenged. There were a couple from the last two categories on the bus, not including myself. One man was having an argument with the bus, the world, himself, invisible demons – who knows? His angry outbursts and mad eye-rolling stares were followed with the smug laughter of a spurned genius. But at least he was smart enough to see that I was a foreigner and failed to direct any abuse at me – no doubt aware that foreigners are a little crazy and there's no telling what they might do.

I think one of the reasons Kending is so popular, and perceived as being more beautiful than it really deserves to be, is that most of the drive down there is so damned ugly. The city of Kaohsiung stretches south into the countryside in a double strip of factories and shops that flanks the road, and the remaining countryside behind it is a mess of dirty fish farms. The little paddles frothing the water in the ponds reminded me of sewage-treatment works.

After an hour blue sky finally started emerging from behind the brown blanket of pollution, and at the end of a second bus ride I got dropped off at botanical gardens that sit on a hill overlooking the peninsula. I had the place practically to myself – a rare treat in Taiwan. And as I made my way to an observation tower the only sound I could hear was that of bird song echoing through the dense tropical foliage. The view from the top was stunning: thick forest canopy rolling down in waves of lush green to the shimmering blue ocean. Ancient volcanic plugs left stranded by time rose up from the forest as strangely shaped mountains. Hawks rode the thermals of late afternoon. Compared to the greyness of western Taiwan, this 360-degree scene was Kodachrome heaven – real colours, clean and vibrant, and a bright azure sky that stayed blue all the way down to the sharply drawn horizon.

Considering that it's a seaside resort, Kending's beaches are rather disappointing. Taiwanese don't seem to mind, though, because they are not big swimmers and what a lot of them call swimming is what we would call paddling. Go in over your waist without a lifejacket and there's a chance the life guards will launch a rescue. For inhabitants of a sub-tropical island a surprising majority can't swim, and even among those who can there seems to be a strange fear of drowning. According to traditional beliefs, people who have drowned become water ghosts who lie in wait at the place of death, ready to pounce and drag an unlucky victim to a watery grave. Some older people still caution against going swimming during the busiest time of the spirit calendar, the seventh month of the Chinese calendar (better known as "ghost month"), which rather inconveniently falls smack in the middle of the scorching hot weather of late summer.

Large notice boards scattered around the Kending area give warning of another possible danger – a nuclear accident at the local nuclear power station – and instructions of what to do in case of an emergency.

I rode a rented bicycle from Kending nine kilometres southeast to Eluanbi, where an old lighthouse stands guard on a grassy hillock with a commanding 270-degree sweep of the sea. The first lighthouse keeper, Englishman George Taylor, lived there from 1882 to 1887. It was an interesting but sad time to be at Eluanbi – the twilight of authentic native life, when aboriginal culture was just starting to be overwhelmed by the modern world and the old ways were coming to an end. Chinese settlers were moving in and military roads were being cut through the forests. The influx of cheap manufactured goods had already destroyed the arts of metalworking and weaving.

Taylor, like Beazeley, worked for the Imperial Maritime Customs, and had already served five years in the Chinese port city of Amoy (Xiamen). He could read Chinese, speak Taiwanese, and he learnt the Paiwan language of the local aborigines. Taylor explored the cape and developed friendly relations with the local people, among whom he moved with ease to the extent that he was even invited to an initiation ceremony for young girls about to become priestesses. We have a wonderful snapshot of those times because Taylor wrote several articles for papers and magazines.

The lighthouse was an absolute fortress, described in a Maritime Customs document as follows: The lantern "had revolving steel shutters to shield the glass in case of an attack, the lantern gallery was loop-holed for rifle fire, and carried a five-barrelled Gatling gun on gunmetal racers.... The staff usually lived in large brick bungalows, each room in the bungalows being connected with the wrought-iron fort by a bullet-proof passage."

The compound was protected by a brick wall, a twenty-foot ditch, a barbed wire fence, and armed with two Gatling guns, a mortar, and two eighteen-pounder cannon. In addition to the ordinary staff, a guard of eight men was employed under a European gunner.

* * *

Taylor liked the local people but thought them much too fond of the bottle. Drunkenness was the "great vice" of the tribe, and those who could afford liquor were "hardly ever sober." Chiefs fell into that category; according to Taylor they were "habitual drunkards," and the most powerful chief in the area was correspondingly the biggest drinker and a drunken "imbecile."

The aborigines lived in a world full of ghosts, goblins, witchcraft and omens. Although the warriors may have been fierce in battle or on the hunt, they were afraid of the dark and young men considered it "a test of courage to pass a night in the woods alone." The most dreaded of ill omens, perhaps a legacy from some epidemic, was sneezing. Should you hear a sneeze you must return home immediately. See an armadillo and you'll have bad luck, touch it and "prepare for a sudden death."

"One who has unpleasant dreams must confine himself to his house for the day. If your dog howls at night, secure the services of a priestess else there will soon be a death in the family. The crowing of a cock just

*Eluanbi lighthouse*

at sunset is an evil omen; the bird must at once be taken to where roads cross and killed."

Taylor was told of a reclusive tribe of red-haired savages who lived far away in the mountains of central Taiwan, made their own brass guns, and spoke a distinct language. The information about them was second hand and he didn't believe it, yet it gives some idea of the unexplored nature of the interior that it couldn't be entirely discounted.

Paiwan youth were free to choose their mates but still required permission from the girl's parents. The young man would take a bundle of firewood and a bucket of water and leave it in front of the house. If the parents consented to the union then they would take in the firewood and water.

Taylor says that for Paiwan men the most glorious way to die was to be gored to death while wrestling with a wounded boar. Young hunters would follow the animal to some thicket, encircle it, then tighten the ring until the animal was forced to break out. Should the animal rush in your direction you had to grab it and hold on with hands and knees, awaiting your friends to move in with knives. This was every bit as dangerous as it sounds, and injuries and deaths were a common outcome, with Taylor estimating that a quarter of the wounds proved fatal. But as he explained, "they laugh to scorn any attempt to dissuade them, saying 'Will not his name be remembered in the songs of the tribe?'"

Priestesses were seen as intermediaries between the human and spirit world, and held a high place in Paiwan society. On one occasion, before travelling with an aboriginal party on a long overland trip through the southern area, the priestesses were consulted. The signs, the women conceded, were favourable but a ceremony was needed to be absolutely safe. The band of seventeen men, "all armed to the teeth," sat in a circle. "The witches, standing in the centre, began waving bunches of reeds over us, and broke into a quick chant." The priestesses placed guava leaves in their hands, then began smearing ointment on the men's heads. Everyone received four sacred beads from the chief to ensure "invincibility." A few days into the march they came across a Chinese man who could have used a few beads – his headless corpse a grim reminder of the dangers of mountain excursions.

Perhaps Taylor's most frightening moment of the trip came at the end of a visit to a tribe that welcomed them by forcing a display of marksmanship on their guests to prove their mettle. When they arrived, there was an exchange of chants between the two groups.

*Sketch of an aborigine by Eluanbi lighthouse keeper
George Taylor, 1880s*

"Who are you of the shining muskets and jingling clothes?"

"We are princes of the blood and warriors from the great confederation of the South."

"If you are princes, you are Tipuns; if you are warriors, you can hit the mark. Prove your tale!"

"We are ready."

A small disc, three inches in diameter, was stuck on a bamboo about sixty yards away, and Taylor given the first trial. His shot blew it entirely away and the other warriors also scored hits. Having passed with flying colours a "drinking bout followed, jar after jar being emptied," then they retired to the chief's house for dinner. Following that, women came forward with betel nuts and tobacco for the men, the chief's widowed daughter showing a fancy to the lighthouse keeper in the liberal quantity of betel nuts she gave him. For manner's sake he chewed one. Later on the widow took out a half-chewed betel nut from her mouth and pressed Taylor to accept it.

The next morning the chief offered Taylor his daughter in marriage, but despite glowing testimonies as to "how many measures of rice she could pound in a day," the Englishman politely declined the offer.

* * *

Nobody offered me their daughter but I still had a great time cycling around the peninsula. I felt twelve years old again, was carried back to those golden New Zealand summer days when I would go riding through the rolling hills and along the beautiful coastline armed with binoculars and a bird-watching field guide. After a full day of exploring Kending on a bicycle I had a brainwave – ditch the plans to do some hiking in the area, buy some wheels, and ride halfway up the East Coast to Yu Shan National Park. I had checked with the authorities and learned the lower eastern areas had reopened to hikers.

The next morning I took a bus to the nearby town of Hengchun and bought a NT$3,000 (US$100) ten-speed bike. From there I rode back to Kending and once more to the lighthouse, then up the coast road on the eastern side of the peninsula through some wonderful rugged scenery of crashing waves, cliffs, and lush-green hills. The mercury was hovering in the high twenties – perfect for cycling. In the steepest sections I had to walk my bike up, then once at the crest I'd come speeding down, the sweat blasting off my body and the brakes squealing in agony. The only problem was that my bike wasn't fitted out with panniers for touring and I had to ride with my huge pack on my back. Oh well, at least it looked macho.

Although my pace was leisurely – making plenty of short stops to admire the view and check my dodgy bike chain – the funny thing was that from midday to early evening I kept running into a nerdy young couple from Taipei who were driving a large off-road vehicle along the exact same route as me. I'd first seen them at lunch sitting next to my table: two drooling love-struck honeymooners in their mid-twenties. The husband had the chubby smooth face of a teenager still waiting in vain for his first shave and was wearing glasses so thick you could've built a telescope from the glass. But walking out the restaurant, Romeo transformed into the Marlboro Man, climbed – with difficulty – into his rented four-wheel drive, and drove off with a throaty V-8 roar.

Unfortunately, the oversized four-wheel drive only accentuated how short he was, and the little cowboy actually had trouble seeing over the dashboard – likewise the doll-sized wife, who was even shorter than him, not withstanding a vertigo-inducing pair of platform shoes. Whenever they drove by me it would seem at first glance that there was nobody behind the steering wheel! The phantom jeep would pull up at a scenic spot and the honeymooners would jump out, literally, and then take turns posing alongside the vehicle while the other snapped away, and all with the urgency of a Formula One pit stop. Then they'd climb back in, drive off, and repeat the process a few hundred metres on, in a hurry to get more pictures for what was obviously going to be the holiday photo album from hell.

Every so often I had to stop and fix my jumping bike chain. What had started out as the occasional skip soon developed into a mechanic waltz; one revolution of the pedal, two, and then on three it would skip, rattle, and I'd be pedalling air for a few seconds until the chain once more caught a sprocket, then one again, two and so on. And just before dusk the waltz was interrupted every now and again by some mad techno-grunge and I was worried my two-day-old piece of Taiwanese junk was dying on me.

As dusk fell I found a wonderful campsite past a line of cliffs in a hollow among some sand dunes just forty metres from the shoreline. It was an epic setting heightened by the knowledge that beyond the horizon lay nothing but thousands of miles of empty ocean. Buffaloes, collared with tinkling bamboo bells, grazed on a hill behind me. A couple of locals fishing from the shore pulled in their lines and wandered off home, overtaking a wizened old woman carrying a haystack-sized load of driftwood.

From atop a sand dune I sat watching the last colours of dusk drain away until the sea turned black and the stars came out. I retired to my tent, lit candles, and tuned into the BBC World Service on my short-wave radio to find that a military coup in Pakistan had interrupted regular programming. Cooling salt-laden showers brought welcome relief from the heat. My bedtime lullaby of large waves pounding the shore, rather than being relaxing, set me to thinking about earthquakes again and the safety of my campsite. How strong would an offshore quake need to be to generate a tsunami big enough to wipe me out?

I found calming distraction in my backpack: a few cans and some well-thumbed photocopies from my favourite book on Taiwan's wild frontier days, *Pioneering in Formosa – Recollections of Adventures among Mandarins, Wreckers, and Head-hunting Savages*, by W.A. Pickering.

# 9

# Days of High Adventure

PUBLISHED in 1898 but describing adventures that took place in the 1860s, *Pioneering in Formosa* is a romantic story of the East straight out of the pages of Joseph Conrad, a beautiful book that makes you wish you were living in more adventurous times, and the inspiration for me to write this book.

It sounds a bit pretentious to describe books as "life-changing" but *Pioneering in Formosa*, and to a lesser extent MacKay's *From Far Formosa*, are a major reason I'm still in Taiwan. It was only after reading about Pickering's exploits that I decided Taiwan's history and landscapes were worth exploring, that I'd wasted time, and should stay longer.

I was hooked from the first line of the first chapter: "In the year 1862 I was third mate on a Liverpool tea-clipper lying off Pagoda Island, in the river Min, some nine miles below the City of Foochow." What names! Pickering had gone to sea at the age of sixteen, and now, six years later, was an experienced sailor ready for a change. He had come to the conclusion that a sailor's life was "but a dog's life even at best. But, more than this, five or six years' voyaging between the many Ports of Burmah, Siam, China, and the Malay Archipelago had fascinated me with the glamour of the Orient, and I was eagerly longing for some opportunity to present itself which would open out for me a prosperous career amongst the people of the Far East."

Fortune smiled on him in the form of a chance encounter with an old Scottish shipmate from his apprentice days, an old salt called Johnson, who possessed a strong "devotion to the national beverage" and an inexhaustible supply of stories. Pickering recalled how he and the other apprentices "would listen breathlessly while he spun interminable yarns of adventure among South Sea cannibals, of revolutions in South America," and other tales from the far-flung corners of the earth.

Old Johnson convinced Pickering to come ashore and got him a job in the Chinese Imperial Maritime Customs service (which Beazeley and Taylor were to later join). Following the Scotsman's advice to master the language as quickly as possible, Pickering used every spare moment to pick up the local Fujian language and spent a quarter of his salary to hire a native instructor to teach him Mandarin Chinese. His hard work and natural ability for languages soon had him speaking both, and he was duly rewarded with a posting to Taiwan, where custom houses were being set up.

The first foreign commercial presence in Taiwan dates back to 1858, when two Hong Kong firms (primarily opium dealers) Jardine Matheson & Co. and Dent and Co. began buying camphor. They operated illegally for a few years, the foreigners initially living on heavily armed receiving ships moored at the ports, then later set up representatives on the island after the Treaty of Tientsin (Tianjin) opened four of Taiwan's ports to trade: Danshui, Anping, Kaohsiung, and Keelung. The main import was opium, and exports consisted mostly of local agricultural products such as sugar, rice, and sesame oil. By 1866 there were twenty-three British citizens resident in Taiwan.

* * *

Pickering first lived in Kaohsiung, from 1863 to 1865. Then, at the young age of twenty-five, he was put in charge of customs in Anping, the port for the city of Tainan and a place he described as a "squalid little fishing village." In 1867 he quit that job to work for a European trading firm. Pickering took every opportunity to go exploring and spent seven eventful years in Taiwan, being personally involved in many of the historic moments of that eventful decade. He was invalided home at the end of 1870.

In Pickering's day the coast around Kending was extremely dangerous and "woeful indeed was the fate of any mariner who might chance to be wrecked upon this inhospitable shore. The Koaluts, [a subgroup of the Paiwan] a savage tribe, would unfailingly make short work of him, for the sake of preserving his skull for a trophy."

The Chinese-controlled west coast of the island was little better. "Cruel were the tender mercies of the Chinese fisher-folk, even amongst the law-abiding population scattered along the sea-coast between Taiwanfoo [Tainan] and Takao [Kaohsiung]. Further north, the wild and lawless settlers cultivated wrecking as a profession," and any vessels unlucky enough to be stranded upon the sand banks near their villages were plundered.

The two most dreaded parts of the west coast were near two pirate villages; one in the north near the present-day Taoyuan International Airport, and the other in the south, a village known as Kok-si-kong a mere six miles north of Tainan. That you could find pirates so close to the capital shows the weakness of the Chinese government at that time. Late in the summer of 1866 a British barque was driven ashore at Kok-si-kong by a typhoon. As the ship floundered, hundreds of villagers armed with long knives boarded it, began plundering, stripped the ship, and then turned their attention to the crew, who were left barefoot and naked. To add insult to injury the sailors "were obliged to promise to pay one of the pirates $600 for showing them the way" to Tainan, just a few miles away.

The Chinese authorities did nothing. In fact, they sometimes encouraged violence against the foreign community. The local officials had been put out by the establishment of the Customs service, as it reduced their opportunities for graft. Though staffed by British personnel, the service worked efficiently and honestly for its employer, the Chinese emperor.

One day about two dozen Europeans, almost totally naked, were brought to Pickering's office in Tainan. They had been wrecked and stripped of everything, and had spent the night covered with sand to keep them warm. The next day they had walked to a small town, where a kind local magistrate gave them food, a small sum of money, rice bags for makeshift clothing, and a guide to take them to the European's house at Tainan. As they were walking back to civilization dressed in sacks they passed through a coastal village where they were robbed of everything, including their new garments.

Early in 1867 an American ship, the *Rover*, hit a rock off the southern tip of the island and sank. The captain, his wife, officers, and crew took to the lifeboats and managed to reach the shore at Kending. All but two – a Chinese cook and steward – were murdered by aborigines.

Pickering was called upon to act as an interpreter for a punitive American expedition. He went ashore at the scene of the massacre with a force of 180 blue-jackets and marines, and accompanied a scouting party into the thick jungle. Unseen warriors opened fire but did little damage with their ancient matchlocks – with one notable exception. The expedition leader, Commander Mackenzie, was shot through the heart by a chance bullet. Unable to find any village, the marines marched back to their boats and sailed away with the intention of returning in the dry season when the jungle could be burned off.

Pickering made another trip down to Kending before then, during the southwest monsoon; this was the summer rainy season and his least busy time of the year. Once again his linguistic skills were put to use interpreting, this time for an American looking to find and retrieve the remains of the captain's wife from the *Rover*. Pickering not only managed to buy the bones but succeeding in rescuing two dozen shipwrecked Spanish sailors.

On his way back from the cape he ran into a group of high officials and the American consul, General Le Gendre, at the head of a large Chinese army on its way to punish the Koaluts. The local Chinese settlers were terrified by the approach of their own soldiers knowing that they would strip the countryside "worse than locusts" and after a few skirmishes would retreat to leave the settlers to suffer revenge from the aborigines. Pickering helped persuade the commander-in-chief that the local Chinese settlers, whom the aborigines depended upon for supplies of guns, ammunition, and salt, would do everything in their power to bring the Koaluts to heel and that the use of force would be counterproductive.

With Pickering and the great chief Tok-e-tok becoming sworn brothers by the mixing of blood, the negotiations got off to a good start, and the conditions of a treaty were soon agreed to. Getting the aborigines to actually physically sign the treaty proved rather more difficult because they had drunk themselves to a state of unconsciousness thanks to the generosity of the Chinese settlers who "in their joy at thus escaping from the ravages of their own troops, had brought quantities of rice whisky, in which the savages indulged to their hearts' content."

It was during this lull that Pickering, one of five to sign the treaty, felt it necessary to preserve European prestige upon which the delicate negotiations relied. He heard from some of the locals that General Le Gendre's cook from Amoy (Xiamen) had been casting doubts on him.

"Pi-ki-ling," one of them said, "we always thought you a great man amongst the barbarians; we understood that your words had weight and power. But that Chinaman over there, the great general's man, he says you are no account at all!"

"Yes, indeed," broke in a another, "he says that over in Amoy, such as you barbarians are just kicked about the streets."

"Come and see," Pickering told the doubting locals as he strode over to the cook and called the frightened man out. "Make room," he shouted at the gathering crowd, "Come along, brothers, and see; I will show you how the red-haired barbarians are kicked in Amoy."

Pickering took the "craven cook by the pigtail, and kicked him energetically round the circle, and round again, giving him a little lesson to respect barbarians in future days."

*William A. Pickering, 1869*

The Englishman, thinking that the sooner the treaty was signed the better, hatched a scheme with General Le Gendre to rouse the drunken aborigines back to the world of the living. The general had fought through the entire American Civil War and was "covered with honourable wounds; above all, he wore a glass eye." Pickering addressed the aborigines, telling them of the general's growing impatience and warned them that he was no ordinary man, definitely not someone you wanted to anger. At the right moment, the general made a great show of indignation; he shouted, stamped his feet, then took out his eye and placed it on a table before him. "The savages were absolutely dumbfounded. They gave us very little more trouble, and the treaty was signed forthwith."

\* \* \*

I was up early to a golden dawn and rode back to the shop in Hengchun where I had bought my bike. Rather than double-back along the coast I took an inland road that went through a few small villages and over some hills. Children, waiting by the side of the road for the school bus, would take a few seconds to get over the surprise of seeing a foreigner, and by the time they had mustered enough courage to shout a belated, "How are you?" I'd already be forty metres down the road.

My bike was quickly developing a schizophrenic personality and couldn't make up its mind whether it was working or not. It would run perfectly for a while then inexplicably start frothing at the mouth. As I neared the bike shop it was on its very best behaviour forcing me into the ridiculous situation of having to ride around the small town in circles for half an hour trying to cajole my chain and gears into failure. I finally managing to tweak a problem from the chain and made straight for the shop.

The bicycle shop owner, after recovering from the shock of seeing me return and the possibility that I might be back to get a refund, performed the cycling equivalent of turning a computer on and off – throwing a bit of oil at the moving parts, and tightening a few things. It helped a little, but the bicycle retained its idiosyncrasies to the end. Nevertheless it was to stand up to the thrashing I gave it pretty well and succeeded in limping its way to the finish line up in Yu Shan National Park.

There were still a few hundred kilometres of cycling before that, though; and now finding myself on the wrong side of the island, I rode north before tackling the road over the mountains to the East Coast.

As I was grinding my bike up a steep bend, a farmer behind the wheel of a pickup stopped ahead of me. "Do you want a ride?" he asked. The kind man meant well enough but he obviously wasn't familiar with the code of the long-distance cyclist – that stubborn will to keep going, the satisfaction of conquering the mountains with your own muscle and sweat, and the heightened appreciation of the natural world around you that comes with the slower pace and expenditure of effort. Neither was I. My bike and I were in the pickup quicker than lightning. The tinge of guilt for "cheating" was more than compensated by the luxury of having my butt resting on a seat bigger than the size of a shoe.

The roads on the east coast were ideal for cycling: fresh air and magnificent blue ocean. At least that's how it looked from the cab of the speeding vehicle. And I confirmed it a little later when my truck ride came to an end and I was once more relying on pedal power. People were very friendly and encouraging; grinning motorists, farmers, and roadside vendors waved, shouted greetings, or gave encouraging thumbs up.

By the second afternoon I'd made my way up the valley road that leaves the coast near Taitung to the small town of Yuli. On I rode through the brilliant green fields of paddy rice squeezed between mountains toward the eastern side of Yu Shan National Park. Popping into the park visitor centre to pick up a map, I got a rude surprise; "Sorry, the park is closed," a park ranger informed me. I stood there exhausted in a state of disbelief, sweat running down sunburnt limbs and creased forehead, my leg muscles – unaware I'd stopped cycling – vibrating madly the whole time. Closed? One of my Taiwanese friends had called several offices to make sure it was open, so this bad news was completely unexpected. I felt like crying.

"I was told this side of the park was open. I've cycled for days to get here," I pleaded, "Can't I just go into the park a short distance?"

The staff conferred in a circle of grim looks and low murmurs. "It's impossible. There's a suspension bridge at the start of the park that may be unsafe," was their consensus. Nearly a month after the quake and they hadn't checked a bridge just half a dozen kilometres up the road! I took my bike and rode and walked up the steep winding road into the park but camped before the bridge, in a wild spot overlooking a sheer drop hundreds of feet to a river below.

The next morning I rode back to Yuli in the rain. After the disappointment of not being able to hike, my previous enthusiasm for cycling had evaporated like a cold lager on a hot summer's day. I packed my bike on a freight train and sent it back home, and I continued up the coast to the town of Hualien, gateway to Taroko Gorge.

* * *

Taroko National Park, established in 1986 as the third of the island's national parks, stretches from the sea to mountain ranges that include twenty-seven peaks above three thousand metres. Taroko Gorge, the heart of the park, is considered Taiwan's premier natural tourist attraction. The Cross-Island Highway, which links Taichung and Hualien, cuts through the gorge, but this was still closed due to earthquake damage, with the exception of a skeleton bus service running up the eighteen kilometres from Taroko to Tianxiang. The highway was built by mainland veterans at a cost of 450 lives: completed in 1960, this engineering feat is almost as impressive as the scenery, and a lasting memorial to the sacrifice of its builders.

I decided to walk up the road. Man's touch, so often intrusive and ugly, was here something of a wonder. One section known as "The Tunnel of Nine Turns" was especially impressive, cutting a zigzag path through solid walls of marble. You step from a sweeping panorama of mountains and river gorge into the monastic coolness and dark of tunnels, quiet save for dripping water, then move into half-tunnels whose open sides reveal a precipitous drop to the raging Liwu River below, and vertical cliffs overhead. Almost the entire first eighteen kilometres of the road is perched in a similarly precarious situation, and any earthquake could bring a mountainside of overhanging rock, or the very ground you're standing on, crashing down. The dangers are very real. A German tourist was once walking along a precipitous mountain trail when landslides fore and aft left him stranded on the trail for days. Luckily he was rescued after being spotted by a Japanese tourist scanning the scenery with a pair of binoculars.

My most exhilarating moment came, not from camping in a secluded area a stone's throw from a cliff, nor from hiking narrow trails in the area, but on a bus trip down to Hualien. The earthquake and continuing aftershocks (or perhaps the bus driver) had frightened off tourists, and there was only one other passenger: a middle-aged Japanese teacher from Okinawa. The driver was a really friendly guy, but his speech disorder and facial er ... irregularities – bulging eyes and over-keen lower jaw – didn't inspire confidence. On our way down the gorge road he kept turning around to talk to us and the bus would lurch so far over to the side that I couldn't see the road anymore, just the river hundreds of feet below.

*Taroko Gorge*

It was a beautiful ride notwithstanding the white knuckles, and I'll resist the temptation to turn it into that crappy little standard of travel writing: "the dangerous mountain ride episode with kamikaze driver." Of course, like all the other authors, I made it or you wouldn't be reading this book. But at the time the safe outcome wasn't guaranteed. Buses not infrequently do go flying off mountain roads.

What a relief it was to reach flat land! And it was nice to have my opinion of the driver confirmed by a third passenger, an old man who boarded the bus. With his long white beard and old-fashioned clothes, the old man looked like he'd walked straight out of a Hong Kong kung fu movie. Before long he was shouting at the driver, calling him an idiot for failing to pick him up on a few previous occasions, and it came to a head as the old man got off the bus. The wiry old veteran brandished his walking stick and brought it down on the dashboard. Thwack! The driver grabbed his umbrella, fended off a few blows, wrestled the old man out, then drove on, quickly forgetting about the incident, and was back to his chatty carefree self in a few moments. Just another day at the office.

*The Qingshui cliffs, near Taroko Gorge, eastern Taiwan*

# 10
# Culture Shock

I HAD been in Taiwan for only a week when a strange rash-cum-sore started growing on my left leg. It didn't help my peace of mind that the news had been full of stories about flesh-eating bacteria; healthy people walking around fine one day, the next amputee-bait. The sore exploded all over my lower leg, and when I showed my boss, Mr. Young, he insisted on taking me to a doctor straight away. His father had been a surgeon and having trained as a dentist himself he knew something of the medical profession. Sensing my apprehension about where he was driving me, Mr. Young sought to ease my fears.

"Don't worry, I know this doctor, he's an expert in treating skin diseases. He's treating my mother at the moment."

"Is he a Western or Chinese trained doctor?" I asked.

"Chinese. Chinese medicine is good," he said, going into the merits of the ancient art, and should've stopped while he had me convinced. Instead, he skewed off into the realms of quackery.

"Some doctors don't even need to use medicine."

"Then what do they use?"

"Words. They say special words," he answered, the straight delivery showing me that he wasn't joking. I choked on a nervous laugh and resisted making any sceptical comments. Unbelievable – an educated man and a strict Buddhist who believed in voodoo. I was being taken to a doctor by a man who believed in witch doctors and voodoo!

The doctor's clinic was simply the ground floor of his house, the consulting room a couple of stools at the front in view of the street. The doctor, an old balding man, shuffled out in flip flops and pyjama-like cotton baggies. He took one look, "Too hairy!" The barbarian had to go home, cut and shave the hair, then return.

Half an hour later I was sitting on a stool, the doctor applying a herbal ointment to my sores, which he had diagnosed as "snake skin," when I noticed a small stuffed deer of great antiquity perched on a tall medicine cabinet. The hair was patchy and dull, worn thin by the passage of seasons, and I guessed it had been handed down from generation to generation so many times they had lost count. Mr. Young explained that the deer was in fact the clinic emblem. I asked about its age. "About fifteen," the doctor answered! Oh my God! If he was unable to preserve a lousy deer skin, how about my leg? Why would you have such a sorry excuse of a carcass on display in a clinic? I regretted not having insisted on going to a proper doctor. After my leg was greased and bandaged, the doctor turned to grinding up some medicinal powder with a pestle and mortar. The resulting elixir was measured out into dosages and placed on little squares of paper spread out over a counter. Mr. Young was watching at the time and made some chance comment about the barbarian being very big, so the doctor suddenly decided to double the dosage! The little pieces of paper were folded into triangle parcels and put in a plastic bag.

"No names or amounts, no instructions?" I asked incredulous.

"It's the Chinese way – doctors don't want to give away their secret recipes," he explained. Thankfully, the recipe included antibiotics and I made a timely recovery.

\* \* \*

My first few years in Dounan certainly gave me an insight into small-town life Taiwanese style. Too much insight sometimes! I remember a glorious Sunday afternoon when one of my adult students – in a not untypical display of Taiwanese generosity and concern for foreigners – gave me his surplus 24-inch television and video player, and helped me sign up for a membership at a local video rental store. The promised land of movies (in English) awaited. I was the only Westerner in town so was often a little starved for conversation and the chance to hear real English. Another six months and I'd have been speaking to invisible friends, or worse – trying to improve my Chinese!

Taiwan only has one English-language radio station, ICRT, but the reception in my area is terrible, squeezed out by pirate Taiwanese stations playing home-karaoke and taxi driver call-in talk shows. I did have a television set, well, of sorts. It was a tiny antique hybrid caught in no-man's land between colour and black and white, and it just had the three local channels serving up a never-ending monotony of soap operas, historical (kung fu) dramas, and mindless variety shows, only broken by commercials for cell phones, scooters and breast enlargement.

Now that I had a video player I could actually watch something half-worthwhile. No more television deprivation. My first video was *Last of the Mohicans* and it sprang to life out of the TV set with a vividness that shocked me. But the smile soon fell from my face. What was that sound? "Ding, ding, ding...." The noise was not ear-splitting, just a quiet but sanity-destroying metallic ping that kept ringing in my ears. Oh no! My video recorder! I put an ear to it but couldn't pinpoint the source. Talk about surround stereo sound – the metallic clink was all around the room, and inside my head like some evil Chinese water torture. I turned up the volume to drown it out, which helped for a while, until the "ding, ding, ding" penetrated through it. When I turned the TV and video off, the sound still rang in my ears. I turned them on and off countless times but I couldn't shake the noise.

Disappointed and irritated, I stepped outside to clear my head. The noise followed me out and became louder. Then I saw the reason – it was coming from a group of monks set up in a makeshift funeral tent in an alley next to the school. They were striking small bells, and they continued to do so, often accompanied by chanting, through the night, and the next day, and the next, until a week of mourning had passed.

In *Harmony in Conflict*, the long-time Taiwan resident Richard Hartzell offers some advice for foreigners who can't handle the noise of funerals: "ear-plugs are generally the only answer, short of moving into a hotel a few blocks (or a few kilometers) away for the duration. One is therefore always advised to keep note of interesting and low-priced hotels in one's not too distant vicinity, where a room can be rented upon need."

During that week my bathroom became the official funeral bathroom, as I found out one afternoon when some of the neighbour's relatives, whom I'd never seen before, came walking up the stairs to my room. Apparently, they were prohibited by custom from making a flame in a house containing a dead body, and because hot water comes from gas-fired heaters that meant no hot showers. To be precise, it meant no hot showers in their place – next door in mine was okay.

It's standard practice to keep the corpse in the house, but the length of time depends on the feng shui master's choice of an auspicious day for a funeral and it could be a week, a month, or even longer. At least it's for a shorter period than it used to be. The first European to write an account of burial practices in Taiwan was the Dutch missionary Candidius. In his time the local aborigines put the dead body near a fire, roasted it dry over nine days while a funeral feast involving dancing and drinking was underway. The corpse was placed in high scaffolding for three years until it had dried thoroughly, then taken down, and after a feast, it was buried under the house.

Another of my introductions to a facet of the local culture also started with a strange noise. I was woken by the sound of clanging metal and loud voices from the street below my room at the ungodly hour of eight o'clock. Well, it was early enough considering the time I'd gone to bed the night before. The beauty of starting work in the late afternoon is that regardless of how much you drink at night it's impossible – apart from the unlikely event of going into an alcohol-induced coma – to not get up in time. Anyway, I opened the curtains, and peering bleary-eyed over the balcony, saw a team of workers erecting an arched iron framework across the small street below. They then covered the frame with a large tarpaulin. Strange. Some sort of political rally I guessed. Electioneering was underway at the time, and there were many small trucks crawling the streets with loudspeakers blasting out recorded messages at ear-splitting volume.

I found out from Mr. Young that all the activity was actually for a wedding reception for the household three doors along and that I was invited, despite the fact that I didn't know the couple or their families.

Chinese weddings proceed based on the theory that bigger is better. The wedding caterers began preparing the food in huge pots and pans on the roadside. A little later three dozen round tables were placed under the canopy, covered with plastic tablecloths, and set with plastic bowls, disposable chopsticks, and small plastic cups. Ten short little metal stools (ubiquitous in Taiwan's cheap restaurants because the discomfort ensures a quick turnover of customers) were placed at each table. Hordes of guests arrived at around twelve o'clock, handed over red envelopes containing money, signed a silk cloth, congratulated the newlyweds, and wolfed down the food. The formal dress of the wedding party cut a bizarre contrast with the setting: stools on a road, plastic dishes, and the caterers who were serving the food dressed in aprons, farming overalls and gumboots. Because most people were fitting the wedding into their lunch hour, there wasn't any time for pleasantries and it was pretty much a case of trying to get your money's worth by wolfing down as much of the MSG-laden food as possible.

I made some comment to Mrs. Young about the incredible number of guests – at least two hundred – and she explained it was actually a "small" wedding. "There aren't many tables – other weddings have four hundred or more guests," and lowering her voice in a conspiratorial tone explained, "That family follows a special religion, Yiguandao, they're vegetarians, and nobody likes to go to a vegetarian wedding."

Perhaps the strangest thing I have ever seen in Taiwan was the noisy double act of a wedding and funeral held at exactly the same hour on the same day, and once again it was small-town street theatre with no better view than my balcony. These two groups, unrelated except for having both chosen an auspicious day, were only separated by twenty metres, each pulling out all the stops to make more noise than the other. The funeral was the full, spare-no-expense rent-a-monk package complete with chanting brethren in Ku Klux Klan robes, bonfires of ghost money, a brass band, a massive convoy of karaoke trucks, and a professional wailer (a woman, hooked up to a microphone and speakers, whose job it was to cry and lament the passing of the old man, unrestrained by the fact that she'd never met him). A little down the road, the wedding hit back with the noise of hundreds of guests, and a singer and musicians performing on the back of a truck fitted out with a monstrous stereo system.

Chinese and Taiwanese love noise and have a word, *renao*, (literally "hot and noisy") that means lively, bustling with noise and excitement, and by implication, fun. It's actually a term of approval. Taiwanese like a carnival atmosphere, so if something is *renao* then it's good. Street markets, weddings, and religious parades are usually *renao*. That's one of the reasons firecrackers are so popular and are used at any auspicious occasions, such as weddings, temple festivals, and opening ceremonies.

Chinese New Year, by far the most important holiday of the year, is actually partly founded on the celebration of noise. A long, long time ago in ancient China a mythical beast called a *nian* would attack villages on New Year's Eve. Over the years, people eventually discovered that the beast was afraid of the colour red, fire, and loud noises, and ever since then Chinese have been letting off firecrackers.

For me personally, Chinese New Year brings a welcome reprieve from noise because it is considered unlucky to sweep the floor during the first five days of the New Year as that might sweep all the good luck (i.e. wealth) out of the house. And that means – oh, mercy of mercies – that Mrs. Su, the cleaning lady, doesn't go on her nightmarish daily cleaning sprees, and I can actually sleep in. On practically every other day of the year she comes a-cleaning. Her approach is signalled by the ominous "jingle jangle" of a thick wad of keys hanging from her belt;

the clang of metal is a cross between cowboy spurs and the chain mail of a knight going into battle, and always reminds me of Bob Dylan's line in Tambourine Man: "In the jingle jangle morning I'll come following you." Cleaning the school is more than her hobby – it's a mad on-a-mission-from-God obsession that is as much exorcism as cleaning. Whether mopping, dusting, throwing furniture or belching, it is always done at maximum volume in an apparent attempt to frighten off evil spirits and ghosts. Sunday morning is not sacred. Neither Christmas day nor New Year's Day – and the first sound of the millennium I heard was her rattling her way up the stairwell with an array of throat clearing sounds and kung fu broom strokes against the metal stair railings.

Another *renao* activity is eating out with friends: this often involves a large group of noisy diners toasting one another and playing finger drinking games, the sounds of children playing, fighting, and crying, and the background noise from other diners and the kitchen. All this "hot noise" is part of the fun atmosphere, and even if they don't like it, Taiwanese are tolerant or desensitized enough to ignore it.

The way people eat tells you a lot about their culture and attitudes to life. The most usual Chinese greeting, "Have you eaten your fill?" accurately shows where their priorities lie. Eating out is more of a group activity than in the West, weddings being one obvious example, and there are numerous banquets, some for business where the focus is on networking and gaining face, and others for a mixture of pleasure and obligation.

Family and restaurant meals are eaten from communal dishes placed in the centre of the table; because of this, there's always room for another person, and as the food doesn't take long to cook and isn't fixed into set portions, a few unexpected guests don't cause too much trouble. By comparison, the Western custom of eating individual portions looks rather anti-social.

The second-worst thing about banquets is the excessive "polite speech," which, for Westerners fresh off the plane, borders on sycophancy and dishonesty. According to Chinese ideas of politeness, a direct refusal, such as an unambiguous, "Sorry, I can't. I'm too busy," in response to an invitation is rude because the person inviting will lose face. The proper reply, even if you have no intention of going, is, "Yes, I will come," or at worst, "Yes, I'll try my best." Diners suck up to each other with polite toasts, compliments, and vague promises. For example, if you were making polite conversation and mentioned that you wanted to learn the local language, Mr. Wang might say that he'll teach you. It doesn't mean he's going to teach you – it's just a nice thing to say, gains both of you some face at the table, and you'll likely hear nothing more about it. As long as there is no intent to cheat or harm, lying is considered acceptable, and often preferable to the truth.

The worst thing about banquets is being dragged off to a KTV at the end. Unless you like the idea of being in a small box-like room watching schmaltzy music videos and listening to lousy singing amplified through stereo equipment, it is well worth trying to fake a medical condition.

KTV is an all-encompassing entertainment activity, popular across all age and social groups. It comes in many forms: from stereos and televisions with built-in karaoke for home use, to cheap KTV parlours with simple cubicle rooms, to plush ones in up-market hotels. Last but not least are the sleazy places that double as pick-up joints for prostitutes.

KTV stands for karaoke television, "karaoke" being a Japanese term that translates directly as "an orchestra without instruments" but which involves a microphone hooked up to a video and stereo. Each song has a video with lyrics at the bottom of the screen, and you sing along to the taped music.

The popularity of KTVs is a reflection of how few opportunities there are for recreation. Something as simple as going for a jog, a bike ride or a simple stroll loses all its appeal when you have to negotiate roads jammed with traffic, sidewalks crammed with scooters, building sites, and piles of trash. With polluted air and uncomfortably hot weather for much of the year, it is little wonder most people choose indoor options. Sports, especially outdoor ones, are unpopular and very few people follow them, let alone participate. Baseball is the national sport, but its popularity has fallen in the wake of scandals involving gambling and thrown games.

# 11

# Gods and Ghosts

A POPULAR dish during the winter months is *huoguo*, literally "fire pot" but better translated as "hot pot." It's a sociable DIY meal best savoured with a few friends and a couple of beers. A pot filled with soup stock is placed on a gas cooker at the centre of the table, to which vegetables, meat, seafood, and other ingredients are added according to the diners' tastes. *Huoguo* is the perfect metaphor for religion in Taiwan because it's likewise a mixture of things thrown together and made to suit an individual's personal preferences. The main ingredients are Buddhism, Taoism, folk religion and a touch of Confucianism – doctrines that are blended into one another and difficult to separate. You can find a Buddhist statue at a Taoist temple and vice versa, and even the more staid Confucian temples contain figures from the vast Taoist pantheon. This bewildering array of possibilities is further complicated by geographical variations – different villages have different gods – and, similarly, by families and individuals favouring certain deities.

I had a quick immersion into this mad smorgasbord of faiths as there were a couple of temples near the school where I lived and my boss, Mr. Young, was a devout Buddhist. He left much of the school's running to his wife, Maggie, in order to spend more time reading ancient Pali texts, and it was not uncommon to find him sitting cross-legged chanting mantras. With each "Namo Amida Buddha" he'd thumb another rosary bead, and repeat the chant, thumb a bead, slipping deeper and deeper into a state of vegetable serenity. Mr. Young had set up a small Buddhist association and converted spare classrooms into a library and a worship room complete with a large statue of Buddha. There was also a Confucian temple nestled in a narrow lane less than half a minute's walk away, and a large and busy Matsu (Sea Goddess) temple at the end of a wide road running past the school. From the school it was just a hundred metres away and I had a brilliant view of the steady stream of religious processions that visited the temple.

What's more, I shared the school building with an old monk and nun. It was pretty obvious that the elderly couple were on the scrounge rather than responding to some higher calling, and when I asked Mr. Young what religious duties they performed he broke into laughter: "Decoration. They don't know anything. Can't even read or write, have no religious knowledge. They just put on robes and shave their heads so they can get rice." His tone softened, "But we have to show respect to monks, they have a hard life."

Except for public servants such as teachers and soldiers, Taiwan doesn't have a national pension scheme so responsibility falls on the individual or family. Monasteries provide an alternative, but with a strict regime of early rises and two meals a day, they are something of a last resort. Unfortunately, the old monk was still very much in the habit of getting up early. He would announce the arrival of each day by banging on his gong, the noise of which would carry through the wall into my room and wake me.

Mr. Young eventually managed to get rid of the old couple, and found an excellent replacement in an outgoing middle-aged nun. She had a sparkle in her eyes, a winning smile and, according to Mr. Young, possessed supernatural powers.

"She speaks a special language, 'heaven language.' It sounds strange – a little like Chinese, Japanese, and English mixed together," he told me in the hushed tones of a man divulging a secret.

"But is it really a language? Can anyone else understand it?"

"Yes, when a few of them get together they can talk to each other. Terrible," he said with a wince as if a chill had run down his spine. I asked a few more questions but he was uncomfortable discussing the topic.

"Don't talk about it!" he warned.

This was dark territory, and although Mr. Young followed a pure form of Buddhism that, in his own words, was from "the source, what Buddha said," he admitted the existence of demons and spirits, but thought they should be ignored.

"Don't go that way," he often cautioned, "We don't need to concern ourselves with that to follow the Right Way."

I had to share the kitchen with the newly arrived nun, which was a little difficult given my dietary prejudices. Mr. Young called me down to the kitchen one day, saying there was a problem with the fridge. He opened the fridge door – layer after layer of offending foods stared out at us in proud bachelorhood: meat, beer, eggs, and the only greens in sight were cans of Heineken. This was truly the Buddhist fridge from hell. Mr. Young decided to give me a small fridge to put in my room.

What would normally have been a very good compromise was rather unfortunate timing because I had just been about to cut down on my liquid consumption. Now instead of having to walk down a few flights of stairs, the amber fluid was now within arm's reach.

The nun cooked some really great meals. It was my first taste of vegetarian food and a pleasant surprise, but the novelty soon wore off and a month later I couldn't stand the sight of it. Her vegetarian food was just too bloody unhealthy! Incredibly, it was much greasier than the very worst of my fry-ups. Because vegetarianism in Taiwan stems primarily from religious dogma rather than health concerns, a lot of the food is actually imitation meat. Plant matter is mashed up, boiled, fried, taken to pieces and glued back together, then fried some more until it looks, tastes, and feels like meat. Of course, by that time, all the goodness has been beaten out of it, and it doesn't help that the food is laced with MSG and served up swimming in oil.

The nun's former teacher, a sly white-haired fortune-teller from Taipei, would sometimes drop by for an overnight stay at the school with a few female devotees in tow. Hospitality was repaid with some prophecy freebies, although it seemed to be a matter of getting what you paid for. One of the schoolteachers – told that her husband was having an affair – duly rushed off home in tears.

My turn came next. After I gave him the time and date of my birth he went into a trance and started mumbling. With a thin black marker, the fortune-teller scribbled unintelligible signs across a large sheet of paper in a wavy shorthand that looked a lot like drunken Arabic. When he had covered the entire A3-sized sheet he handed it to the youngest and most buxom of his followers, who then translated the "heaven language" into Chinese, and in turn Mr. Young translated it into English for me. It was all rather vague stuff, a few statements about my personality and background that moved on to a few predictions; "you like writing," and "you'll be old before you marry, not before thirty-five," were about as good as it got. Still, the vagueness meant that there was less than a third that I could actually say was wrong. I tried telling Mr. Young as politely as possibly that it was crap, but he thought it was closer than mere chance would allow: "Like clouds covering mountains, you can't expect him to see all of it clearly at one time."

About six months later I once again had the kitchen refrigerator to myself. The nun went off on some pilgrimage and never came back. In fact, to this very day, we've neither seen nor heard from her. Mr.

Young's guess was that "she went crazy," and after making a couple of unsuccessful attempts to contact her, thought that her mysterious disappearance was better left unsolved.

Mr. Young gradually lost interest in his Buddhist association because it was really little more than a social club for elderly women, and he spent more time at home looking after his ailing mother and reading his Buddhist texts. He had enough money from rents on a number of inherited properties not to work, and could have easily afforded to hire a nurse, or send her to a hospital, but stayed by her side twenty-four hours a day and did the job himself. It was rather strange to visit his house at that time because his mother, a lovely old lady going on eighty, was a WWF (World Wrestling Federation) fan. I would sit chatting to Mr. Young about Buddhist precepts while his mother watched the TV action, muscular hulks in underwear body slamming and choking each other.

Despite the nun's absence, and Mr. Young not wanting the responsibility of looking after any more clergy, there were still more than enough religious activities going on around the school. I've literally seen (I should say heard!) thousands of processions filing past the school on their way up to the Matsu temple. Have you ever seen an old-fashioned tiger hunt on TV, where the bearers spread out, and with pots and pans, gongs and horns, try to flush out any tigers? Okay, imagine a tiger hunt concentrated into a single mob, then add a couple of stereo systems, a ton of firecrackers, and for good measure throw in a couple of sexy dancing girls and some bare-chested men who go into trances and strike themselves with weapons until drawing blood. There are countless variations: giant puppets on stilts, dragon and lion dancing, kung fu troops, and marching bands, but there is a basic motto "make as much noise as possible" and a method to the madness. Your stripped-down, no-frills procession is as follows:

Several buses and a truck pull in alongside the school. Men wearing yellow tracksuits and red caps jump out and start unloading equipment: a music cart (large drums and gongs on wheels) and a sedan chair containing an image of the god. The music begins and followers pour out of the buses. A medium takes his shirt off and goes into a trance. His assistant stands by ready to grab him should he fall, and takes out a sword from a small trolley with a selection of weapons. The medium swings the sword around and strikes himself to draw blood, usually on the back between the shoulders, or the forehead. Meanwhile a herald takes a long bamboo with a banner and starts down the street, waving the procession's arrival. The music cart is wheeled after him, drums and gongs getting hit on the run. Then follows the medium in a drunken walk, and the sedan chair, which is jerked about by the bearers to show the power of the deity.

At the rear come the followers holding incense sticks in their hands. Reaching the temple steps, the herald and medium do various manoeuvres, the sedan chair swings around and around, fireworks being let off all the while. The sedan chair enters the temple, a signal for the followers to rush in, place their incense in the altar burner, pray, then straggle back to their buses.

At any one time, there can be as many as twenty-five buses parked along the street, their air-conditioning noisily purring away. The biggest processions are for Matsu's birthday and for funerals, at which time the processions travel around the town rather than just up to the temple, and there's almost always a lot of activity on Sundays. I remember one weekday afternoon not long after I'd arrived in Taiwan when a huge carnival procession marched by the front of the school. At the rear was a convoy of gaudily decorated karaoke trucks with a little stage at the back where young ladies in sleazy outfits were singing and dancing.

"What's this for?" I shouted above the noise at Mr. Young, who was sitting at his desk reading Buddhist scriptures. The music was so loud that I had to go over to him and repeat the question.

"A funeral," his lips answered.

"A funeral? What kind of –" I asked before giving in to the noise and waiting for the procession to pass on its way. Knowing Mr. Young's dry sense of humour I thought he must be joking – what kind of religion would pay homage to the dearly departed by driving around in vehicles blasting out pop music with girls in mini-skirts.

"No, it's really a funeral," he insisted. "The truck covered in imitation flowers was the funeral vehicle."

"And the girls?"

"To please the Gods."

My stream of questions were dismissed with a shake of the his head, "It's low-level religion, nonsense."

Mr. Young and I would sometimes sit drinking "old man tea" and talking about religion, and I think he had hopes of a teacher-student relationship developing between us so he could pass on his learning to me in the same fashion his elder brother, a professor of Buddhist theology, had passed it on to him. At the very least, Mr. Young thought, I should study Buddhism. He always looked irritated whenever I asked him to go into the details of folk religion, in his mind useless distractions, and he would reproach me for "wasting intelligence on the wrong way." It was only after knowing him for over five years that I found out his family connection to the two nearby temples.

"My father built both temples. First, the small one."

"The Confucian temple?"

"Not just for Confucius, it's also a Guan Gong (the patron saint of soldiers) temple. People think the two together – a scholar and a strong warrior – are powerful. A little over thirty years ago a *tang-ki* (spirit medium) from that temple went into a trance and used a willow to write a message. He said my father should build a Matsu temple; it cost NT$2 million," Mr. Young explained with a typical Taiwanese mention of the cost tagged on.

"I could be the leader of that temple now," he puffed himself up in a mock display of self-importance then brushed it away with the sweep of his hand, "Useless!"

I respected Mr. Young's disinterest in the trappings of religion, the lack of pretension, and his un-Chinese straight-talking manner, which – although causing offence to many others – I found refreshing.

"Buddhism is very simple. There are three bad things: greed, hatred, and ignorance. Follow the Dharma, do not follow people. Study, use your mind, not the church. I was a vegetarian for twelve years, then went back to meat. Buddha never said not to eat meat. Food is only for the stomach, not the mind. No connection – it's rubbish."

Mr. Young's insistence in always going back to the earliest scriptures was such that he'd actually taught himself how to read Pali, "It's like taking milk directly from a cow – pure, original milk; if you buy it from the merchant, it's been watered down, changed. The right way, there is only one way, it may not be a straight line, but it's the way. Maybe next life, the life after, or many more, to become a Buddha."

"You don't believe," he asked, sensing my scepticism.

"The reincarnation part."

"Simple," he pointed at a bed lying at the back of the room. "As my brother told me, you go to sleep and wake up, every day is a new life, waking up is being reincarnated – open your eyes, new life."

"But you can't test it."

"You don't need to put your hand into a fire to know it will burn you. You need to have faith in your judgement, in your wisdom. You know Armstrong has been to the moon but you haven't seen it with your own eyes. You know that you had great-great-grandparents but you've never seen them."

According to Mr. Young, monks were too caught up in the practice of religion, and not devoting enough time to the study of the scriptures. It was the wrong way around, "Study, then apply, not enlightenment through practice." Meditation and fasting were peripheral things, unnecessary – none of your forty days and forty nights in the wilderness stuff for him, "Buddha did it for us, we don't need to do it. Have faith in him, follow him. You don't need to learn everything in the world by yourself."

* * *

Officially about half the population, split almost evenly between Buddhists and Taoists, is classified as religious, but in reality all but a handful of Taiwanese participate in some religious activity, whether going to a temple, having an ancestral altar at home, or making offerings to gods and spirits on important occasions.

Almost every house in Taiwan has an altar. This is a high narrow table placed against the back wall, with a photograph or portrait of the recently deceased, a statue of a god or two, religious paraphernalia, an incense pot, and the ancestral tablets, which are wooden blocks with the name of deceased family members inscribed on them.

One of the startling things for people coming from a Christian country is the religious tolerance that allows seemingly contradictory beliefs – for example worshipping ancestors when they've already been reincarnated – to exist side by side. Except for some monks and nuns virtually nobody receives any formal religious education and people know surprisingly little about what they are worshipping. I remember asking one of my adult students whether she ever went to a temple.

"Yes, if I have a problem, mostly before an exam," she answered.

"What god do you pray to, what type of temple is it?" I asked.

"I don't know how to say it in English."

"Say the Chinese name then."

A long pause followed, "I don't know," she admitted.

I was dumbstruck – a young cosmopolitan graduate worshipping a god she didn't know!

With such ignorance it's little wonder then that religious fraud is so common, in fact an everyday occurrence. There is a ready market for magic potions, lucky charms and the like which offer shortcuts to health and happiness, and there can be few people living in such a technologically savvy country who are more susceptible to a religious scam than the Taiwanese. A recent case in my neighbourhood involved a con artist setting himself up as a religious guru. Followers of this self-described Taoist master could reach a higher spiritual level by following his teachings, having sex with him, and giving him money. When police finally raided his apartment, they found aphrodisiacs and electrical sex equipment.

Not a few religious frauds involve followers having sex with their spiritual leaders. The connection between sex and religion is not as bizarre as it first seems. Sexual activity is an important thread that runs through Taoism's and China's long history.

The belief that regulated sexual activity could improve health and prolong life was an important part of court life in imperial China. You would've thought that being a Chinese emperor – surrounded by the most beautiful and charming girls – must have been like living in some kind of sexual wonderland, but the reality is a little disappointing. What happened between the sheets was governed by suffocating rules of etiquette, and it was reduced to a health and breeding routine. A man's semen was his most precious possession – life itself – and the emperor had to save it and build up his power for copulation with the empress. That was the theory anyway. Being an emperor, spoilt from birth as a semi-divine being, didn't exactly help engender the development of self-restraint and there must have been quite a few "failures."

According to Taoist sexual practices, you have to take yourself to the brink then reign in your little buddy using mental discipline, or physical means such as compressing the seminal duct with your fingers, or "simultaneously inhaling deeply and gnashing your teeth." The *yang* essence, now intensified by contact with the woman, will then flow up the spinal cord to the brain. A man derives energy from a woman's secretions because they contain *yin* essence, so he should have sex with different women without emitting semen and thereby increase his *yang* force.

As detailed in R.H. van Gulik's pioneering classic *Sexual Life in Ancient China*, for most of their long history the Chinese were very open-minded about sex. It was seen as something natural, even sacred, neither dirty nor sinful, and definitely not something to feel guilty about. Although the society that Westerners encountered upon China's opening after the mid-1800s was one they found promiscuous in its attitudes to homosexuality, prostitution and polygamy, China was actually at its most prudish. (This change was a result of the conservatism of the ruling Manchu elite and a reaction to the prevalence of venereal diseases.)

Sex handbooks in China date back nearly two thousand years. They were illustrated with pictures showing various positions, and the text was usually written in the form of dialogues between teachers and students. The books contain wonderfully imaginative names to describe the various positions: Reversed Flying Ducks, Bamboos Near the Altar, Phoenix Holding Its Chicken, Goat Facing a Tree, Wailing Monkey Embracing a Tree, and Hounds of the Ninth Day of Autumn, to name but a few.

According to one rather overoptimistic sex manual: "Those who can exercise the sexual act scores of times in one day without once emitting semen will thereby cure all their ills and live to a great age. If the act is performed with a number of different women, its benefit will increase. It is best to engage in the sexual act with ten or more different women on one night."

With all this Taoist sexual activity herbal concoctions were often needed to put the wind back in a man's sails. One such medicine was called the "Bald Chicken Potion." A seventy-year-old prefect who partook of the potion had three sons and was supposedly so active with his wife that she developed a vaginal disease and was unable to sit or even lie down. He threw the medicine away and a cock ate it. The supercharged bird leaped on a hen and continued copulating for days without rest, picking at the hen's head until it was completely bald. Thus, the name.

On a more serious note, van Gulik concluded *Sexual Life in Ancient China* with his assertion that Chinese sexuality was one of the great strengths behind the civilization and that it was the "careful balancing of the male and female elements ... that caused the permanence of Chinese race and culture. For it would seem that it was this balance that engendered the intense vital power that, from remote antiquity to the very present, has ever sustained and renewed the Chinese race."

*Procession approaching Matsu temple, Dounan*
*(photo taken from the author's roof)*

# 12

# Tracking Matsu

I REMEMBER turning on the television one winter morning to find, instead of the usual program, a live news broadcast from the tarmac of Chiang Kai-shek International Airport. Hitting the channel button showed all three channels had the same broadcast. Behind the excited news reporter was a plane, just landed, and groups of dignitaries, monks, dancers, and musicians churning out a cacophony with their drums, horns, and gongs. What was happening? Who was visiting? Obviously someone very important to get this kind of red carpet treatment, but who would dare visit Taiwan and provoke the ire of Beijing? It did turn out to be an important figure – none other than an eight-hundred-year-old wooden statue from China of the Goddess Matsu, protector of seafarers.

Matsu is said to have lived on Meizhou Island, in China's Fujian Province, during the tenth century. Blessed with special powers, she most famously put them to use to rescue her fishermen brothers and father from a typhoon. There are various versions of the story, but most involve her spirit leaving her body to travel to their boat and carry them away. She died when she was in her twenties, and a Matsu cult spread along the southern coast and into Southeast Asia. Over time Matsu evolved from the patron saint of fishermen and sailors to an all-purpose goddess.

Temples in Taiwan have Matsu statues that are several hundred years old, but the Meizhou Matsu is the oldest and most sacred. It went on a hundred-day tour of Taiwan, drawing millions of followers and a fortune in donations. But of course any exchange between Taiwan and China has political overtones, and this goodwill gesture from Beijing was no exception. The statue was escorted by Chinese politicians, who stressed how Matsu was a symbol of cross-strait unity and unification. It was also good business. Worshippers gave generously, not deterred by the accusations that it was a fake – indeed the statue was in unbelievably good condition for its age, perhaps a sign of its power!

A few years later, when I had gotten used to the noise of the local Matsu temple and no longer cursed it from between pillow earmuffs on Sunday mornings, I actually went looking for more of the same, and joined a Matsu procession winding its way around the central area of western Taiwan. From Chiayi, my Taiwanese friend Jenny and I drove northwest along a road lined with scantily clad betel-nut girls that led us into a messy semi-rural landscape of rice fields, poultry and pig farms, vegetable plots, and factories. It was early in the morning – well, too early for me anyway, and a sharp reminder to myself that I'd done the right thing in giving up on the hope of making a living from photography. As I explained to Jenny we were up early because the early bird gets the best pictures: the lovely warm tones of morning, the clear skies, and the sun's low angle to bring out the relief. My words had a hollow ring to them because the heavens hadn't complied – it was the same damn suffocating weather we'd had for months, the same overcast sky sweating grease that gave the landscape a dull flat sheen which is the photographic kiss of death.

Every spring a procession of Matsu devotees travels about three hundred kilometres through central Taiwan on an eight-day pilgrimage that starts and finishes in the town of Dajia near Taichung, goes down to Xingang near Chiayi then turns around and heads back to Dajia. The newspaper's times for the route I'd read were wrong; when we arrived in Xingang, the pilgrimage was long gone, having started on its homeward leg ten hours before. Jenny asked for directions but nobody knew the exact route. With the pilgrimage zigzagging its way through obscure back roads, we were going to have problems finding it.

We soon realized our fears were unwarranted when we found a tidal mark of garbage lining the road leading out of town – plastic cups, containers, and sheets of unburnt ghost money – which continued into the countryside, and it was just a case of following the trash. We slowed down at intersections to see what road had the most trash.

"Ghost money – this way, turn right," I instructed.

"You should be grateful that Taiwanese are so messy – otherwise we would be stopping all the time."

"A holy sign from above!"

"Don't say that!" Jenny cautioned me. She was in her own words "not superstitious" but didn't think it wise to tempt fate.

Five, ten, twenty kilometres! On we went following kilometre after kilometre of religious debris, until the trash petered out to a few pieces of ghost money every twenty metres or so, then after another ten kilometres dried up. We had gone too far, somehow had shot past the pilgrims by mistakenly following the old trail the procession had used travelling south, and we realized that they must be using a slightly different route to go north.

"I knew that was too clean for Taiwanese," I quipped.

We doubled back and rejoined the fresh trail of ghost money, then took a short cut to a small village awaiting Matsu's arrival. In front of people's homes were tables laden with food offerings and incense, piles of fireworks at the ready, and the residents were busy feeding paper money into burners. We drove out to some fields for a nice backdrop and waited.

The procession resembled a medieval pageant assembled in the fashion of some ancient army. At the forefront came Matsu's messenger announcing her arrival, a rather redundant message considering the noise, and a column of standard-bearing troops dressed in brown military pyjamas. Then followed more marching troops bearing inscribed wooden paddles, a convoy of religious floats, and a palanquin carrying the Matsu. The more devout of the worshippers standing at the roadside came forward and lay face-down on the road, prostrating themselves with outstretched praying hands before the palanquin so Matsu would pass over them and thus bestow her blessing.

Behind the core of the procession came hundreds of pilgrims on foot, bicycles, motorbikes, and a long line of cars. We slotted into the traffic jam and crawled at walking pace through the narrow streets of a small town. Heart-pounding fireworks and the naked flames of burning piles of ghost money threatened to set the car on fire.

As we drove on, we saw several entertainment floats by the sides of roads, including a puppet-show truck and a karaoke music truck. At the back of the music truck a female singer wearing a racy version of the traditional *qipao* dress was going through the motions of some old love song.

"Ah, lucky. A sexy girl for you," chided Jenny.

"You know, I can never understand how Taiwanese can have some hot KTV girl involved in a religious activity. And don't give me any 'it's for the Gods bullshit!'"

"That girl," she laughed, "that's nothing. Sometimes the girls are naked."

Naked! I'd heard people mention girls "with no clothes," and always thought it was an exaggeration, that the girls had stripped down to their underwear. From my experience of seeing them cruise past my house in Dounan, a very short miniskirt and tank top was as wild as it got.

"Naked? You mean in their underwear?" I checked.

"No, completely naked! I've seen them with my own eyes more than four times, at weddings and during Matsu's birthday."

I thought I'd seen enough of Taiwan not to be amazed anymore, but obviously not, and my head shook in disbelief. Now, when you think "wedding" don't imagine some wild stag night in a private club in the early hours of the morning – think small-town wedding reception, hundreds of people having lunch outside under a large tarpaulin in broad daylight.

"The wedding was out on the street, set up in front of the family's house. The girl was up on the back of a music truck. She was wearing a bikini, but after she finished singing she took it off, and walked around to each table and toasted the people."

A naked woman walking around amongst men, women, and children! I had to ask her to repeat her description, but sure enough there was no mistake.

"And how did people react?"

*Pilgrims on the annual week-long Dajia Matsu procession*

"The men liked it, eyes coming out of their heads – the women felt really embarrassed."

"Not angry?"

"Nobody said anything. At that time it wasn't that unusual. It was like a craze for a while, about six or seven years ago. For two years running there were naked women in the procession for our local Matsu temple. On Matsu's birthday they take the statue from the temple and walk around in a procession. There were women wearing see-through gowns, but totally see-through, dancing on the back of a truck, and there was always a large group of *ojisans* (old men) following the truck."

We drove ahead and caught the pilgrimage further on. If you ignored the farcical religious element and just took it as a carnival, then it was an incredible spectacle, and a lot of fun. Taiwanese normally avoid walking like the plague so it was quite moving to see the pilgrims, not a few of whom were middle-aged women or physically handicapped, struggling on. There were also a large contingent of the mentally challenged, but it wasn't always easy distinguishing mad looks from fatigue.

\* \* \*

Jenny and I met up with the slowly moving pilgrimage two days later near Taichung and once again the atmosphere was good-natured. The pilgrims were in worse physical condition, footsore and numb with weariness; yet when I took advantage of a brief halt to talk to some of them they said they had been doing it for years and would be sure to be back again next year, although perhaps on a bike. An old man on a motorcycle alongside me politely interrupted to announce that he had been on the annual pilgrimage thirty-five times. His bike was covered in charms and banners, luggage at the back, and a statue of Matsu from his family altar strapped to the handlebars. In fact, quite a few pilgrims had brought their idols along for the ride. Seeing the little gods, the piles of ghost money being burnt and littered, and once again, the people prostrating themselves on the ground for nothing more than a wooden statue of Matsu, to a non-believer like myself, left a bad taste at the back of the mouth.

"I can't get over it," I grumbled to Jenny. "Parading a piece of bloody wood around the countryside for a week – like putting a doll in a chair and carrying it around, people following it. It's crazy."

"You're more crazy! You're following the people who are following the statue. That's worse!" came Jenny's cutting reply.

\* \* \*

Spirits can lead a comfortable enough life as long as their descendants provide them with all the necessities of life: food, alcohol, clothing, housing, and especially money, and these things are routinely offered to them. But should there be no descendants to take care of the dead the spirit will be slowly reduced to poverty, growing more pitiful, desperate and angry, until it attacks humans. These "hungry ghosts" are euphemistically referred to as "Good Brothers," and when offering sacrifices to gods or ancestors something has to be set aside to placate them.

This ancestor worship explains much of the Chinese bias in favour of boys and why failure to bear a son was once legal grounds for divorce. After marriage, girls became part of the husband's family, looking after the man's parents and worshipping his ancestors. If you wanted to be taken care of in old age and have descendants to offer sacrifices after death, it was vital to have sons. This idea still holds true for the more conservative-minded. But should your wife be unable to produce a boy, there are several possible courses of action short of taking a new wife – you can adopt a son, or get your daughter's husband to take the family name.

The hungry ghosts are not the only ones to worry about; spirits of those who have committed suicide, been murdered or executed, and those who have drowned can also be troublemakers. The most dangerous time is during Ghost Month, the seventh month of the Chinese calendar, which falls in August or September, when the ghosts from hell walk the earth – a time when the prudent refrain from travelling, swimming, moving house, or making any important decisions or purchases. Ghost money is burnt and offerings made in large quantities, as usual to bad as well as good ghosts, which seems like nothing less than bribery on a massive scale.

When evil cannot be kept at bay by such simple measures, you can call in your local Taoist priest-cum-exorcist to purify your village, house, family, or body of the malignant forces causing illness and misfortune. Taiwanese love colour and noise, and these exorcists usually put on a good show that includes chanting, purification by fire, driving stakes into the ground, fire-crackers and so on.

Taoist spirit mediums, known by the Taiwanese term *tang-ki*, are frequently called upon to communicate with the gods. One of the methods is to use a divination chair carried by two men holding the legs or supported by poles carried by two or four bearers. The small wooden chair is believed to seat a god, invisible to us but its presence is obvious by the bouncing and jerking motion of the chair despite the best efforts of the *tang-ki* to contain the force. A question is put to a god. The god takes possession of the chair, which is dipped in ink, and writes something on a sheet of paper, or scratches marks in sand. The unintelligible squiggles and blotches that result are then translated into something meaningful.

Self-mutilation is another *tang-ki* specialty, a powerful demonstration that the medium is genuine, and something I could see most Sundays from the comfort of my building. Traditionally five weapons are used, ranging from a ball of nails to, most dangerous of all, an axe. The *tang-ki* hits himself with a weapon to open wounds on the upper body (and sometimes the forehead) that produce a lot of blood. The cuts are mostly superficial – not much worse than a bad early morning shave – and heal after a couple of days. The only time I've seen them going at it hammer and tongs was for Matsu's birthday when a group of young *tang-ki* were standing in a circle covered in so much blood that at first glance I thought it was tomato sauce. They kept their wounds flowing with constant blows and before long there were a few healthy puddles of blood on the street.

* * *

If you should ever find yourself travelling down some rural back road in Taiwan and see a red envelope lying on the road, the kind used for gifts of money at weddings or Chinese New Year, keep on walking. It's most likely bait put down to trap a would-be-husband for a ghost! A family that finds itself plagued by sickness and misfortune may suspect a malignant spirit at work inside the household, perhaps the spirit of a girl who has died in childhood. Other times the ghost will make a direct appeal, appearing in a family member's dream and announcing her wish to be married.

A red envelope is strategically placed to tempt a passer-by, and the family wait in hiding. Someone stops to pick up the envelope and out pounces the family, who inform the lucky guy that he has just become the bridegroom. Refusal could mean the ghost seeking retribution for the snub, and incentive is given in the form of a dowry offered for acceptance of marriage. The wedding ceremony is as much like a normal one as possible, the girl represented by an ancestral tablet, and sometimes by a dummy made out of wood, paper, and cloth, and dressed in a wedding gown. The husband doesn't have any obligations to his in-laws but he must keep the ancestral tablet of the bride on his family altar and provide it with sacrifices.

There aren't any cases of male ghosts wanting to get married – and it's not simply that they like the free and easy bachelor lifestyle; the reason lies with the nature of ancestor worship and the Chinese line of descent being through men. If a woman is to be worshipped, she needs to have a husband and children; in this way, a ghost marriage is a lot like a girl being adopted into a family.

One of my acquaintances, Fred, a forty-year-old factory owner from Chiayi County, is married to a ghost. I met up with him one afternoon to hear the full account. The plastic furniture, canned pop music, and bright fluorescent lights of the setting – the basement of a Kentucky Fried Chicken outlet – didn't really set the right mood for a story of the supernatural, but at least the lousy cell-phone reception ensured the place was almost empty.

"I was nineteen and studying at an agricultural college in Pingtung. One day my brother arrived at the school and told me the news that my girlfriend had been killed in a car accident! I cried all the way back. I saw her lying in a coffin at her house, and promised to marry her."

Fred was comfortable enough to recount the story with a laugh or two, but I could see his eyes glassing over at the memory of his sweetheart, who was the first and greatest love of his life. He obviously still loved her very much. They had been together for three years and would have gotten married in a few more.

"About a month after the funeral her grandmother suddenly died. This was very strange because she was very healthy. A feng shui master said that the coffin had been buried on the wrong day and in the wrong place. They dug her up, but the problem was that they needed to wait about a month for an auspicious day, so the father had to stand guard over the coffin, which was sitting on the ground in the cemetery. It was terrible," he said shaking his head, "chasing away cats and dogs for all that time!"

"Did your girlfriend speak to you in a dream?"

"She first appeared in my mother's dream. My mother is a spirit medium so she consulted her deity, the Goddess Matsu, with the use of a divining chair. She and another person took the sedan chair and it started shaking around. The arm of the chair scratched marks on a table spread with incense ash. Matsu said that my girlfriend was sad because she was in 'ghost jail.' Young people who die go to jail to wait until they are older and can leave. We had to burn ghost money for her, and also for her jailers, bribe them the same way we bribe officials, who would then treat her better and maybe let her out early.

"A strange thing happened while I was still at college. I got a rash and red spots all over my body. The doctor at the hospital said there was nothing wrong with me, but gave me an injection anyway. It didn't work. When I called my mother, she said she'd dreamt about my girlfriend a few days before. My mother consulted Matsu again, who speaking through the chair, wrote some words on paper. These papers were sent down to me and for three or four days I had to burn the paper and pass it all around my body, and also to mix some of the ash with water and drink it. After three days the rash disappeared."

"So at that time you were still single, huh? When did you actually marry your dead girlfriend?"

"I married her the afternoon before my real wedding, and that was when I was thirty."

I did a quick subtraction, "Eleven years! An eleven-year engagement!"

"It was my promise to marry her first and I kept it."

"And what did your wife have to say?"

"I explained everything to her from the beginning, and she understood and could accept it."

"And the wedding itself?"

"I took the girl's ancestral tablet from her parents, carried it in a bamboo basket and under a black umbrella because ghosts should not see the sun. I took it to my house, talked to her, tried to make her feel comfortable, and shared a meal with her."

"And what are your duties to your ghost wife?"

"To worship her every year and on Tomb Sweeping Day, April 5, go to her grave and tidy it. It's strange, you know. A couple of weeks before Tomb-Sweeping Day I dream about her, imagine having sex with her. It's different from a normal dream, so lifelike, and the strange thing is that she has not aged, always as she was before her death – but I keep getting older. Not fair!" he laughed.

"Doesn't sound like too much work."

"Not much trouble, and people say that being married to a ghost brings good fortune. You will become rich."

"Okay, that explains your Volvo."

Fred went on to tell me that his brother was also married to a ghost. "Five years after getting married he became very ill, and had to marry the ghost of his wife's sister, who had committed suicide when she was a girl."

The strange thing about Fred's ghost marriage is that in the years between his girlfriend's death and their wedding he had experienced a change of heart about religion and superstitions, and had doubts about whether ghosts were real or simply self-delusion.

"I think it was a reaction against my mother's superstitions. All my life, ever since I was young – this ghost, that god, that message, and warning me not to go out at night because I might meet a ghost. I got sick of listening to it."

This was a bombshell. I asked him whether he believed in all the religious things he had done. "In the beginning but not later. I wanted to marry my girlfriend because I loved her and because I'd promised it. And also for a peaceful feeling. Even if you're not sure something is true it makes you feel better."

# 13
# Peach Town

THIRTY minutes south of Dounan lies the city of Chiayi. According to a local tourist publication, it is "an old cultural city full of art and passion," that once went by the nickname of "Peach Town" because of the shape of the city walls. Chiayi's original name was actually Chu-lo but this was changed by the emperor Qianlong in appreciation of the citizens' loyalty during a revolt to the present name that means "the great and renowned city of the Yi people." Today the city of 264,000 inhabitants is an ugly expanse of concrete and iron shacks, with pollution levels that defy its small size. Despite being known as the "Gateway to Alishan," Taiwan's premier mountain resort, the beautiful backdrop is invisible for most of the year. The city's other modest claims to fame include a scaled-down Statue of Liberty in a traffic roundabout, and the fact that the Tropic of Cancer lies just a few kilometres to the south (something that is celebrated by a bar called the "Cancer Pub"). There is also a 2-28 Peace Memorial Park commemorating victims of a massacre in 1947. Although killings took place throughout the country, Chiayi – where people were gunned down across from the train station – probably suffered the highest number of casualties.

The fertile Chiayi area was one of the first regions in Taiwan to be opened up by the Dutch in the 1600s, resulting in the inevitable "red hair" place names such as "Red Hair Reservoir" and "Red Hair Well." In 1704 Chiayi became the first city in the island to have a wall built around it, though nothing remains of it today. A Chinese work, *Statistics of Formosa*, from the early eighteenth century, described the surrounding area as having very rich soil, and that the settlers were, "fond of abusing and fighting one another," but were also friendly and generous: "Benighted travellers can gain admission at the first door they apply at, and few will refuse them shelter."

* * *

During the summer, when the southwest monsoon was blowing and no vessels dared approach the coast, William Pickering (an employee of the Chinese Imperial Maritime Customs in the swashbuckling 1860s) often spent his free time exploring the countryside around Tainan on horseback. This was a lot more dangerous than it sounds; the highways were infested with bands of robbers, and villagers felt so insecure that they grew large stands of bamboo around their villages to form stockades.

Pickering had an amusing encounter with bandits on a trip from Tainan to Chiayi. He was travelling with a European friend, a few servants, and some townsfolk who, deciding that there was safety in numbers, thought it a good opportunity to tag along and take some merchandise to Chiayi. The little caravan, the two Europeans on small horses, the others on foot, followed the "high road" north. The road, the country's main north-south artery, consisted of "a single line of rough granite slabs, laid down more or less imperfectly on the top of a mud bank which sloped down to the paddy fields on either sides."

As they approached a dangerous section, the guides and coolies began warning that they were "sure to be stripped of all their clothing." Pickering saw a group of people in the distance moving from the village toward the road, and never being one to wait and see, he made up his mind there and then that they were bandits and took action against them.

> With a British yell, we fired our revolvers, and gal-
> loped into the middle of them, crying "The red-haired
> barbarians are coming!" ... and the brave banditti
> scattered back into their village, crying, "Run, run!
> Ayo, ayo! They are not men! They are red-haired bar-
> barians. They may be bears or they may be tigers!
> Run!" The road was clear.

There is nothing in Chiayi that Pickering could recognize today. Apart from uncontrolled development and the fact that there weren't many good old buildings to start with, Mother Nature has wiped out her fair share of history. A large earthquake hit central Taiwan in 1906, devastating Chiayi and the surrounding district. Whole streets were laid to waste, 1,258 people killed, double that number seriously injured, and over thirteen thousand houses destroyed.

My first job in Chiayi, teaching English to adults, was a memorable one. Despite the school's handy downtown location – the seventh floor of a high rise across from the train station – there were surprisingly few students and it wasn't uncommon to have just two or three in a class. I soon found out that the building was reportedly haunted. Eleven people staying in a hotel a few floors above the school had died in a fire a couple of years before, and students were still afraid to come back. There was also talk that one of the two elevators was haunted because several people had died in it during the fire and it had a tendency to make jerky movements.

William Campbell, the first Western missionary to establish a mission in Chiayi, also had problems with haunted premises. When Campbell and a small group of Taiwanese followers first arrived in Chiayi shouts went up that a "red-haired barbarian" had come, and the innkeepers closed their doors. To prevent the missionary from establishing a mission, a town crier was sent around the streets announcing that anyone renting, leasing, or selling land for a church would be seized and buried alive. Nevertheless, the power of money prevailed and a small house was purchased. After a few months a larger much more suitable building was offered for sale; not until later did Campbell learn it was a haunted house, and that the "neighbours were constantly alarmed at midnight on hearing loud screams, and the rattling of iron chains being dragged from one room to another."

On a later visit to Chiayi, Campbell found the area suffering from "a severe outbreak of plague." The usual offerings and prayers had failed so the locals turned to special means to supplicate the Gods: a renowned Buddhist priest brought over from the mainland who, by climbing a ladder of knives with bare feet, would gain merit for the people and save them from calamity. Campbell was among the large crowd that gathered. Two long ladders were set up with the tops tied together and the bottom ends set about twenty feet apart.

> The Priest in gorgeous robes then slowly advanced, put off his outer garments, and began his ascent with great deliberation. He paused from time to time, and gave rather overdone signs of undergoing a tremendous strain, but seemed soothed on witnessing the exertions of those beneath him, who kept pounding on the drums, gongs, and cymbals they had in readiness. When the summit was reached, he rained down handfuls of little pieces of red paper, having charms written in Chinese characters. There was a mighty scramble to pick these up, the idea being that,

if carried on the person, they would afford protection against all kinds of mental and bodily distress.

Campbell says that the rungs were indeed long knives but with the blunt ends facing upward and the blades placed at an angle, and he was later informed by a friend that the priest had pasted strong bank-note paper to the soles of his feet as protection.

On another visit to Chiayi he arrived "to find the people engaged in their absurd periodic custom of stone-throwing." This "custom" had been going on for thirty years when Campbell wrote about it in his *Sketches from Formosa* (1915). It had started with boys from the South Gate pelting those of the West Gate with fruit. The projectiles escalated from fruit to stones, adults joined in, and for several days the two groups pelted each other. There were many injuries and some deaths, yet it was all strangely amicable as if it were a sports match, and the city officials did little. From that time forth, every anniversary of the stone-throwing was celebrated by hundreds of people taking part in a huge fight.

Although William Campbell was, like George MacKay, a Presbyterian, and despite the fact that the two men were contemporaries, they seldom crossed paths. Travel between the south and north of the island was so difficult, time-consuming, and dangerous that the two churches might as well have been in different countries. Relations were friendly, but missionaries from the two areas only met every few years or so. Nonetheless, Campbell was the first missionary to visit MacKay, and years later made a second trip, on which they went touring the villages and towns preaching the gospel together. They agreed to spend ten days without speaking English but on the first day Campbell had had enough and turned to his friend, "MacKay, this jabbering in Chinese is ridiculous, and two Scotchmen should have more sense; let us return to our mother tongue."

Campbell had arrived in Taiwan in 1871 a few months before MacKay. It took more than six weeks to sail from Liverpool to Hong Kong, where he had to change to a small coasting steamer, whose captain it was said "could not properly navigate his ship unless he was half-tipsy." As if to prove the point, the captain took out two pairs of boxing gloves, and was much displeased that Campbell refused to go a few rounds up on the deck. In Amoy (Xiamen), Campbell changed to a small, "evil-smelling" sailing ship that took him across the Taiwan Strait, but not before crashing into a large fishing junk. Writing over forty years later he said that he could still "hear the yells of those poor drowning Chinamen." Outside of Kaohsiung port Campbell had to climb down a rope into a bamboo catamaran, which then took him ashore. One final boat trip up the coast saw him safely to his destination, Tainan, the capital and the oldest and largest city on the island.

His first impressions of Tainan were that the streets were "narrow, winding, ill-paved, and odorous," and full of begging lepers. He thought the Buddhist priests "poor effeminate looking creatures" and the Chinese literati conceited, but was struck by "the extreme civility of the common people." The Presbyterian chapel was in one of the busiest streets and there was always a thick throng of the curious looking in on the services; "They keep coming and going during the entire service; so that beggars, priests, shopkeepers, coolies and all sorts of people may be found there at times, jostling one another...."

The missionaries' dwellings were a ten-minute walk away, still inside the city walls, and possessing a deep well with "cool, excellent water." From the part of the city wall nearest his house (about five hundred metres away from where the train station is today) he could get a great view.

> Looking eastward the eye travels over a wide plain, which, with the exception of roads and a few temples, may literally be spoken of as one vast field of sugar-cane.... The rising ground commences a few miles east from Taiwan-fu [Tainan], and gradually ascends into range upon range of hills which culminate in the majestic peak of Mount Morrison [Mount Jade / Yu Shan]."

Campbell, while admiring his early Dutch counterparts, thought their mission work unsuccessful. It was a failure, he reasoned, because it collapsed as soon as the Dutch left. The priests had been too aggressive in getting a high quota of converts who had but shallow faith. For Campbell there was "no cheap, superficial, and rapid method of enabling masses of converts to stand the test of insidious temptation or fiery persecution."

He established a school for the blind, became a great authority on the early history of Taiwan, wrote several books, translated others, and did extensive mission work. On one of his trips into the mountains he became the first European to reach Sun-Moon Lake and named it Lake Candidius after the first Dutch missionary.

*Reverend William Campbell with native workers*

One afternoon when passing through a remote village he saw a group of animated children happily munching on lumps of meat and bones. Campbell found a woman inside a large hut cooking the remains of two human bodies! He was unable to contain his disgust but the woman felt no shame, and actually lost her temper and replied angrily, "Why should we not eat them? They beheaded my husband, they beheaded my nephew, and it serves them very well to be treated in this way."

Another time when touring in the mountains he saw a party of armed aborigines pass by:

> A stout lad was trudging wearily after them carrying some sort of a bundle dangling down behind him. On reaching the hut, where they were to pass the night, I got a closer look of the little fellow, and found that the bundle he was carrying consisted of two fresh-ly-cut Chinamen's heads, which he had fastened by

the queues held over his shoulder. Poor, dear, innocent wee chap! I tried to speak a few kindly words to
him, but he was too fagged out to listen to talk of any
kind. He threw the two heads on the ground, made a
pillow of them by coiling the hair on the top, and was
fast asleep in a minute or two.

Children seemed to get a taste for headhunting at an early age and,
as Campbell saw first-hand, aboriginal children played "Indians and
Chinese," taking turns to play the various roles. The "Chinese" would
walk along, get ambushed by the aborigines, and have their heads cut
off. Then they would swap roles.

Campbell's narrowest escape came when he went to investigate
reports of attacks on converts at a village southeast of Chiayi. He spent
the night in a hut near a newly built chapel but was woken after midnight by the sounds of a mob of armed men who, with their black-
ened faces, "seemed like demons." Before long the bedroom was on fire,
but when Campbell tried to get out the door he was met with jabbing
spears, and forced to retreat into a small smoke-filled room. Spears
came thrusting through the thin lattice walls, one missing his heart by
an inch, another cutting him badly in the leg, all the while the sound
of exploding bamboo echoing around him like gunfire. As the smoke
and heat grew overwhelming, the mob backed off, waiting outside the
burning building for Campbell to come out.

He sprang from the hut as a great gust of wind drove his pursuers
back, and was able to escape. He crawled through a hedge, tumbled
down a bank, and then made his way through an area of tall grass. The
mob spread out with torches and searched for the missionary, eager to
collect on their leader's promise of a dollar each if they brought back
his head. Campbell lay low until they had departed, then walked and
ran back to Chiayi, arriving bedraggled and bloodied at the south gate
in the morning still in his night shirt.

* * *

Foreigners like Campbell, Pickering and MacKay complained about
the intransigence and hostility of Chinese officials, but there was more
than just cause for the anti-foreigner sentiment. Europeans in Taiwan
and on mainland China were uninvited guests who had forced themselves on unwilling hosts by military power. The freedom for MacKay

and Campbell to live and preach in Taiwan was the result of a series of dirty little wars.

In the late 1700s, even more so than today, the trade imbalance between China and the West was a cause for concern. Porcelain, silk, and the increasingly popular beverage of tea, flowed from the East, but with scant demand for European goods, these imports had to be paid for with silver. The British soon found another currency: Indian opium.

The fast-spreading use of opium in China caused alarm at the imperial court, and the emperor chose to enforce the existing ban against its use. A scholar-official called Lin was sent to Canton to put an end to the trade. The foreign traders were blockaded in their compounds. When the merchants eventually capitulated, they were expelled, and their opium confiscated and destroyed.

Rich opium interests in England were able to lobby the government for retaliatory action and drown out the words of protest from Protestant missionaries and others. Britain dispatched a fleet of warships and captured several ports. The Chinese forces were no match for the British. The embarrassingly one-sided hostilities were brought to an end with the Treaty of Nanking. It opened up five cities to the British for residence and trade. They were also given the island of Hong Kong and compensation for expenses and losses incurred. Future prime minister William Gladstone, then a young Liberal politician, was scathing in his criticism, "A war more unjust in origin, a war more calculated to cover this country with permanent disgrace, I do not know and have not read of."

The Second Opium War (1856–1860) was a larger-scale replay of the first and ended in similarly humiliating fashion for the Chinese with the Treaty of Tientsin (signed in 1858 and ratified in 1860). Additional treaty ports were opened, including four in Taiwan: Danshui, Tainan, Keelung and Kaohsiung. Missionaries were given the freedom to preach Christianity throughout China.

* * *

While early Europeans in Taiwan faced some hostility at least they had the support of their governments, and the threat of gunboats to back them up. The local population mellowed in their opposition, and Westerners certainly fared a lot better than Chinese living in the West, who – even if they kept their heads down, worked hard and avoided trouble – could still face persecution.

A succession of bloody internal rebellions in the mid-1800s, and the accompanying famine and social upheaval, drove millions of Chinese to move overseas. Some chose the island frontier of Taiwan, now fully opened up to settlement; others tried their luck in Southeast Asia, Latin America, and the west coast of the United States.

The California gold rush of 1848 drew the first large wave of Chinese to America. Having arrived too late to stake claims on fresh ground, they scratched a living by reworking abandoned sites, then moved on to other areas and other occupations: market gardening, laundry shops, stores, sweatshops, and railway construction. Although America was a country of immigrants, the Chinese stood apart from the others in many respects – from the obvious racial difference and their strange appearance heightened by the Qing queue (pigtail), their horrible-sounding language and inability to speak English, to their "idol worship" and strange customs. The fact that the migrants were virtually all men, and took solace in prostitutes, gambling, and smoking opium, and congregated together in triads that were often feuding, gave fuel to rumours of Chinese depravity, just as in mainland China rumours circulated of how missionaries engaged in depraved sexual activity.

The belief that Chinese dragged down wages caused resentment and fear among white workers. Chinese immigration, particularly fears of a flood of arrivals, became a hot election issue. In 1882 Congress passed the Chinese Exclusion Law, which barred entry of workers, thus bringing to an end the great American dream of making the nation a refuge for all the world's dreamers; "Give me your tired, your poor, your huddled masses yearning to be free ... but no Chinks." This didn't overly worry the Chinese population living in the States because their version of the American Dream was to leave the place, and by 1920 there were only about sixty thousand left. The Chinese Exclusion Law was not overturned until 1965 by President Johnson.

# 14

# Cannibals

FROM the many well-thumbed history books about Taiwan that are piled high on my shelves and desks the most incredible thing I've come across are references to cannibalism, perpetrated not by the aborigines but by the Chinese.

Pickering, who lived and travelled widely in Taiwan in the turbulent 1860s, said that it was: "a common custom, upon the execution of a notorious rebel or hardened malefactor, for the executioner to abstract the liver of his victim, fry it, cut it up into small pieces, eat a portion himself, and sell the rest to the bystanders who desire to be imbued with the hardiness and courage of the man who has been beheaded. During the persecution of 1868, an unfortunate Christian convert was torn to pieces by a Chinese mob near Taiwanfoo [Tainan], and his liver was treated in the manner I have described."

Canadian missionary George MacKay also described this Chinese cannibalism. During a trip to the Yilan Plain he witnessed the execution of an aborigine before a large crowd gathered to watch the entertainment. Two executioners cut off the prisoner's head, tied it to a bamboo pole and put it on the town's west gate. "Scores were there on purpose to get parts of the body for food and medicine. Under such circumstances, or if a savage is killed inland, the heart is eaten, flesh taken off in strips, and bones boiled to a jelly and preserved as a specific [remedy] for malarial fever."

Cannibalism is a controversial subject. The idea of people eating people is abhorrent because it shows man stripped of all his layers of civilization and humanity, given over to animal lust to the extent that his fellow man is no more than a meal. This is especially true for non-survival cannibalism, where eating human flesh is not a matter of life and death.

When I was at university in the 1980s the anthropology professors and textbooks minimalized cannibalism; it was either some rare non-routine ritual or merely a fabrication of the imperialists designed to justify domination over primitive peoples. Accounts of cannibalism were dismissed as propaganda by missionaries and capitalists keen to stress the moral degradation of primitive people and their need for conversion and civilising. The academics had a point in questioning the bias and factual basis of early reports, but their studies were an example of academic revisionism gone too far, part of a reverse black and white prejudice of seeing ethnic minorities as victims, and the white settlers and missionaries as evil racists. The evidence for cannibalism is overwhelming from around the world.

\* \* \*

"So, did any of Taiwan's aborigines eat the brains of their victims?" I asked Professor Chen as I took a seat in his university office. Not a good first question! The smile vanished from his face and he looked back at me as if I'd just slapped his face, recoiling into a defensive crossed-armed position. He was adamant, "The aborigines were not cannibals!" He insisted that there was not a single scrap of evidence to prove otherwise. This was obviously a very touchy subject. Headhunting was a sensitive enough topic, but at least aboriginal apologists could partially justify it as a self-defence mechanism against the encroachment of the Chinese. The accusation of eating human flesh was really moving into darker territory.

There is actually some reasonable evidence that Taiwan's aborigines ate the brains of their headhunting victims. The Scottish Presbyterian missionary William Campbell was crossing the mountains one day when he came upon a riverbank with blood splattered about, and lying abandoned was a netted head-bag – part of the basic headhunter kit. Inside the bag were brain-glue tablets. According to Campbell: "some of the Formosan tribes boil down every head brought in to a thick jelly, from which thin oblong cakes are made, for being nibbled to inspire fresh courage when another murderous attack is to be made upon the invaders of their country." He sent these rare specimens to the Imperial Museum of Ethnology in Berlin.

MacKay was offered jellied brains "as a rare treat" while among the Atayal. He noted that while they didn't eat the flesh of victims it was "common enough to boil the brain to a jelly and eat it with vengeful relish."

The two missionaries were honest, capable and meticulous men with decades of experience in Taiwan – in short, they were reliable witnesses. But the professor did not want to know.

Regardless of the truth about the aborigines' culinary habits, what some of them may have done pales in comparison with what the

Chinese routinely did. As inconceivable as it seems, the Chinese, members of one of the world's great civilizations, ate and traded in human flesh. In *The Island of Formosa* (1903) the American reporter-turned-consul James Davidson says that:

After killing a savage, that head was commonly severed from the body and exhibited to those who were not on hand to witness the prior display of slaughter and mutilation. The body was then either divided among its captors and eaten, or sold to wealthy Chinese and even to high officials, who disposed of it in a similar manner. The kidney, liver, heart, and soles of the feet were considered the most desirable portions, and were ordinarily cut up into small pieces, boiled, and eaten somewhat in the form of soup. The flesh and bones were boiled, and the former made into a sort of a jelly. The Chinese profess to believe, in accordance with an old superstition, that the eating of savage flesh will give them strength and courage.... During the outbreak of 1891 savage flesh was brought in – in baskets – the same as pork, and sold like pork in the open markets of Tokoham [Taoyuan] before the eyes of all, foreigners included; some of the flesh was even sent to Amoy to be placed on sale there. It was frequently on sale in the small Chinese villages near the border, and often before the very eyes of peaceful groups of savages who happened to be at the place. The savages, bad as they may be, are not cannibals, and though the victim's head is severed from the body, it is carried away as a certificate of the warrior's prowess, and the body remains untouched where it falls.

\* \* \*

The twentieth century saw various episodes of "survival cannibalism" during times of extreme famine, but I don't know of anything to compare with a mass frenzy of officially sanctioned cannibalism that occurred in southern China in the late 1960s. This little-known history was brought to light by a Chinese dissident writer called Zheng Yi. He carried out his research from 1986 to 1988, and completed a book while in hiding and on the run from the authorities. The English translation of his book, *Scarlet Memorial – Tales of Cannibalism in Modern China*, is an abridged form of the weighty Chinese original.

For Zheng Yi the tragedy was more than some local anomaly. Cannibalism, he argues, was the extreme outcome of political fanaticism, the ultimate destination of totalitarianism, but also connected to the cannibalism practised in ancient times by the Zhuang, the local ethnic minority. Cannibalism also had more recent precedents – it had been justified against the Japanese during the Second World War and against the KMT during the civil war.

The cannibalism took place a short distance from the tourist Mecca of Guilin in the Guangxi Autonomous Region, an area long famous for its magical scenery of towering limestone outcrops. In the five small areas that Zheng Yi investigated, he found evidence that hundreds had been eaten and that thousands had taken part in the eating.

As elsewhere in China during the Cultural Revolution (1966–1976), mass "criticism meetings" took place in Guangxi. Names would be read out, followed by criminal charges such as being a counter-revolutionary, a spy, or a revisionist. The victims stepped forward, were publicly criticized, "subjected to dictatorship" (in other words, beaten to death) and then carved up.

Once a person fell to the ground the crowd would rush in with their knives and strip the body clean. Some of the mob had preferences for different body parts; one elderly woman with failing eyesight always hovered around the killings waiting for a chance to move in and dig out the eyeballs with her knife, and several old men had a taste for human brains, which they satisfied by driving small pipes through the skull and they would kneel on the ground together sucking out the contents. One party member, a young woman, had a taste for penises. For most people hearts and livers were the preferred flesh because of their assumed medicinal value. A schoolteacher who had heard that eating the heart of a beauty could cure disease singled out a beautiful young teenager for denunciation. She was "subjected to dictatorship." He cut out her heart and took it home to eat.

The more radical revolutionaries encouraged "hands on" killings and the mobs were told to use clubs, stones, and their fists, rather than conventional weapons. A director of a county revolutionary committee responsible for many deaths organized the carnage to the point of giving out quotas for beatings and deaths; "one third or at least a quarter of the social dregs must be bludgeoned to death during this campaign." Despite his responsibility for thousands of horrible deaths he went unpunished and was in fact promoted.

Position was neither a barrier to being eaten nor for joining the cannibal orgy. Zheng Yi cites the description of the director of the local Bureau of Commerce walking home nonchalantly with "a human leg on his shoulder, which he was taking home to boil and consume." In another appalling case a school principal was killed and "each person present ripped off a piece of flesh, and together they started an impromptu campus barbecue."

One of the most startling and depressing things is that people faced death like lambs. There was not a single act of heroism, not one case of someone fighting to live. The author only came across two cases of partial resistance where victims protested their fate. Compassion was also in short supply – in the upside-down world of the Cultural Revolution it was a sin. A widow, crying for her dead husband, was accused of showing sympathy to a class enemy and beaten to death.

The more people killed the easier it became.

"On campuses, in hospitals, in the canteens of various governmental units at the brigade, township, district, and county levels, the smoke from the cooking pots could be seen in the air. Feasts of human flesh, at which people celebrated by drinking and gambling, were a common sight."

* * *

The anarchy of the Cultural Revolution is still felt today in that it scarred China's current leaders. Fearing a return to chaos, their priorities are order before human rights, and authoritarian rule to stop China from breaking up. And for Taiwan that's not necessarily a bad thing. If China were to break up or suffer from internal turmoil and have factions vying for power, then an attack against the "renegade province" would be more likely. The military or a hawkish wing of the Communist Party could use it as a nationalistic rallying cry or a diversion in the same way the Argentinean junta used the invasion of the Falklands to divert public attention away from the disastrous economy.

# 15

# Japan's Showcase Colony

JAPANESE colonialism in Taiwan is not a story of blacks and whites. It was a mixture of militarism, harsh rule, and economic exploitation, counterbalanced with progressive, honest, and efficient government. In many ways, Japanese rule was superior to the Chinese governance that came before and after it, and old people still speak of the Japanese occupation (1895–1945) as a time of law and order, a time when there was no need to lock your door. Colonization on the beautiful isle was the least harsh of Japan's overseas adventures and today the legacy is as much goodwill as animosity. The president, for example, works in the Japanese-built Presidential Office Building, formerly the colonial headquarters. By comparison, its counterpart in Seoul was levelled by order of the Korean president. Japanese culture – everything from music, food, and fashion, to cartoons and comic books – is very popular, and there is a steady flow of tourists between the two countries.

Japan's acquisition of Taiwan came about as part of its Meiji-era expansion into the northeast of the Asian mainland and southward into the Ryukyu Islands (a chain of islands extending in an arc from Japan to within 110 kilometres of Taiwan). In 1871 a Ryukyuan ship was wrecked on the wild east coast, and fifty-four members of the sixty-six-strong crew were murdered by aborigines. Peking would accept no responsibility for the actions of non-Chinese citizens in an extra-territorial region like eastern Taiwan. Another deadly shipwrecking incident prompted Tokyo to take matters into its own hands, and in 1874 a large punitive force landed near Kending. Relations between the two countries were stretched to breaking point, but war was averted by diplomacy.

The Japanese incursion and another wake-up call ten years later, this time in the form of a French naval blockade, made the Chinese government rethink their former neglect of the island. In 1885 Taiwan was upgraded in status from a mere district of Fujian to a province and more resources were put into developing the island.

The Japanese generals had already had their eyes on Taiwan for a while when an opportunity came to secure it by indirect means. A struggle between Japan and China over control of the Korean Peninsula flared into the Sino-Japanese War of 1894–1895. After a series of battles in Korea and Shandong Province in which, true to recent form, China lost in humiliating fashion, the Treaty of Shimonoseki was signed. Japan, proving a good student of the Western imperial powers, copied what its role models had done in the preceding half century and with the agreement acquired some new treaty ports, damages, and the island of Taiwan "ceded in perpetuity."

On May 23, 1895, some Taiwanese officials and the military, unhappy about being handed over to the "dwarf pirates," declared the founding of the Democratic State of Taiwan. Independence was short lived; a week later Japanese troops landed. Taipei fell immediately, and Tainan in October. Seven thousand Taiwanese soldiers were lost in the conflict; the conquering army suffered very light casualties in action, but thousands died from disease. The heavy losses to disease deterred the Japanese from sending large numbers of settlers, and despite population pressures at home, very few Japanese farmers immigrated to Taiwan. As a result, the bulk of Japanese residents in Taiwan were officials, soldiers, and businessmen.

The island's new masters were seen by most resident foreigners as an improvement on the Chinese, though some merchants were annoyed at their profitable trade passing into Japanese government monopolies.

Taiwan was Japan's first taste of being an imperial colonizer, and its government was determined to show that they were equal to "the great and glorious work" of civilizing backward nations. They looked to European powers like England and Germany with admiration, and sought to adopt the best aspects from the West such as modern schooling and medicine.

One of the most glowing testimonials from the Japanese era is Owen Rutter's travelogue, *Through Formosa – an Account of Japan's Island Colony*, based on a brief trip the Englishman and his wife made in 1921. They arrived in Kaohsiung, travelled up the west coast to Taipei, and departed from Keelung. At that time, the country was virtually closed to tourists, but Rutter, a colonial administrator in Borneo, was able to get an official invitation through a friend. He came away greatly impressed by the cordial welcome and – with the exception of the pacification of the aborigines – Japan's colonial experiment.

"During the twenty-eight years Japan has been in possession of the island she has succeeded in developing it in a manner which must be almost, if not quite, unparalleled in the history of civilization."

*Owen Rutter with Japanese guide and rail push car, 1921*

He thought that they had done a great job after starting from scratch with a wilderness that was without an education or health system, had poor transportation, and was plagued by corrupt government, bandits, and hostile tribes. The Japanese had invested heavily but made it pay in a short time.

Rutter was given rose-coloured glasses in the form of a guide-interpreter, and a carefully controlled schedule designed to show the colony at its best. It included tours around schools, a prison, a sugar factory, a model aboriginal settlement, and some of the usual tourist sites. He and his wife also received a free train pass and red-carpet treatment: officials meeting them at train stations, invitations to dinner, and an endless exchange of cards and little cups of tea.

The Englishman had a keen eye for the details of administration, but his account often gets bogged down in tedious descriptions about accommodation, food and drink. On the steamship from Borneo to Taiwan he described the hardships thus: "We found dining at 5.30 a little trying, but fortified ourselves with biscuits before going to bed, doing our best to make each other believe that it was good for us to get out of the conventional rut of 8 o'clock dinner for a while."

His senses were overly offended, and he vents his annoyance on petty things with patronizing comments. Clothing, for example, was an ill-matching mixture of East and West such as kimonos worn with caps or bowler hats: "A bowler when worn with an ordinary lounge suit is ugly enough; with a morning coat and brown boots it is an offence, but with a kimono and geta [wooden-soled sandals] it is an outrage."

Everywhere the Rutters went they found themselves being stared at. There were only a handful of resident Westerners – mostly missionaries, teachers, diplomats, or merchants – and although the majority were based in Taipei, even there the one European club had a paltry membership of twenty.

\* \* \*

Rutter's stage-managed travels to the aborigines, brief as they were, couldn't prevent him from seeing that Japan's handling of the tribes was a failure. The problem stemmed, he thought, from a lack of sympathy because at heart the Japanese despised the aborigines as savages. Rutter believed in a more paternalistic approach, that "a native should not be treated as a savage, but rather as a child."

The Japanese had underestimated the stubbornness of the aborigines to come into the fold and found the very problem itself degrading – a hundred thousand natives tying up half the country from development. And unfortunately the "native problem" didn't draw the best and brightest government workers. In contrast, in an English colony the romance and adventure of the challenge would actually have attracted more able young men than needed. As a former district officer in Borneo, Owen had personal experience of a successful model for dealing with aborigines. District officers would visit the villages in their area of responsibility on foot, live among the people, learn the language and customs, settle legal disputes, and protect them from exploitation.

In the north of Taiwan a guard-line – cleared zones through the mountains with guard posts, mines, and even electrified wire fences – was used to cage in the recalcitrant Atayal. The guard-line very soon became an offensive line, moving further and further into the mountains and often meeting with stiff resistance. Punitive expeditions razed villages to the ground and the inhabitants were killed or forced to flee. The Japanese forces, the majority of whom were local Taiwanese soldiers, suffered heavy losses; between 1898 and 1909 alone over four thousand were killed.

In the 1920s the guard-line stopped and a system of reservations was established. Resentment against forced resettlement boiled over into revolt in 1930. Atayal fighters descended on the police station at Wushe and killed more than a hundred policemen and their families. The Japanese retaliated many-fold, and stepped up their resettlement and assimilation programme by moving highland groups into more accessible areas, improving transportation, and introducing schools.

Not all Japanese, however, were happy to see their culture supplanting tribal ways. An idealistic interpreter-turned-researcher called Mori Ushinosuke, who risked his life to venture into the mountains and study the aborigines, cared so passionately about preserving their dying cultures that he eventually took his life out of despair. Mori was born in Japan in 1877. He was a strong-willed but sickly child whose doctor predicted he wouldn't reach twenty. Chafing at the mollycoddling treatment of his mother and sisters, the sixteen-year-old Mori quit school and ran away from home to live the life of a vagabond. Two years later, he made use of the Chinese he had learnt at school and enlisted as a translator, arriving in Taiwan with the Imperial Japanese Army in 1895.

The young daydreamer was fascinated by the tribal areas and quickly made up his mind to learn about the aborigines. Mori managed to become an assistant to Japanese researchers and anthropologists, then later worked on his own. In the face of great danger and hardship he travelled on foot, unarmed and without a military escort, throughout the entire country, including unexplored areas. Three decades of research produced a massive amount of work; so many botanical specimens that he has over twenty plants named after him, an extensive photographic record of the aborigines, and the first dictionaries of the tribal languages. He also wrote many newspaper and magazine articles, and several academic publications. Although Mori became a well-known figure amongst the tribes, he never received the proper recognition he deserved from the government or the academic community because of his lack of formal qualifications.

In his later years, saddened by what was happening to aboriginal culture, Mori turned his attention to creating a reserve high up in the mountains. Failure brought depression and in 1926, at the age of forty-nine, he jumped to his death from a steamer offshore Keelung.

\* \* \*

A gutsy American, Janet McGovern, had the rare opportunity to spend time with the aborigines during her two-year stay from 1916 to 1918, and she was a critical witness to the aboriginal population's "benevolent assimilation" into the Empire of the Rising Sun. She was actually the first white woman to go among some of the tribal groups and later wrote of her experiences in *Among the Headhunters of Formosa*. McGovern had no love for the Japanese, and personally saw "instances of the most hideous cruelty on the part of the Japanese toward the Chinese-Formosans, and of barbaric torture, officially inflicted, as punishment for the most trivial offences." Her sympathies lay entirely with the tribes, and "after the mask-like stolidity of both Chinese and Japanese" found their sincere emotions refreshing. She thought them a fine people and downplayed the grisly practice of headhunting, which was then on its way out among the three tribes still practising it, by comparing it favourably to the mechanized mass murder of World War One. "What is war between 'civilized' races, except head-hunting on a grand scale," she asked.

For her the tribal villages were a socialist utopia where, "from each according to his ability, from each according to his need" was reality, where people helped each other, a person's word was sacred, and prostitution was unheard of. She was a romantic, yes, but shrewd enough to see the irony in people living a so-called primitive life in harmony with nature being far from carefree. It's tempting to imagine a return to natural living as one of freedom, breaking conventions of society, and individual indulgence in natural passions, yet the reality is that tribal behaviour is often extremely conservative and rigid, and strict laws are enforced with harsh punishments.

McGovern was interested in the matrilineal and matrilocal nature of some of the tribes, (the former being the descent of the name in the line of the mother, and the latter referring to the residence of newly married couples with the bride's tribe). However, after spending time in Hawaii, the Philippines, and with Native Americans, she had given up on finding a "true matriarchate" where women had real power. That is exactly what McGovern mistakenly believed she had found in Taiwan, and she consequently thought that Taiwan's aborigines offered a fascinating glimpse into a lost age at the dawn of civilization when, according to some anthropological theories, the world was ruled by matriarchies. In time these earth-worshipping societies were replaced by sky-worshipping patriarchies ruled over by an order of "heaven-sent" male god-kings.

It has also been argued that Chinese society was once matriarchal, and traces have survived two millennia of strict Confucian patriarchy in old myths and legends where women are imbued with special magical powers. And in sex handbooks, which date back over two thousand years, women, without exception, are the repository of knowledge and the teachers, while men are the ignorant students. Is there any significance that *yin* comes before *yang*, and that the trigram for completion of the sexual act is water over fire (i.e. a woman on top of a man)?

McGovern's view of empowered aboriginal women doesn't fit with the assertion of the first Dutch missionary, Candidius, that although the female priestesses commanded power this didn't correspond to female dominance in all areas and that the women were "complete drudges" who did most of the agricultural work.

It was Taiwan's great beauty, first seen from the ship on her way to Japan from Manila, that had interested McGovern in visiting the island. She spent several years in Japan teaching English and studying Buddhism without thinking anything more about Taiwan, as it was off limits to anyone not on business and the handful of travellers who did manage to visit were kept under strict Japanese supervision. A lucky break came while she was studying in Kyoto in the form of an offer from a Japanese official to teach English in a Japanese government school in Taipei. She eagerly accepted the invitation.

As a foreign teacher McGovern was ranked as a "two-button" official, and thereby entitled to wear two buttons on the sleeve of her coat and carry a short sword with a white handle. Most teachers were "one-button officials," who had to make do with a single button on their sleeves and a sword with a black handle. McGovern would have gladly traded places because "two-button" teachers had to attend government functions, while one-buttons "escaped these honours."

School holidays and a four-day work schedule left McGovern with plenty of time for exploring. The Japanese officials frowned on her vagabond ways, which they thought unbecoming a proper lady and tried to pressure her into doing what normal white women did: attend tea parties, take rickshaw rides around the city, play tennis and hand out Bibles. Her forays caused something of a scandal and one day the Director of Schools gave her a stern talking-to.

"Why you want to walk?" he asked. "Japanese ladies never walk; only coolie-women walk."

McGovern replied that if the distinction between being a coolie-woman and a lady was determined by whether they walked or not, that she "much preferred being classed in the former category." The perplexed director scratched his head, then came back with a cunning argument.

"Ah, but they will say you are immoral, and Christian ladies do not like to be thought immoral."

"Yes, and who is likely to think me immoral?" she asked.

"Oh, everybody. And they will publish it in the papers – all the Japanese papers in the city, and in the island, that you are immoral. And, anyhow, you must do in Rome as the Romans do."

On a conciliatory note her Japanese superior said that it would be all right if he accompanied her on trips into the mountains. McGovern warned the director, a married man, that he himself would be in danger of scandal if he travelled with a single woman while his wife was at home. And of course, McGovern, using his words, reminded him that Japanese women, "did not walk."

"I am afraid," she said, "I must continue to go my wicked way without the protection of your companionship, and if 'they' – whoever 'they' may be – annoy you with questions as to the object of my excursions into the mountains, or if they are inquisitive as to whether I go there for the purpose of a romance, legitimate or otherwise, tell them that I am one of those who like to 'eat of all the fruit of the trees of the garden of the world.'"

The director put his hands to his head in dismay, while she continued, "Tell them, 'Yes,' to anything they ask about me."

Listening to a female subordinate talk back to him in such a manner was too much for the man, and he could contain his anger no longer.

"I'll tell them you are immoral, that's what I'll tell them –" he snapped as he tried to rise and leave. However, the director was rather fat, unaccustomed to sitting in a chair, and his sword had become stuck in the wickerwork, so that when he stood up the chair rose up with him. It was not a dignified exit.

Some of the Western residents also had trouble accepting McGovern's interest in local culture. One day, absorbed in singing some aboriginal chant, she walked straight past a missionary acquaintance without acknowledging her. McGovern, realising her error, turned around to apologize and explained that she was returning home after having just visited a Chinese friend and his three wives.

"Disgusting heathen!" exclaimed the woman, and, no doubt worried that McGovern was "going native" implored her to be more careful about wearing her sun-helmet in a tropical climate. "If one does not, something might happen to one – to one's head, you know," adding gravely, "and it would be a terrible thing in a heathen country...."

McGovern was surprised to find that all the women of Chinese descent "except those of the despised Hakkas" had bound feet. She had understandably supposed that the custom was restricted to the upper classes. In fact, it was still considered essential for marriage, as she found out one day when her house-boy came begging his "Shining Lord" to lend him seventy yen to buy a "lily-footed bride." His father had told him it was time to marry but with savings of only forty yen he would only be able to afford a "big-footed" wife, which would make him a laughing-stock.

Luckily for McGovern two sympathetic officials gave her the necessary permission to make trips into the mountains. She mostly travelled by push-car railway, and would then set out on foot. The warm receptions she invariably received and the close relations she managed to forge so quickly with the aborigines were, she believed, due to the fact that they regarded her "as the reincarnation of one of the seventeenth-century Dutch, whose rule over them, three hundred years ago, has become a sacred tradition." Oral history said that the Dutch had treated the aborigines well, and even taught them to read and write their own dialect in the "sign-marks of the gods" (i.e. romanized script). McGovern was told that there were old books written by their ancestors, but they had been confiscated by the Japanese. The time of the Dutch was remembered and cherished as a Golden Age although no evidence remained except for the vague memories of culture given by "fair gods who came over the sea in white-winged boats" or "came up out of the sea." McGovern also relates a belief among some of the tribes that a reincarnation of a former "Great White Chief," who she speculates could be Candidius, would return and help them kick out the Chinese and Japanese.

During her first New Year vacation McGovern visited the Ami tribe along the East Coast. It was impossible to travel overland so she embarked on a small coastal steamer in Keelung that was headed for Kaohsiung. The coastal scenery north of Hualien is truly spectacular, sea cliffs that rise straight out of the ocean, and McGovern was suitably impressed, calling it "one of the most imposing sights" she had seen in all her wanderings around the world.

On the second day a storm broke, making it too dangerous for the ship to put in at McGovern's intended destination, the southeastern town of Taitung. When several Ami canoes braved the wild seas to row out and barter with the steamer, she saw her chance. She could go back in one of the canoes. The Japanese captain, who happened to speak

English with a Scottish accent, didn't want the responsibility of her death and forbade it. After much argument he gave up and lowered a ladder so the spirited woman could scramble down into the Ami chief's craft. Stormy weather whipped the sea up into a mass of waves, and the canoe was swamped. The chief, unfazed by the situation, motioned her to get on his back and he swam to shore with McGovern – a poor swimmer – clinging on for dear life.

During her next winter vacation, spent in the mountains of the Atayal, she was crossing a swollen stream when an aborigine appeared and carried her across. They continued on to a group of villagers who, made homeless by torrential rains that had destroyed their bamboo huts, were sheltering under a great tree. This tree was sacred, the dwelling place of their ancestors, and the village priestesses had just been praying to the spirits including the "Great White Fathers of Long Ago." The arrival of a white woman was interpreted as an answer to the prayers and both men and women fell on their faces, and some of the children fled shrieking in terror.

McGovern believed the fact that she had "come to them out of the water" on two occasions also impressed the people, "made certain in their minds the conviction that I was the spirit of one of the beloved white rulers of old, returned from the elements."

*Paiwan skull rack, 1901*

McGovern's stay in Taiwan coincided with the twilight years of headhunting; the Japanese were trying hard to stamp it out, and the practice was in sharp decline. Some of the more bloody customs associated with headhunting continued with substitutes for human flesh. The Paiwan, for example, had a game – played once every five years – in which a bundle of bark was tossed in the air and warriors tried to lance it, the winner being the first warrior to catch it on his bamboo spear. Formerly an enemy's head had been used.

* * *

The neighbouring Piyuma tribe had an annual ceremony in which a live monkey was tied before the bachelor dormitory and young men killed it by shooting arrows into the unlucky creature. An offering of alcohol was thrown thrice to the sky and earth by a village chief, a signal for singing, dancing, and feasting to commence. The tribal elders explained that in the good old days a prisoner, some unfortunate from a rival tribe, was used but now they had to make do with a monkey. And the animal was a lousy substitute because it couldn't act as a messenger to the afterlife, whereas with the human sacrifice each of the arrows carried a message to an ancestor in the spirit world.

The marriage ceremony usually involved the bride and groom squatting back to back inside a circle of relatives and friends. Sword-yielding priestesses danced around the couple chanting and slashing the air to drive away evil spirits. The marriage ceremony had a rather macabre conclusion, the bride and groom drinking together from a skull, preferably one the man had collected himself. Surprisingly, McGovern found that the majority of Atayal grooms had indeed taken heads. Men in other tribes made do with skulls taken by their father or grandfather. The Ami and Piyuma substituted with monkey skulls, "for which effeminacy they are held in great contempt by the Taiyal [Atayal]."

A practice common among the teenage boys and girls was the removal of two upper incisor teeth. Tattooing started even earlier – boys and girls around the age of five had several horizontal lines tattooed on their forehead. A tattoo on the chin signified that the man had taken a head.

McGovern saw no trace of the infanticide mentioned by Candidius, but says that illegitimate babies were killed. Adultery was considered a heinous crime and in those tribes uncivilized by Japanese and Chinese, the offender, be it man or woman, was punished by death. McGovern not only found that prostitution was unheard of among the mountain tribes, but that she couldn't even explain the idea of prostitution to them.

*Atayal woman with facial tattoo. Only girls who had proved their skill in weaving could have their faces tattooed*

One of Janet McGovern's goals was to determine whether there was any truth to the rumour of the existence of a pigmy tribe. Not surprisingly, no such group was found although she did come across a few very short women in Atayal territory that she conjectured might be remnants of an ancient population of pygmies. The three woman had "negroid" features but not the dark skin and crinkly hair to go with them. These "pygmy women" were probably just anomalies, yet there is an interesting "dwarf" legend among the small Saisiyat tribe bordering the Atayal. Folklore has it that three-foot dwarfs taught them how to farm, sing and dance. Things went wrong when the dwarfs started making moves on the Saisiyat women. The aborigines invited the dwarfs to a ceremony and on the way pushed them off a cane suspension bridge into a deep ravine. Every two years since then, and to this very day, the Saisiyat in Miaoli hold "the Ceremony of the Dwarfs" to appease the souls of the murdered dwarfs.

# 16
# The Hell Camp of Kinkaseki

A LITTLE over an hour's drive from Taipei around Taiwan's northeast coast takes you to Jiufen, a historic mining settlement that clings to steep denuded hills overlooking the Pacific. After gold was discovered the town boomed, and by the mid-1930s it was known as "Little Shanghai:" a place of bright lights, windfalls, whoring, and desperate toil. A decade later the gold was gone and so were the lights and people. Today Jiufen is a tourist town full of arts and crafts shops and traditional teashops catering to Taipei day-trippers. A few minutes further along the coast at the bottom of steep hills strewn with abandoned mining buildings and gravestones, lies the sleepy village of Jinguashi. During the Second World War, when it was known by the Japanese name of Kinkaseki, it was the most notorious POW labour camp on the island and the final resting place for hundreds of British prisoners.

The Kinkaseki POW saga began in Malaysia. A Japanese task force first landed on the northeast coast on December 8, 1941, which brings up a little known point. Japan's entry into the Second World War did not start with the attack on Pearl Harbour; the air strike on the Hawaiian naval base was on the seventh of December but the time difference meant the Japanese had actually attacked Malaysia about an hour earlier.

The Japanese air force was equipped with faster, more manoeuvrable planes flown by better-trained pilots, and the army boasted hardened troops who had been trained for jungle warfare. Britain was tied up fighting the Nazis in Europe and North Africa, and the Allied troops in Malaya were inexperienced and ill-prepared. The British air force was a shambles, and the absolute necessity for air support in modern warfare was dramatically shown two days after the invasion when the battleships *HMS Prince of Wales* and *HMS Repulse*, operating without air cover, were sunk.

The British fought a running retreat down the Malayan Peninsula to the "impregnable fortress" of Singapore, surrendering to the Japanese on Chinese New Year's Day, February 15, 1942. It was a fatal blow to the colonial empires in the East as it shattered forever the assumed superiority and invincibility of the white man. British Prime Minister, Winston Churchill, called the fall of Singapore "the worst disaster and largest capitulation in British history."

Summary executions of the local Singaporean population began in earnest; all male Chinese between eighteen and fifty were ordered to assemble, tens of thousands of whom were taken away, tortured, and killed. Some civilians – women and children as well as men – were roped together, taken out to sea, and pushed overboard. Those who didn't drown were shot.

The fall of Singapore and the ordeals of the "hell-camp" of Kinkaseki are chronicled in *Banzai You Bastards!*, a suitably defiant title from its tough Welsh author, Jack Edwards, a sergeant in the Royal Corps of Signals. After the surrender of Singapore, Edwards was in a work party assigned to drag dead bodies from the beaches to mass graves: a grisly job made worse by the fact that the corpses were often entangled in barbed wire and decomposing under the equatorial sun. The killings and burials continued for three weeks.

Toward the end of 1942 Edwards and his comrades were shipped to the Taiwanese port of Keelung, then marched to a camp at Kinkaseki and put to work mining copper. On his first day down the mines Edwards felt as if had descended into hell; carbide lamps provided feeble lighting as, bent over in the tiny shafts, they descended down steps, level after level, hotter and hotter the lower they descended until they were nearly two hundred feet below sea level.

The guards, who soon earned themselves nicknames like "the Beast" and "the Madman," took every opportunity to beat prisoners. Whenever prisoners saw or went past camp personnel, even the lowest-ranking Taiwanese guards, they had to stand to attention and bow. Failure to do this quickly enough, or to the guards' satisfaction, resulted in a beating, which could be anything from a slap or punch to being beaten unconscious with a rifle butt. The more sadistic guards took pleasure in catching out the POWs by rushing into huts so they wouldn't have enough time to come to attention and bow. Beatings were lashed out for offences as trivial as lying down in bed before the official nine o'clock "lights out." Even in sleep there was no rest from beatings thanks to an order that blankets couldn't be pulled over their heads; offending prisoners were often rudely awoken from their dreams on cold winter nights with a rifle butt, slapped around and forced to stand for an hour as punishment.

High rank and illness were no protection. Officers and hospital patients also came in for vicious beatings. Major Crossley, the highest-ranking prisoner, kept – at great personal risk – a secret diary in which he recorded some of the worse beatings. Here are extracts for February 1943, taken from *Banzai You Bastards!*.

> *2nd February.* A Taiwan soldier known as "The Nasty Carpenter" went into the officers' billet and there was a terrific beating-up. Many officers were knocked out completely.

> *8th February.* Eight Taiwan soldiers (the "Runabouts") entered the officers' billet and made straight for Captain A. Sewell, MC, RA. They proceeded, each in turn, to beat him for an hour, and finished up with a sentry with rifle, holding the butt end, hitting him on the head with the bayonet. The officer concerned was in a very bad way when this brutal, savage beating was finished.

> *18th February.* Inspection of the whole camp. All Taiwan soldiers appeared with sticks, and beat up all the sick men left in the camp after the mine workers had left.

> *20th February.* The Camp Commander walked into the prisoners' cook-house and ordered four of the cooks to beat each other with fists for half an hour. The Japanese NCO of the guard ("Mussolini") had a terrific day, beating up all and sundry."

While one out of every twenty British prisoners in the POW camps of Nazi Europe died, in Japanese camps that figure was one out of every three (and that doesn't include those that died soon after from ill health). The difference in the rates was a result of tropical diseases and harsher treatment that stemmed from the Japanese despising their prisoners. According to the warrior code of the samurai, they should have died in battle or committed suicide instead of surrendering.

Despite the hard physical labour at Kinkaseki, the prisoners were on starvation rations; it took an iron will not to talk or think about food. Some men tormented themselves with imaginary menus and meals, a sign they were on their way out. Edwards proudly recalls that "the vast majority looked after their mates" and that "knowing that someone cared, the love of one individual for another, is what enabled us to survive." For him the key to survival was "courage, self-respect, and mutual respect between the men."

One of the biggest morale-boosters was news from the outside world and the prisoners took considerable risks to scrounge a few scraps. To facilitate the running of the camp and mines, the guards had beaten a handful of Japanese numbers and commands into the prisoners. Edwards didn't need any prompting and took advantage of every chance he had to pick up the language, which he put to use in gathering news. He befriended a Taiwanese coolie who he had overheard singing "Onward Christian Soldiers" in Taiwanese. The man had been to a Christian school and hated the Japanese. In a mix of Japanese and English the worker gave Edwards the latest news, and a little while later smuggled in a two-sheet Japanese newspaper reporting the Allied landing in France. That was the first of many newssheets either stolen or brought in by sympathetic civilians. Prisoners were always searched going to and from the mine but the resourceful Edwards never got caught. Back in the camp he would hand the papers over to a couple of the officers who could read enough Japanese to translate the newspapers.

The news about the fighting in Europe was reasonably accurate, but that from the Pacific was pure propaganda. There was even a story about Japanese airmen who had brought down two enemy planes by throwing rice balls at them. Still, reading between the lines and noting how the glorious Japanese victories kept getting nearer and nearer to Taiwan confirmed that Japan was losing the war.

Edwards was befriended by an American-born Japanese mine policeman who had come to Taiwan in 1940 and been stuck there against his will. The Allied sympathizer said he would try to get news of the prison camp off the island through friends in Keelung. Edwards never saw him again, but heard later that a spy had been caught and executed near Keelung – presumably the same man. No news of the hell-camp ever got off the island.

The first definite sign that the war had turned was the first sighting of American fighter-bombers in October 1944. It was a much-needed morale-raiser: "To know that at last someone was hitting back for us gave us our best feeling since we had been taken prisoner. We felt that every bomb dropped was a blow in retaliation for our persecution."

A few weeks later there was a much bigger raid on Keelung – a night Edwards would never forget. As the prisoners lay in their beds listening to the bombs explode they gave vent to their anger, and cursed the guards who were hiding in shelters. When the guards returned and asked Edwards who had shouted, he pleaded ignorance, and was punched, knocked to the ground and kicked. He was taken away for a bashing with a bamboo fencing stick, then forced to kneel on stony ground, and whenever he moved – even made the slightest adjustment to bring relief to his aching legs – he was hit with a stick or fist. Edwards felt his life drifting away as the guards stepped up the torture. On regaining consciousness, he found himself lying half-dead in a hut. Now weakened, he felt his "turn" was close at hand.

The following month brought some good news. The camp commandant explained that, "out of concern" for the prisoners' health, a tunnel "short cut" had been dug. This tunnel saved the men from the tiring climb over a hill, which was often made in rain and took an hour either way. The good news soon took on a macabre aspect. The POW officers learnt from some sympathetic Taiwanese that there were official orders to kill all the prisoners in the advent of the Americans landing on the island. Only Edwards and five others knew this, and lived with the knowledge of this axe hanging over their heads, afraid to tell the other men lest it break their will to live. A closer inspection of the short-cut tunnel revealed heavy metal doors at either end that made it suitable for holding all the prisoners. Edwards had to go to work and back with the knowledge that the "short cut" would most likely become his tomb.

Days dragged on through the wet winter, and the death rate worsened as years of slave labour, beatings, disease, and starvation took their toll. One day Edwards collapsed in the mine and woke up in a small sick ward known as the "Death Hut" because so few returned from it. He managed to recover and left the living nightmare of broken men raving and sobbing away their final days of life.

Trying to escape from the camp would have been fruitless but one small breakout occurred in another camp at Taichung. The two escaping soldiers were quickly caught, tortured, made to dig their own graves, and beheaded. Their foolhardy attempt brought harsher treatment for that camp and others throughout the island.

In March 1945 work stopped in the mine, rations were cut, and the following month the prisoners were moved to a jungle camp south of Taipei, where they spent the last four months of the war. On their journey there they saw extensive bombing damage and preparations for an invasion. The final leg was a seventeen-kilometre uphill trek from Xindian that was so gruelling that even some of the guards collapsed. The POWs' job was to build a camp from scratch on a disused and overgrown tea plantation. They were set to work planting, building, collecting materials from the jungle, or portering supplies up from Xindian. Racing to an impossible deadline made for endless beatings and despite the work being safer than in the mines they were "never hungrier, worked harder, or beaten more." Their only solace was seeing daily flights of American bombers passing overhead to bomb Taipei.

Edwards later wrote: "Those of us who survived those four weeks are convinced we were walking on the narrow edge between man and animal. All of us looked ghastly, eyes sunken, mere skeletons, covered with rashes, sores, or cuts which would not heal. Others too far gone to save were blown-up with beri-beri, legs and testicles like balloons."

On the sixteenth of August normal work duties were suspended amid rumours the war had ended, and on the eighteenth the Camp Commander informed them that peace talks were underway. They left the camp the following week – sick men carrying those sicker yet on foot down the mountain – and then travelled by truck to Taipei. The Japanese surrendered meekly to the arriving Americans and the British POWs were evacuated by the U.S. Navy.

Although Edwards returned to the camp in 1946 as part of a war-crimes investigation team, and later made two other trips back to Jinguashi, it took him over forty years to write *Banzai You Bastards!* because he was "too traumatized by the experience" and would become overwhelmed with emotions whenever he attempted to put it down on paper. A trip back to Taiwan to make a documentary film helped banish some of the ghosts and hardened his resolve to write his book. It was published in 1991, followed by a Japanese version two years later.

\* \* \*

I tracked down another former POW from Kinkaseki, Jack Butterworth, a retired printer from Manchester, and talked with him over the phone. Despite his age, eighty-three, he was as sharp as a tack, comfortable discussing his experiences, and could recall details in an instant. Trying hard not to sound condescending, I asked how he had kept his mental facilities so intact.

"Music. I play the clarinet and when you're a musician you can't miss a single note." He also played the saxophone, oboe, and flute, and had been a bandsman in the army.

I felt bad making the old gentleman talk because he had trouble breathing and would draw in raspy breaths between sentences.

"What happened after you surrendered at Singapore?" I asked of his unit.

"*We* didn't surrender! The *generals* did!" he answered with a fierceness that shocked me – fifty-eight years obviously hadn't erased the anger of not being given the chance to fight. "We were disgusted when the order came through. It was a terrible mess. There wasn't a single plane in the sky!"

After being taken prisoner at Singapore, Butterworth was shipped to southern Taiwan and spent his first year in a camp picking up rocks and carting them away in canvas stretchers.

"Oh, it wasn't that hard really compared to Kinkaseki. The only thing was that I picked up malaria, which they didn't have up in the north. I spent nearly two years at Kinkaseki then I was put on what they called a 'thin man party,' those that were too sick to work were moved on to easier camps."

"And what work did you do at Kinkaseki?"

"Down in the copper mines. It was extremely dangerous because we dug up rather than in, and as the roof went up we had to raise the floor with rubble. Debris often came crashing down, and many men were injured. You had to bring out twenty-four bogeys of good cooper ore per day for a four-man team. If you didn't get that you were lined up and beaten."

"Beaten with what?"

"Six or eight strokes with a stick, a hammer shaft, and it was called 'getting the hammer.' You'd look at the rock at the beginning of the day, decide whether to go for the twenty-four or not. Sometimes it was better to get the beating."

"And were the Taiwanese guards less harsh than the Japanese?"

"Just as cruel. They emulated their masters very well. The guards would strike you for the most trivial things. You had to stand to attention while they hit your head with their fist. If you didn't, trying to dodge it, then you'd end up with a rifle butt on your head, on the ground –" he was stopped by painful wheezing fit, "Sorry, I suffer from asthma," he explained then continued, "on the ground getting kicked. I saw them murder a man, hit on the head with a sword scabbard – he died that night from the wounds."

"Do you still hate the Japanese?" I asked.

"Not now. Of course, at first everything Jap was bad, but you can't live with hate in your heart. I lost many close friends so I still feel hatred towards the camp guards but not the Japanese people. Some men still do though, mostly those who lost brothers in the camps."

"And how was the morale and camaraderie?"

"It was marvellous really. If you lost the will to live, two or three days and you were gone. I never ever thought I was going to die."

"Your willpower saved you?" I asked while Mr. Butterworth drew a couple of wheezy breaths.

"No. It was the atomic bomb what saved us. The Japanese had plans for disposal of all the prisoners, with discretion given to the camp commander whether to bury, drown, or shoot them. It was planned for the eighteenth of August 1945, but news of the surrender came through on the sixteenth, two days short of us being disposed of. I have copies of those documents if you'd like to see them."

\* \* \*

War-crime trials were held in Japan, but the majority of war criminals escaped justice; and since then, in sharp contrast to the continual prosecution and retribution sought for Nazi crimes, there has been little or no investigation. The Japanese got off very lightly after the war because attention quickly turned to halting the communist threat. Chiang Kai-shek actually recruited some Japanese officers and soldiers into the KMT army, one notable example being the commander-in-chief of the Japanese invasion army, Yasuji Okamura, the man who had come up with the idea of the "comfort women" program. (Historians estimate more than 330,000 women were forced to work as prostitutes, but Tokyo continues to deny official involvement.) Okamura was appointed as a secret military advisory by the KMT, and helped form a group of Japanese military advisors that trained tens of thousands of soldiers in Taiwan from 1949 to 1968.

The only compensation the POWs have received was a meagre seventy-six pounds from the British government at the end of the war. Jack Edwards and others continue to press the Japanese government for compensation but Japan has stubbornly refused to admit guilt, and it seems to be simply waiting for all the old men to die off. Indeed, Jack Butterworth passed away just six weeks after speaking to me (and several months short of his planned trip to return to Kinkaseki).

# 17

# The White Terror

WITH Japan's surrender Taiwan once more became part of China. The reunion was not a happy one. After suffering fifty years of discrimination under harsh Japanese rule, the Taiwanese were glad to be free; but their hopes were quickly dashed. The island was placed under military rule and the hard-liner Chen Yi appointed governor-general. The army commandeered material and buildings for its own use and the island was stripped. Rice supplies were seized and sent to troops fighting the Communists in China. The resulting shortages caused severe hardships. Prices skyrocketed, black-market profiteering flourished, government services broke down, and disease flourished. Moreover, many of the soldiers who arrived from China were a sorry sight – little more than an undisciplined, uneducated, and dishonest rabble. In short most Taiwanese began to feel that their fellow Chinese "liberating heroes" were actually worse than the Japanese.

The antipathy was two-way. To the Chinese arrivals, the Taiwanese were Japanese collaborators; more than two hundred thousand of them had served in the Imperial military, and despite a policy to send them to Southeast Asia, some had served in Japanese units fighting against Chinese forces. Taiwanese people spoke Japanese rather than Mandarin Chinese, and had adopted much of the fashion, etiquette, and culture of their conquerors.

All that was needed to ignite this powder keg of animosity was a small spark. It came on February 27, 1947, in the unlikely form of a middle-aged Taiwanese widow selling cigarettes without the required licence. Agents from the Tobacco Monopoly Bureau tried to confiscate the woman's cigarettes and money; she resisted so they beat her. Outraged bystanders protested. The agents fled the scene, shooting as they did so. A man in the crowd was hit and died the following day. On February 28, rioting broke out and spread throughout the island.

To the military authorities, what was a leaderless and unorganized spontaneous protest looked like a rebellion, and Governor-General Chen Yi reacted with an iron fist. Reinforcements were brought in from China and a brutal crackdown ensued. It was government-sanctioned mass murder, rationalized as suppressing communists but in fact revenge for Taiwanese violence against the mainlanders. And at a time when a life-and-death struggle for the Chinese homeland was underway, any anti-government action was seen as traitorous.

The exact death toll will never be known; but a very conservative estimate would be about ten thousand. In 1992 a KMT report put the number between 18,000 and 28,000. More devastating for Taiwan than the sheer number was the calibre of the victims. Lists were drawn up of lawyers, landowners, businessmen, academics, doctors, journalists, artists, and students, who were then rounded up and executed. The cream of a generation was wiped out. Although Chiang Kai-shek replaced Chen Yi with a moderate, the "White Terror" continued, martial law was imposed in 1949, and Taiwan became a police state.

History was suppressed for nearly forty years; textbooks made no mention of "2-28," and it was a taboo topic – to the extreme that just talking about it in public could send you to prison. This only changed after the lifting of martial law in 1987 and the death of Chiang Ching-kuo (Chiang Kai-shek's son) a year later. In 1995 President Lee Teng-hui made an official apology, and in 1997, fifty years after the incident, 2-28 was made a national holiday.

* * *

One of the least-known facts about the first decades of KMT rule in Taiwan is how intricately the party was bound up with the drug trade. It was actually the KMT that turned the infamous Golden Triangle – the tri-border junction of Laos, Thailand, and the wild Shan States of Burma – into the world's premium source of heroin. Before the KMT set up operations in Burma the country produced a modest thirty tons of opium (from which heroin is derived) a year for local consumption. After five years production had exploded to two hundred tons a year, and it continued rising.

Following their defeat in the "Opium Wars" of the mid-nineteenth century the Chinese line on drugs became, "If you can't beat 'em join 'em." Within decades poppies were being cultivated on a large scale in the southwestern provinces of Sichuan and Yunnan. This "import substitution" helped the balance of payments but only exacerbated the social and health consequences of drug use. The fall of the Qing dynasty in 1911 ushered in a chaotic period that saw warlords vying for power, civil war between the KMT and CCP, and invasion by the

Japanese. All these players, Chiang Kai-shek included, utilised the drug trade as an easy means to shore up treasuries for military expenditure.

With the defeat of the KMT forces in China, Chiang Kai-shek, like Koxinga three centuries before, retreated with his forces to Taiwan, from which he hoped to retake the mainland. Some of his troops, however, were stuck far inland so instead of crossing the Taiwan Strait they retreated southward to Yunnan. The KMT planned to establish a base there but were pushed across the border into the mountainous Shan States of Burma. So began Taiwan's secret war. Contacts were made with the local Chinese community in Burma and northern Thailand, a base established, and an old airstrip upgraded for supply planes flying in from Taipei and Bangkok. The Burmese government was too busy suppressing ethnic and communist insurgents to forcibly eject these uninvited guests.

The Americans, deciding that opium was a lesser evil than communism, turned a blind eye. They gave covert assistance to the KMT in the Golden Triangle. A small freight airline, Civil Air Transport (later renamed Air America), was bought and used as a CIA front to take in military supplies from Taipei and Bangkok.

Although pressure from the international community and Burmese military attacks forced the KMT to repatriate most of their soldiers to Taiwan in 1954, several thousand troops remained behind and continued their drug running and secret war.

\* \* \*

Chiang Kai-shek's son, Chiang Ching-kuo, is an interesting character who is difficult to tie down. He was caught up in many of the major twists and turns of the century – was at one time a communist, ran a police state in Taiwan, and presided over the island's economic miracle. During his presidency, from 1978 to his death in 1988, he also laid the groundwork for democracy, although his critics argue it was more a case of just reacting, and slowly at that, to events and the tide of history.

Chiang Ching-kuo was the first and only child of Chiang Kai-shek's first wife, a woman his father physically abused and later divorced. From the beginning Ching-kuo had a stormy relationship with his father, and it only became worse as the young Chiang became involved in left-wing politics and publicly criticized his father's actions. Chiang reluctantly gave Ching-kuo permission to go to the Soviet Union to study. At that time the KMT was still in an alliance with the Chinese Communist Party and receiving aid from the Soviets. Shortly after

Ching-kuo graduated from university in Moscow, his father launched a purge of the Communists. Ching-kuo was appalled and condemned his father as a counter-revolutionary and a traitor. It was only in 1937 that he returned to China and a reconciliation took place. Now disillusioned with communism the young Chiang worked diligently under his father.

Chiang Ching-kuo can either look good or bad, depending on whether you compare him to his father or to his successor, Lee Teng-hui. Doubtless Chiang Ching-kuo was a savvy and experienced politician who, with the help of some outstanding staff, transformed Taiwan for the better, but he was an old-fashioned authoritarian who crushed any political dissent and repressed Taiwanese language and culture. Despite cultivating a folksy image as a hard-working public servant – lots of tours around the country to small towns in baseball jackets and caps – and as a quiet-living man, there were more than a few skeletons in the Chiang Ching-kuo closet.

In the early 1980s a naturalized American journalist, Henry Liu, wrote a short biography of Chiang Ching-kuo, revealing embarrassing information about his extra-marital activities and illegitimate children. Taiwan's ruling family was not amused. The intelligence agency was given the job of silencing Liu. The dirty work was farmed out to the criminal Bamboo Union Gang.

Things did not go to plan. The gangsters – who turned up on bicycles at Henry Liu's house on October 15, 1984, and shot him dead – were quickly tracked down and the plot exposed. Among the gaffs was a phone call made by the killers to Taiwan's defence intelligence bureau to boast they had done the job. The call was picked up by American intelligence, and before long the whole sorry story had been pieced together. Strong pressure from Washington led to a couple of high-ranking scapegoats doing time, but it is thought that the order to murder Henry Liu had actually come from Chiang Ching-kuo's second son, Alex Chiang (Chiang Hsiao-wu).

Alex Chiang died in Japan in 1991 at the age of forty-six. Chiang Ching-kuo's children – three boys and a girl by his Russian wife – were the only third-generation Chiangs. People have offered a variety of explanations for the bad luck of the third generation of Chiangs; it was the bad karma from their father and grandfather's misdeeds, or it was because Chiang Kai-shek's body was not disposed of properly. His body was not buried but lies in a heavy sarcophagus in his former country house near the Shimen Reservoir, a temporary resting place until political relations allow a return home.

* * *

The 2-28 massacre had wiped out the Taiwanese elite, silenced a generation, and turned people away from politics. It wasn't until the 1970s that a new middle class began to emerge and started demanding freedom and democratic rights. Taiwan's democratic transformation has been dubbed "the quiet revolution" and in keeping with the peaceful and gradual nature of change there were few landmark events. The major exception is the Kaohsiung Incident of December 10, 1979. It was a watershed event for Taiwanese self-identity, and the careers of many of today's leading politicians can be traced back to it. The incident started with a rally organized by *Formosa Magazine*, a front for the then-illegal opposition political party. The rally, held to observe Human Rights Day, turned violent.

A crackdown ensued, and among the arrested were eight leading pro-democracy figures soon to become known as the Kaohsiung Eight. They were tried by court martial on charges of sedition, a charge carrying a mandatory death penalty. Their nine-day trial received intense coverage and provided a rare opportunity for the activists to promote their causes: the end of political censorship, the end of martial law, and the replacement of one-party rule with democracy and free elections. Their well-presented arguments and common sense together with their self-sacrifice won a lot of public sympathy.

Future president Chen Shui-bian was then the youngest lawyer on the defence team, and one of the most outspoken. The twenty-nine-year-old maritime lawyer was taking a huge risk – it could have ruined his successful law career, and it was only his wife's prompting that pushed him to take up the challenge.

Chen and the other lawyers lost their cases, but it was something of a victory that none of the Kaohsiung Eight were sentenced to death. Even Shih Ming-te – though daring the authorities to execute him – was given a life sentence instead; the others received sentences of ten to fourteen years.

Two infamous murder cases occurred shortly after the Kaohsiung Incident; they remain unsolved to this day, though many suspect the authorities were responsible. On February 28, 1980, the mother and daughters of Lin Yi-hsiung (one of the eight) were brutally murdered at his residence while he was in jail. The following year the badly beaten corpse of Chen Wen-cheng, a Taiwanese-born math professor visiting the island, was found on the campus of the National Taiwan University. The police determined that the cause of death was "suicide" out of remorse for having criticized human rights violations in Taiwan.

# 18

# Island Fortress

As the small aircraft taxied out to the runway past military hangars, workshops, and bunkers, Taiwan's first line of defence – F-16 fighter jets – came into view. They were parked under camouflaged roofs shaped like hillocks, and ready to scramble at a moment's notice. This was Shuishang Airport, an air force base that doubles as a domestic airport for the nearby city of Chiayi. I kept an eye open for my "blood brother" (it's too long a story to tell, but I was very drunk at the time), an old student and friend of mine who was in charge of loading missiles at the airbase. My friend, Book (a strange enough name to begin with, even more so for a man of such few words) did have something to say on the topic of flying – rather worryingly he was afraid of getting into aircraft of any kind, military or civilian.

Speaking of planes and strange names, two of Taiwan's domestic carriers have rather unfortunate ones. Who was the genius who though up the name "U-land"? Is it a guarantee that you will indeed land (as opposed to exploding in mid-air) or do you actually have to land the plane yourself? Then there's Far Eastern Air Transport, which shortens itself down to the acronym FAT.

I'd given my fellow passengers the once-over back in the waiting lounge and it was obvious this was no ordinary flight; most of the passengers were young soldiers, about half of whom didn't have enough backbone to sit up straight and had slunk so far down into seats they were nearly horizontal. They could have learnt a thing or two from a pair of likely prostitutes sitting ramrod straight, their shoulders back, chests out, and heads held up. The two women were in their early twenties; one had the darker colouring and rounded eyes of an aborigine and was pretty. Both were very self-conscious, and kept touching their hair and faces, and rearranging their clothing as if they were models having one last look into a mirror before a fashion shoot. From their dyed and permed hair to their high-heel shoes they had transformed natural good looks into cheap plastic sex appeal, what Taiwanese call "spice girls."

The fashion in Taiwan these days is for a busty look rather incompatible with most Chinese girls' slight frames. Padding makes up the deficit. Like some kind of cold war arms race, it seems the bras get bulkier and more sophisticated every year, and these two ladies heading to the frontline were wearing state-of-the-art ones that had so much padding that they could've doubled as mattresses. A few of the younger soldiers watched the two women out of the corner of their eyes with a mixture of fear and excitement. Away from home for the first time, and with a bit of money in their pockets, they were no doubt looking forward to their first bit of action. The other passengers I guessed were Kinmen residents by the honest-looking faces you can only get from working outdoors and living on an island that gets pummelled by fierce winds for nearly half the year. I was the only tourist, foreign or local.

The plane took off. Our destination was Kinmen, a small island right on China's front door, literally just a few kilometres away, and one of the most heavily fortified pieces of real estate in the world. The island, which has been the scene of major battles, was under strict martial law until 1993. Residents had to endure decades of artillery bombardment and an evening curfew that meant total darkness outside after nightfall, and they could use inside lights only if the windows were shuttered. Islanders were prohibited from moving to Taiwan because of the entirely realistic fear that the entire population would leave.

The flight over the Taiwan Strait took just fifty minutes. Engineers in China, looking ahead to a time when relations between Taiwan are normalized, have drawn up tentative plans for a tunnel that would link both sides. The tunnel would have a staggering 125 kilometres underwater, making it over three times longer than the world's longest, the Channel Tunnel between England and France, which has a thirty-eight-kilometre underwater section. Given the cost and various technical problems, it won't happen anytime soon, if ever.

Back in 1984, the attraction of crossing the strait proved a fatal one for a flamboyant French aristocrat, Baron Arnaud de Rosnay. The thirty-eight-year-old attempted to windsurf to Taiwan from the Chinese port city of Quanzhou. De Rosnay was an expert windsurfer with some major open-water crossings under his belt; he had windsurfed from Florida to Cuba and across the Bering Strait. He set off alone on November 24, quietly slipping past the Chinese coast guard and navy. He was never seen again, and what happened to him remains a mystery.

\* \* \*

As the plane came in low to land, a great view opened up of farmland dotted with little villages and clusters of old-fashioned houses sporting curved tiled roofs. That first impression was confirmed on the ground. Kinmen is a pretty and surprisingly peaceful little island blessed with unspoiled (by Taiwanese standards) rural scenery and historic architecture that Taiwan so sorely lacks. The roads are good, the traffic light, and the island is clean. The military presence is low key largely because most military buildings and armaments are underground; everything from bunkers and a huge auditorium for concerts and movies, to a hospital, has been carved out of solid granite.

Having about thirty thousand soldiers stationed on Kinmen has meant a ready supply of labour for public works such as planting trees, cleaning streets, and reconstructing historical buildings – cheap labour, too, because most of the soldiers are conscripts doing their compulsory two-year military service and earn only a small stipend. In addition, the military zones and the designation of the island as a National Park have mostly prevented the type of ugly development so common in Taiwan.

Today the military situation is still tense, but how typical that one of the hot spots of the cold war and current frontline area should be a local tourist attraction. Luckily, I saw only a few dozen Taiwanese tourists and no foreign ones during my three-day visit. It was the result of careful timing; it was mid-week, the start of the off season, and, in keeping with my knack for having major natural disasters precede my visits, the island had just been ravaged by a typhoon.

Kinmen, which is Chinese for "Golden Gate," is the shape of a double-headed axe head, about seventeen kilometres wide, and varies from three to twelve kilometres from north to south. The folk who settled Kinmen must have had a very good sense of humour or come from one of the flattest places on earth because every second anthill-sized pockmark is called a mountain. Not surprisingly my first trip was to an absolutely flat village called Beishan (North Mountain). I got off the local bus and walked along the edge of town, which overlooks a lake teeming with bird life. It was mid-afternoon and the light – rich, soft, and warm – was a perfect match for the earthy colours of the old-fashioned brick houses. I felt as if I'd walked into an impressionist painting of an oriental Monet. At every turn of the narrow winding lanes there were some new architectural details raised to the level of art by design and craftsmanship: courtyards, stone walls, brightly painted wooden

183

doors, mosaics, tiled roofs, and curved rooflines with upturned eaves. There was a nice sense of continuity – newer dwellings built in the old style side-by-side with the authentic ones worn smooth by countless winters when cold salt-laced winds blow from the north. This was no museum, actually people's homes and, where the European counterpart might have been too tidy and sterile, there was just enough Taiwanese disorder to give it a comfortable, lived-in look.

Among the unique features of the Kinmen landscape are the "Wind Lions," statues, usually several feet high, that are used to guard against the ferocious winter winds. Villagers place offerings before them, and dress the lions in capes, which makes them look like some bizarre Asian superhero – move over Batman, here comes "Super Wind Lion."

I walked through the village and down a tree-lined road to the Kuningtou War Museum as the sound of explosives and small-arms fire carried over embankments. The museum is built on the site of an important battle that was fought between the Communists and the KMT in 1949. As I began working my way around large oil paintings lining the walls that told the story of the battle, a young fresh-faced soldier stepped alongside me, and in fluent English, offered his assistance. I was the only visitor in the building so he gave me a personal tour around the building.

"You're lucky," he explained. "We just reopened yesterday. The military's first priority is to help the civilian population and we have been busy cleaning up the damage from the typhoon. I think about eighty thousand trees were knocked down."

In the early hours of the morning of October 24, 1949, ten thousand People's Liberation Army (PLA) soldiers boarded two hundred fishing boats and set off for Kinmen. The Communists had been routing the Nationalist troops in battle after battle, and at the beginning of the month Mao had stood on Tian'anmen Square's Gate of Heavenly Peace and declared the founding of the People's Republic of China. Now his troops were mopping up the remnants of the KMT army. Kinmen seemed doomed to fall and become a stepping-stone to the grand prize of Taiwan.

As the boats neared the shore, Chinese artillery batteries on the mainland opened up to give some covering fire. The Communists managed – at great cost – to secure a foothold. The KMT forces drove them into the area where the museum now stands. The arrival of another PLA battalion failed to turn the tide, and surrender came fifty-sixty hours after the battle had begun. It was a bloody engagement of fierce artillery and hand-to-hand fighting that left fifteen thousand dead.

"The difference was the ROC air force and navy – the Communists had neither," my guide explained.

"And being on an island there was nowhere to run to!" I said, and regretted doing so a moment too late. My sarcasm, which was a reaction to the jingoistic tone of the displays, only drew a smile in response so I carried on in a similar vein.

"Do you think Chiang was a good military leader?" I asked.

"I'm a soldier so I can't answer but if you were to ask my family they would say 'No,' and if you ask me in two months then –"

"So, you're –"

"Yes. I'm a conscript soldier. I graduated in international trade. I've just got two months to go."

"Your job seems okay."

"This job itself is easy, one of the best, but Kinmen is just about the worst posting. It's better than prison, but only just – and in some ways worse. We spend so much time underground we call ourselves 'gophers.'"

"And how about free time – are there any places where you can go fishing or swimming?"

"We can't do anything – fishing and swimming are prohibited, the punishment for it is seven days in the detention centre." He pointed to a large map of Kinmen we were standing next to. "You see how small Kinmen is? But we're not supposed to travel around the island. And that small island, we call it Little Kinmen – you can visit it but soldiers aren't allowed to."

An old man suddenly stepped forward, his rasping northern Chinese accent thick enough to saw through stone, and almost as if he had understood our conversation, began to admonish today's soldiers for being soft and spoilt.

He turned to me, "How old do you think I am?" he demanded.

"Sixty-five."

"Eighty. Look here," he opened his wallet to show his ID card and an old black-and-white photograph of him as a handsome young captain.

"I was there in the thick of it," he bellowed, pointing at the wall map. In a whirl of hand movements, lists of military units, and long-dead comrades, he relived the three most intensive days of his life. His son, after watching awhile from a distance with a mixture of pride and embarrassment, stepped forward, wrapped an arm around the old man's shoulders, smiled an apology and led him away.

The Chinese PLA would have mounted another invasion and taken Kinmen and gone on to take Taiwan had it not been for the outbreak of the Korean War. For Chiang and Taiwan the invasion of South Korea in 1950 by the communist North was heaven sent. The American government, which had decided to wash its hands of Chiang Kai-shek after wasting billions of dollars of aid on him, now chose to make the KMT a strategic Cold War ally and turn Taiwan into an unsinkable aircraft carrier. President Truman ordered the seventh fleet into the strait to protect the island. Others in the United States, notably General MacArthur, wanted to do more. MacArthur, who was supreme commander of American and U.N. forces in Korea, wanted to use Taiwanese troops in Korea; but Truman rejected the proposal for fear it would widen the conflict. That's exactly what the hawkish MacArthur intended: a war to retake China using the newly invented atomic bomb to nuke the Commies into submission. Truman believed that China was far less important than the threat of a Soviet invasion of Western Europe and relieved MacArthur of his command.

Mao's forces made further attempts to take Kinmen in 1954 and 1958, but the Americans threatened to come in and the Chinese didn't follow up their artillery bombardments with ground troops. The second of the two engagements came in the wake of a secret visit to Beijing by the Soviet Union leader, Nikita Khrushchev. Mao was furious with the Russian "revisionist" who had denounced Stalin and wanted to avoid confrontation with the West. Mao's reply was blunt. In August 1958, the PLA unleashed the full force of its artillery against Kinmen – nearly half a million shells fell over forty-four days. The Taiwanese fired back and the American navy arrived. After a brief cease-fire shelling resumed. Mao offered to limit his bombardment of Kinmen to alternate days if the Americans kept their ships away. Although the Taiwanese and the Americans refused at first, the resumption of continual shelling persuaded them to rethink the offer. Taiwan and China came to a gentleman's understanding and henceforth took turns blasting each other. Taiwan shelled the mainland on Mondays, Wednesdays, and Fridays while the PLA fired their artillery on Tuesdays, Thursdays, and Saturdays. They both had Sundays off. And rather than using live shells they switched to "propaganda shells" containing leaflets urging surrender. This situation continued until 1978.

The islanders have made a good business turning swords into plough-shares, using the scrap metal from the shells to make butchers' cleavers. These hefty knives along with *gaoliang*, a potent locally-brewed spirit, are the two quintessential Kinmen souvenirs – surely not the safest combination! *Gaoliang* is the Chinese word for sorghum, the drink's chief ingredient. The island's poor soils and low rainfall make rice cultivation impossible, but sorghum grows well and one of Kinmen's trademarks is the sight of the spiky heads of this poor man's wheat spread out to dry on the rural roads. Farmers thresh the sorghum, put it in sacks, and then send it to a large local distillery. *Gaoliang* drinkers claim that despite the drink being 58 percent alcohol, it doesn't give a hangover because the fermentation process is very simple, and nothing is added, not even water or sugar.

Kinmen looked the perfect size for cycling so I rented an old one-speed rattler from a bicycle shop and spent two days touring the island. With perfect autumn weather of blue skies and a cooling breeze, quiet roads, picturesque rural architecture, and no aftershocks, it was some of the most idyllic travelling I've experienced in Taiwan.

One of my longest rides took me to Ma Shan (Horse Mountain), the island's closest point to China and the site of a broadcasting and obser-vation station. I handed over my passport at a military checkpoint and walked through a series of tunnels to a bunker from where the main-land, just two kilometres away, could be seen through horizontal slits. Scanning the opposite shoreline with a large pair of binoculars revealed a strangely mundane landscape without any obvious military flavour.

Because of Ma Shan's proximity to China it was from here that pro-paganda was once broadcast to the enemy. Huge loudspeakers, said to be the largest in the world, blasted political messages across the water. The Chinese responded in kind. The noise from this duel of loudspeak-ers must have been mind-numbing – butchers' cleavers and *gaoliang* were starting to make sense.

Cycling back to my hotel, I rode past a detail of about a dozen sol-diers clearing branches from the roadside. One of them, a cocky-look-ing jerk, screwed up his face at the sight of the foreigner and turned to his friends, and sure enough, when I was gone a safe distance, I heard a mangled English "Fuck you," followed by laughter.

A flash of Celtic anger shot through me. I slammed on my brakes and my bike screeched to a halt. So typical that the coward had waited until I had my back turned to talk tough. I've lost count of the times some loser in a group has amused his fellow buttholes by hurling an English expression at me while I'm walking away – just like the chicken-arse street dogs that cower while you walk toward them then transform into rottweilers from hell once you're gone.

I looked at the soldiers and let off a few choice expletives at the one I guessed had insulted me. I was fuming. The scrawny punk had the gall to insult someone the size of a fridge, and a fridge with a right jab that would drop a horse. The soldier was in dire need of a kicking.

Then the voice of doubt entered my head: "What if you kill him? One right cross, he's out, falls badly on the road, hits his head, dies, I get locked up. Or what if all his friends join in? Or if he's some kind of kung fu star?" I pictured myself either behind bars or lying on the ground holding my family jewels and grovelling for mercy. The offender, who looked like he was hosting similar visions of being kicked around, said a nervous "Ha-lo" and I returned the greeting with my best Clint Eastwood squint.

My anger dissipated as quickly as it had come. I got on my bike and rode on, angry with myself for being such a bad-tempered bastard. Still, it was an improvement on the last time someone had bothered me on my travels. That time, in Mongolia, it had ended with me abandoning my donkey to go sprinting over the grasslands in pursuit of a drunken local for a fistfight.

Taiwan's total military force is currently about 380,000, down from a peak of 600,000. In the 1950s and 1960s there were a couple of hundred thousand soldiers on Kinmen and the Matsu Islands further north. Although the islands were of limited strategic importance they symbolized the KMT's claims to China, and kept alive the myth of retaking the mainland.

The island's fifty thousand residents still seem to be running on curfew time; and unlike the rest of Taiwan, Kinmen closes down pretty early. There's a decided lack of nightlife. Before arriving I had thought that having hordes of young men on the island would have meant lots of loose women and drinking, or at least drinking. The place certainly had a reputation for whoring before – there was even a government-run brothel called the 821 Brothel. It got the name, not for being the 821st brothel, but because its telephone number was 821. The place was closed down for health reasons in 1992. I heard a story that while it was up and running women sentenced to prison were given a choice between doing time in a normal prison or having a much-reduced sentence if they worked there. Quite a few chose to do their patriotic duty and came to Kinmen, closed their eyes and thought of Chiang Kai-shek. Actually, you can still stay at the 821 Brothel, now called the Mantingfang (Fragrant and Bountiful Yard) Vacation Center, which a travel guide describes as having small but comfortable rooms.

\* \* \*

Soldiers on Kinmen and Taiwan were on a heightened state of alert following an escalation in cross-strait tensions because of an interview President Lee Teng-hui had given on a German radio station. Lee had said that any negotiations on reunification should be carried out on a "state to state" basis. Those few simple words took him halfway to declaring that Taiwan was independent from China – an act that China has long warned would bring military action. Lee's statement came in face of mounting pressure from China for an interim agreement on unification, which would be negotiated under the straitjacket confines of the "one-China policy," with Taiwan reduced to the status of a local government. The consensus in Taiwan is that the country is already an independent sovereign state so it doesn't need to formally declare independence. Lee's defiance of the myth of "one China" was a reaction against China's use of the principle to isolate Taiwan by preventing the country from joining world organizations and establishing diplomatic links.

Chinese leaders responded to the interview with verbal attacks on President Lee, warning him against "playing with fire," and that he should "rein in at the brink of a precipice" or else! Xinhua, the official news agency, usually content to refer to Lee Teng-hui as a "splittist" or "the so-called president," described him as a "deformed test-tube baby cultivated in the political laboratory of hostile anti-China forces."

The reaction in Taiwan was mixed; the stock market plunged 20 percent, but most people were blasé and got on with what they do best: working hard, studying, making money, and buying Hello Kitty dolls.

Unfortunately, the threat of Chinese military action needs to be taken seriously. Bringing the "renegade province" back into the fold is a popular issue in China, and no leader can afford to go against. China's military options are a naval blockade, a missile bombardment, an air war, retaking offshore islands such as Kinmen, or an invasion of Taiwan. The mainland doesn't currently have the military capability for the latter, but it probably will in another decade.

# 19
# Liquid Gold

A MONTH after the September 21 earthquake, aftershocks were still a daily occurrence but their strength had subdued to the point that people took little notice. I decided to try my luck hiking in the mountains at the southern end of the island. On the morning of October 22, as I was busy packing my equipment – bang! – the school building was rocked by a powerful jolt. As I rode out the swaying motion I wondered whether the weakened structure could take another beating. It didn't help that the very day before, I had read in the *Taipei Times* that Dounan Township was one of eleven areas affected by liquefaction, a phenomenon where the shock waves from an earthquake cause the soil to act like quicksand.

News came through that the quake was 6.1 on the Richter scale and centred at nearby Chiayi. Miraculously, the railway was soon operating again and I took the first train south. My carriage, in fact the whole train, was packed with gorgeous young women from the Chiayi area. It seemed that the city officials were saving the good breeding stock and getting them to safety first.

After arriving in Kaohsiung (Takao or "Beat the Dog," as the city of over 1.5 million was formerly known), I checked into a sleazy hotel near the central train station.

"Go and explore the city," I told myself. "You're going to write a book, but you don't have the 'walk the length of Taiwan' angle, so you need to go and find some interesting stuff – eccentric characters, historical relics of old Taiwan – or at least get some good physical descriptions."

My devil voice had other ideas: "Don't bother – it's a little artificial to go scouting around for episodes for the book. It's much more honest just to wait for things to happen naturally. Anyway, there's nothing to bloody explore anyway. Kaohsiung is just your typically awful Taiwanese urban landscape: noisy, crowded, polluted, and ugly as hell. Face it – the place is a shithole! Just stay in and watch TV – your set has been broken for a while so you needn't feel guilty about it."

I double-checked my guidebook to see if there was anything of interest. It offered up the usual attractions: temples and pagodas, none of them of great age, and the rather bizarre Twenty-five Virtuous Women's Tomb "dedicated to twenty-five women who are said to have committed suicide to avoid being raped by pirates." The devil voice's argument seemed pretty convincing so I went with the couch-potato option. I stayed in my room drinking beer and watching movies on cable TV, but made the one concession of a trip to a bookshop, during which I encountered some local colour in the form of a near-fatal scooter accident.

The next morning I took a bus to the small town of Sandimen and wandered around for quite some time trying to find a taxi or a taxi stand. I could easily have asked for directions. It was purely a male ego thing, some ancient hunting instinct that made me feel embarrassed for not being able to track down my quarry. And as far as quarries come, taxis are pretty big and not exactly camouflaged. I eventually found an empty taxi parked in the ground floor of someone's house and stepped off the road into the house, crossing that tiny two-metre zone in Taiwan that divides the busy street from people's living rooms. When the driver was woken up from his siesta, I introduced him to a new concept: the map. We came to a price and drove off into the countryside. Now it was the taxi driver's turn to do an "ancient hunter – I don't need to ask for directions" routine and we disappeared off the margin of the map I was navigating with. It was a "short cut" he assured me. The rural landscape was green but looked ugly under a dull synthetic sky that kept the mountains hidden and gave a dirty sheen to the hodgepodge of farm plots and buildings.

Half an hour later we reached an aboriginal village where a church wedding was in progress. The driver told me this was my destination. As a light rain began falling I politely explained that this couldn't be Wutai because it was in the wrong location and had a completely different name. He finally admitted defeat and radioed a dispatcher. "Oh, *that* Wutai!" he groaned, and after sulking for a while summoned up the gall to ask for more money. I figured the guy had made an honest mistake so I agreed on the condition that he avoid any contact with the police. We snaked up a long narrow mountain road that was a series of steep S-bends and managed to slip past two police checkpoints where I should have shown a mountain permit.

For the solo adventurer today the red tape involved in getting permits is the biggest obstacle to reaching the high alpine areas. Things were a little different in the 1860s when Pickering made his first visit to "the savage tribes" of the mountains. He and a sea captain set off on foot from Kaohsiung armed with revolvers and double-barrelled fowling pieces (i.e. light shotguns). On the third day, they received dire warnings that the lower slopes of the mountains were wracked by feuding and that the higher mountains were full of murderous headhunters. Given a better than even chance of death should they continue deep into the interior, the two Englishmen reluctantly turned back.

The mountains can still be dangerous. The steep topography and thick underbrush make falling or getting lost real possibilities. In December 1998, a twenty-three-year-old New Zealander went missing near the mountain resort of Alishan. His body was never found despite extensive searches. The heavy monsoon rains of summer cause landslides and flash flooding, and in winter hypothermia is a threat. There are also a handful of venomous snakes, such as the colourfully (and erroneously) named hundred-pacer snake – so called because that's supposedly how far you get before dying. Statistically though, you have more chance of choking to death on a spring roll than dying from a snakebite, and the animals I have always put the most effort into avoiding are people.

Vacations and weekends see the city traffic jams move to popular mountain spots, but at other times the mountains are relatively quiet. And once you arrive in a scenic area the average Taiwanese sightseer's disgust of walking means you usually only have to tread a short distance away from the concrete footpaths and food stalls to leave the tourist herd behind.

As I began walking up the twisting mountain road from Wutai there were only a handful of farmers tending their orchards. Afternoon cloud kept visibility to about a hundred metres. Rather like being on a treadmill, the view never changed and it felt that you weren't really getting any higher despite all the effort. Somewhere overhead loomed my target, the beautiful 3,092-metre North Dawu Mountain, which shoots straight up from the lowlands like a Tahitian volcanic peak rising up out of the Pacific. The mountain is sacred to the Paiwan tribe as their legendary birthplace. The Mutan, a sub-tribe of the Paiwan, have a legend that in ancient times a length of bamboo on Dawu Mountain split open, and snakes came forth. In time the snakes transformed into human beings. The most sacred snakes are the hundred-pacer snakes; Paiwan clothing and artwork is adorned with the colours and triangular patterns of this beautiful creature.

After two hours of walking I came upon an aboriginal roadwork crew. As I stopped to ask about suitable campsites, a small group began forming around me. My hiking plans were answered with a chorus of disapproval, "Very far, too far, too hard ...," and after everyone had put in their two cents' worth and made lots of thoughtful nods, the consensus was reached that I should return down to their village to spend the night. A better suggestion came from a leathery-faced man who handed me a cup of moonshine with the instruction: "Drink." I took a couple of cautious sips. It was pretty rough stuff – drinkable but not the kind of thing you really want to have when you're stone-cold sober. By the bottom of the cup I had acquired a taste for it, and gave the thumbs up, "Not bad!" Faces stared at me with a mixture of surprise, admiration, and disappointment. They had obviously been expecting me to choke on it. My new-found status was further elevated when I told them that I brewed beer back in New Zealand. In danger of becoming their new chief, I begged my leave, thanked them for their concern, hoisted my pack over my shoulders, and carried on.

A few farmers were walking down from their fields and a wizened old man stepped toward me and, without saying a world, gave me a walking stick. A moment later I turned around but he had disappeared into the mist. Very strange indeed – maybe it was just the grog. At least I was holding his walking stick as proof that it was no hallucination.

When darkness came I still hadn't found a decent campsite, which was becoming something of a habit. The discovery that my torch wasn't working properly – in fact, it was so weak that it would have had trouble attracting a sex-starved firefly – forced me to pitch my tent by the side of the gravel road. I broke camp before daybreak and reached the trailhead for North Dawu Mountain. Monkeys announced my arrival as I entered the lush forest. In places the trail was knee-destroyingly steep and I was starting to regret having equipped my backpack with its anti-theft feature; that is, making it too bloody heavy for anyone to steal. My bodyweight also had me worried about the more dangerous sections, where there were ropes to hold onto and safety nets to break any fall. Some of the sheer drops offered one-step death (or at least dislocation) so I concentrated on my footholds and on the way up to a campsite below the peak I spent more time looking at my feet than the forest. As I put up my tent, the thick cloud, which had kept me on the treadmill of hidden mountain scenery all day, started spitting raindrops.

There was a simple mountain hut at the campsite nestled amongst the trees on a mean patch of level ground. I was surprised to find that it was full of hikers from various hiking clubs as far away as Taipei. It turned out this southern peak was the only mountain open to trekkers, and after a month of earthquake-compelled inactivity they had all decided to head here. Some of the hikers came and talked to me. The succession of questions was rather predictable.

"Where are you from?"

"New Zealand."

"How long have you been in Taiwan?"

Resisting the temptation to say "Long enough to get a taste for Taiwan Beer," "Nearly two years," I lied. I thought it better to slice a couple of years off because my Chinese is too embarrassingly bad. Even then, the next question always brought up my language ability.

"Where do you live?"

"Dounan, Yunlin County."

"So you can speak Chinese?" they asked assuming that living alone in such a hick place would have meant learning the local language.

"Well, I think it was a choice between Chinese and drinking. I went with the second option."

\* \* \*

As the early twilight thickened, the rain was still falling, the air damp and cold. The rain, lack of alcohol, and the 2,600-metre altitude made for a long, cold, and uncomfortable night in my tent. I lit a couple of candles and began lustfully eyeing my lighter, holding it against the warm flames and watching the lighter fluid sway back and forth. I absentmindedly picked up my "multi-fuel" stove, and as I sloshed the fuel around I wondered why chemists couldn't come up with a truly multi-purpose fuel so if you didn't need it for cooking you could drink it; strictly for warming purposes, of course. And it couldn't be too much worse than some Chinese brews on the market, such as the red wines churned out by a wine counterfeiting ring in Chiayi. When policed raided the secret brewery they found two thousand litres of "wine" that had been made from flavouring, sugar, and pigeon feed!

It took me two long years to acquire a taste for Taiwan's most popular beer, the imaginatively named "Taiwan Beer." I've often been told by locals, who consider it a brew of some international standing, that it is "famous." In real English this translates to something like "world famous in Taiwan, unheard of anywhere else." At least it tastes better than the mock Taiwan Beer brews (swill sold in Taiwan Beer-style cans almost identical in every detail except for the bizarre names such as Good Cornmeal Beer, I Want Beer, and Superior Beer).

I took moral support in my preoccupation and earnest devotion to the amber beverage by telling myself that I was actually following in the noble tradition of the many ancient Chinese poets and scholars whose drinking abilities earned them the name, "drunken dragons." The most famous was Li Bai (699–762), one of China's greatest poets. He is said to have died under the influence, trying to embrace the reflection of the moon whilst in a boat floating on a lotus pond. He fell overboard and drowned but his words live on:

> The rapture of drinking
> and wine's dizzy joy,
> No sober man deserves to enjoy

During the third century there was a group of eccentric Taoists called the "Seven Sages of the Bamboo Grove," who, after hours spent discussing philosophy, would hit the local taverns. The biggest drinker of the seven was a poet called Liu Ling, who wrote all his poems under the influence. Wherever Liu went his servant would follow with a jug of wine in one hand and a shovel in the other to ensure an immediate burial in case he drank himself to death.

\* \* \*

Bad weather meant that I never got to the top of North Dawu Mountain; but I was more than compensated a week later with a magical trip along the Southern Cross-Island Highway that cuts through the southern part of Yu Shan National Park. Under the gorgeous blue skies of crisp autumn days I enjoyed five days of heavenly travel, walking along the highway that climbs to a height of 2,728 metres and making side trips up mountain tracks. Landslides and earthquake damage to the road had reduced traffic to a handful of vehicles, and I was left alone in quiet solitude. The scenery was *The Lord of the Rings* with sunshine: mountains squeezed together in impossible folds, and climbing higher, swirling mists swept past craggy peaks swathed in pines and conifers that seemed more suited to Switzerland than a sub-tropical island.

From the summit of the highway looking east lay a breath-taking view – range after range of mountains receding into the distance that floated on a sea of clouds as dusk fell. As I wound my way down the twisting mountain road early the next morning dawn broke diamond-sharp over the wildest, most beautiful scenery I have ever seen in Taiwan. Great waves of green forest rolled unbroken to the blue of the far horizon – a landscape so wild and untouched that it was difficult to believe I was in Taiwan. This was Formosa before the fall, a precious glimpse of the beautiful island that Pickering and MacKay knew and loved.

\* \* \*

Pickering made a second trip into the mountains in 1865 with Dr. Maxwell, a medical missionary of the English Presbyterian Church who had just been forced out of Tainan by angry mobs stirred up by local doctors. His practice had been a little too successful; operations for cataracts and the use of quinine – the nineteenth century's wonder drug – had seen the sick arriving from near and far. In response, local doctors put about rumours that the barbarians were killing patients and using the victims' brains and eyes to make opium.

The two Englishmen set off from Tainan in November with servants and three coolies carrying supplies, gifts and medicines. As usual on his travels Pickering wore a kilt as he found it more practical than trousers. After two days they reached the foothills, where the memory of the Dutch still lived on in the hearts and memories of the aborigines. Pickering was touched by the warm welcome, and particularly by one old woman's words:

"You whitemen are our kindred. You do not belong to those wicked shaven men, the Chinese. Yet what kind of people do you call yourselves? Ah! For hundreds of years you have kept away from us, and now, when our sight is dim, and we are at the point to die, our old eyes are blessed with a sight of our 'red-haired relations'!"

They continued on up into the higher ranges beneath a snow-sprinkled Jade Mountain and at the last "tame" village found a guide and escort to lead them to a mountain valley at the foot of the great mountain. The path took the party through thick undergrowth and gorges that were prime ambush sites, so they travelled in silence, refrained from smoking tobacco, and had their weapons loaded and cocked.

They arrived tired but safe, their guide announcing them thus: "Hoé, hoé! Come out and see some of our red-haired relations, our relations

197

of long ago, the men of whom our forefathers have told us!" A feast – pork washed down with generous quantities of local booze – was held, and the aborigines ended up in drunken heaps on the ground. The area was a patchwork of tribes in networks of alliances or at war, and there was plenty of evidence of fighting hanging from the walls of the bachelors' house in the form of the skulls of enemy tribes and Chinese scalps.

\* \* \*

*Central Cross-Island Highway in winter*

A year later Pickering made another trip further up the wild western slopes of Mount Jade to investigate tea and cassia bark resources. Steep trails took him through virgin forests where it was all but impossible to see the sky. As always he was a great source of curiosity, the aborigines fascinated by his white skin and continually asking him to take off his shirt. Pickering got close to the summit of Mount Jade but a couple of men had been killed there recently and it was judged unsafe. A bout of dysentery brought his trip to an end, and rather than wait it out, he decided to head back for medicine.

The driving force for Chinese frontiersmen heading into the wild aboriginal areas was camphor. Camphor comes from a large evergreen tree of the same name that grows in mountainous areas. The trees were felled and cut up into chips that were then boiled in pots and the vapour collected in crystallized or oil form. Camphor was once an important material; it was used to treat rheumatism, and in the manufacture of mothballs, combs, umbrella handles, gunpowder, and celluloid. Taiwan accounted for over half of the world's production of camphor.

This "white gold" was instrumental in pushing back the limits of the wilderness, because once trees were cut down the woodsmen had to head further inland to find new ones. Aborigines often took violent exception to these intrusions. Camphor workers could also lose their heads to the government; in the year 1720 nearly two hundred people were decapitated for illegally chopping down camphor trees and thereby infringing on the government monopoly.

Most of the camphor workers, indeed many of the Chinese settlers living and working in the dangerous hill country, were Hakkas (*Kejiaren* in Chinese, meaning "guest people"). This persecuted minority from China's southern Guangdong Province were easily distinguished from other Chinese by their women's unbound feet. There are about two million Hakka in Taiwan today.

After leaving government service to work for a foreign trading company, Elles & Co., Pickering became involved in the camphor trade; perhaps "camphor smuggling" would be more accurate because this trade was in contravention of the government monopoly. The British traders found Taiwanese sellers willing to risk the wrath of the authorities because the profits were much higher and the smuggling difficult to control. Pickering established warehouses and agents at a small port near Taichung. The clan then monopolizing the trade didn't take kindly to the competition and fighting broke out between them and the clan in the employ of the barbarians. Pickering made a trip to the depot to investigate the theft of some camphor. Although the governor refused to give him permission to travel, he set off regardless, racing there by sea, whilst two hundred soldiers marched from Tainan. Pickering found the warehouses besieged but his seven-shooter rifle and two boat guns soon drove off the occupiers. When the soldiers arrived, the clan on Pickering's side deserted, leaving him holed up in a fort alone save for a leper and a Malay employee of the firm who was "worth many a Chinaman in a fight."

Given a guarantee of safety, Pickering, accompanied by his two helpers, left the fort for an audience with an official, and as usual he was armed with a copy of the Treaty of Tianjin to show his trading rights. Pickering was in a belligerent mood and refused to leave town. While making their way back to the fort, a group of soldiers went for them. The unlikely trio opened fire and ran at the attackers, who promptly fled for their lives. "Some of the soldiers actually held children up before them as shields, behind which they fired after us; but fortunately they were too terrified to aim correctly."

A long standoff at the fort ensued as Pickering awaited instructions from Tainan. After a week a courier arrived with a secret message from the British consul warning that the governor was planning to have Pickering poisoned, or failing that, have an accident arranged. Informed of the news, the Malay servant became downcast, and taking a special amulet, which he wrapped around his wrist, he told his master that their situation was hopeless; "Let us 'amok,' and kill as many of the Chinese beasts as possible before we die." Pickering replied that he did not believe in "amoking" and wanted neither to kill nor be killed.

They managed to escape by boat, but a gale and heavy seas meant their ordeal was far from over. The Chinese sailors proved up to the task and so surprised Pickering "with their skill, their endurance and patience" that he was left shaking his head at the contradictions of the Chinese character. "The Chinaman is an unfathomable creature! A mixture of every best and every worst quality in human nature."

The wrangle over camphor spread to an anti-foreigner purge throughout the island – European firms were looted, mission houses burnt and plundered, and Christian converts persecuted. The British fleet in China sailed from the Yangtze; but when they arrived things had already been settled by a single gunboat and a small party of British marines that took the port of Anping and pressed the government to take action.

Pickering had further run-ins with the authorities, for a time becoming Taiwan's "most wanted" with a $500 reward on his head, but it was poor health that finally defeated him. A life-threatening bout of fever and chronic dysentery forced a return to England in the summer of 1870. He went on to serve the colonial government in Singapore, and when he wrote *Pioneering in Formosa* he had lived nearly forty years amongst Chinese people, and had a high regard for them, if not their officials.

Pickering was an arch-imperialist who lamented the missed chances for enlarging the British Empire. Like many others at the time he believed China was on its last legs and would inevitably be carved up by the European powers, and thought England should secure "her proper share." If he had had his way, Taiwan would been a British colony, and he was angry that Britain "has had several opportunities of annexing Formosa, but has, with a culpable supineness, foregone the opportunity of possessing a fertile island and in the Pescadores (Penghu Islands), a point of vantage for her fleets."

# 20
# Snakes and Lagers

AFTER returning from the mountains I paid a visit to the "King of Snakes," a former crocodile farmer who now breeds cobras and runs a small reptile zoo. The king was no snake expert, having – as he admitted with some pride – learnt by the rather painful method of trial and error. Indeed, he was recovering from a cobra bite on the day of my visit, so his son David, an amiable thirty-year-old, showed me around the enclosures.

"Did any of the animals behave strangely before the 9-21 quake?" I asked.

"Oh yes, these caimans panicked," he pointed down into a pit with dozens of the sleeping creatures. "They became very excited and all gathered in the corner, climbing on top of one another, and one of the caimans climbed over the wall into the crocodiles and was eaten."

"And the Chiayi earthquake?"

"About two hours before, the crocodiles started making a loud noise ... oh terrible," he demonstrated with a deep honking sound.

David was positive that the timing of these "signs" was more than just coincidence. Some scientists believe that before a quake electrical current or chemicals are produced that can be detected by animals but not by humans. It sounds reasonable enough yet surprisingly there is no solid scientific proof to back up the anecdotal evidence that animals can "predict" quakes. The claim of sensitivity to earthquakes even extends to a few humans. A while after the 9-21 earthquake an American woman, describing herself as "a biological sensitive," contacted the *Taipei Times* to warn that her "body symptoms" indicated a large earthquake was about to hit, and suggested people buy a US$20 subscription to her internet quake-alert service.

The snake I had specifically come to see was the hundred-pacer (sharp-nosed pit viper or *Deinagkistroden acutus*). I was not disappointed; a beautiful metre-long specimen lay sleeping in a coiled position safely behind glass. It had an exquisite colouring scheme, a pastel batik of triangles in shades of orange, cream, and brown. The hundred-pacer is an alert and irritable snake that strikes without hesitation when alarmed, and David needed considerable persuasion before sliding up the glass panel about four inches so I could take some pictures.

David was rather more casual with the Chinese cobras, and took out a five-foot specimen for me to have a closer look. It struck a classic defensive pose, rearing up and spreading its hood. The cobra is not an aggressive snake; biting is a last resort, and it frequently strikes with the mouth closed. The *Encyclopaedia Britannica* gives a nasty list of the effects of being bitten by a cobra, beginning with pain and swelling around the bite then "numbness, drooping of the eyelids, head, salivation, difficulty in speech, muscular incoordination, weakness, respiratory distress, blindness, incontinence, convulsions," and finally death. An anti-serum is available. David's father (the King of Snakes) joined us and did his party piece by toying with a cobra, unperturbed by the fact he had been bitten just the week before and was actually nursing a swollen finger. It was his ninth bite and instead of taking the anti-serum was drinking a special herbal-wine concoction based on an old Chinese recipe.

George Taylor, the English lighthouse keeper resident at Kending in the 1870s, reported that there were "professional suckers" who treated snakebites and were usually successful except in cases involving the deadly hundred-pacer. When a man was bitten, the area would be searched and the first snake found tied up. Should the man succumb to the poison – the usual outcome – then the snake would be roasted to death; but if the man survived the snake was set free.

I took a break in the zoo's small restaurant and tried some snake dishes – fried snake skin, snake meat, and snake soup, but passed on the medicinal snake-gall wine, and snake-blood wine. There was a large jar on the counter with snake penises and testicles preserved in a solution. David explained that because those parts had a lot of "hormones" they made the wine a powerful sexual potion.

"And how often do you drink that stuff?"

"Every day."

"Wow! You must be some kind of superman."

"Twin-turbo, like twin-turbo car," he laughed, alone. "It made me hairy," he offered as way of proof to the hormones, pointing at a bit of fluff on his chin. I tried not to laugh – he was, after all, talking to the hairiest man in Dounan.

\* \* \*

Apart from the snakes and other reptiles, the private zoo was home to some sorry-looking Asian bears, a cockatoo, and a sulking orangutan. Doing solitary confinement in a tiny cage as it was, the poor orang didn't have much to be happy about. David came alongside me and turned on his tour guide spiel, "The girls love him, say he's cute and want to hug him. But we can't let them, because he grabs their clothing – he's very strong, and rips off all their clothes!" He mimed the action.

"A pervert orang?"

"Oh yes! One time he had sex with a chicken!"

"And how did you get him?"

"He was a pet but the family couldn't take care of him anymore. He kept ripping girls' and women's clothing off."

The obvious question, but not a story I wanted to pursue, was how the orang had developed this habit; had his owner been perverted enough to actually train him to do it, or was it from watching too much Japanese porn on cable TV?

In many ways it was better to have the orang locked up instead of set loose in the bush, as is often the case with unwanted exotic pets. This problem was recently highlighted by an attack on two hikers that occurred on a trail near the city of Taichung. The two elderly men had been taking a morning walk when a male orangutan approached them, apparently asking for food, then turned violent. It pulled one man's pants off and tried to grab his genitals during a tussle that lasted almost twenty minutes. The orangutan then let go and turned his attention to the other man. This time the "embrace" lasted over an hour. Both hikers suffered injuries to their limbs and one to his genitals, and both wound up in intensive care after being found by other hikers and sent to a nearby hospital.

The zoo had another psycho animal in the making – a baby howler monkey dressed up in diapers that was given a free run of the place. What would happen to it when it was older? The love of all things "cute" gives Taiwanese people a distorted view of wild animals as being little more than stuffed toys. When two koalas arrived at the Taipei Zoo in 1999, the island went crazy. In the first week nearly 350,000 visitors braved 38-degree heat and queued in lines stretching up to four kilometres long for a twenty-five-second glimpse of the sleeping marsupials. Then visitors joined another queue at the souvenir shop selling every koala-related product imaginable. The appetite for koala products was so great that the zoo even thought about selling jewellery inset with koala droppings – until objections from the wildlife sanctuary in Australia that had sent the koalas.

Thinking wild animals are cute can get you removed from the human gene pool. There have been several cases of Taiwanese tourists getting mauled in African game parks because they got out of their car to get their picture taken with the wildlife.

\* \* \*

One of the strongest impressions from my trips into the mountains was the extent of alcoholism. These observations are backed up by statistics that reveal about 40 percent of aboriginal males to be excessive drinkers or alcoholics. Various reasons have been put forward to explain the drinking problem: modernization breaking down the traditional drinking rules, the hopelessness of a people unable to adapt to the outside world, and an escape from unemployment, low social status and low self-esteem.

Professor Chen Mau-tai, an expert on the Atayal – and whose given name incidentally sounds like a powerful spirit, *maotai*, which must be pretty impressive for doing research up in the mountains – believes alcoholism came with the breakdown of the traditional order.

"They drank wine made from millet, but with their simple agricultural techniques it was difficult to grow enough millet to meet their needs. They only made a little, and brewed it for specific occasions, and shared it out amongst everyone. The social and religious significance to drinking was lost after Christianity was introduced."

I decided to get an opinion from a German missionary, Father Weber Anton Josef of the Catholic organization Divine Word Missionaries, who has worked with aborigines for more than thirty years. In these politically correct times, in these days of relativism where nothing is absolute, the Western missionary is a relic of colonial arrogance. Critics ask what right an outsider has to tell people their beliefs are wrong and that they should convert. I'm an atheist but admire much of the work foreign missionaries have done in Taiwan. Besides spiritual sustenance they have provided schooling and health services, and have also done much to help preserve aboriginal language and culture. And on a personal level, old missionaries are some of the most interesting and down-to-earth people you could hope to talk to.

I found the Father in good spirits. The Vatican had been expected to switch diplomatic recognition to China, but Beijing had just snubbed the Pope with the Chinese Catholic Church ordaining five new bishops without Vatican approval and timed it to upstage the pontiff's own ceremony. After the Communists took power they kicked out foreign missionaries and forced Catholics to renounce the Pope as their spiritual leader. The authorities allow worship under the state-controlled Patriotic Catholic Association, but about four million of the devout prefer to risk punishment and attend the underground Catholic "house churches."

"I've been rather preoccupied with how to explain a possible diplomatic switch to our people, so I'm very relieved. And there are encouraging signs because the Chinese wanted to ordain twelve but could only find three people that were willing," he told me with a warmth and expressiveness that didn't seem to match the Teutonic features of blonde hair and blue eyes. You could tell in an instant that Father Weber was a lovely old man. He was modest about his experiences, talkative in fits and starts, and as he told stories stopped to laugh, and wave away thoughts and reminiscences.

Father Weber left southern Germany in 1965, aged twenty-eight, to follow Father Fisch, an old German priest working in the mountainous area around Alishan. He studied Mandarin for two years, then headed to the mountains where he spent sixteen years amongst the Tsou people. With only about five thousand members the Tsou is one of the smallest of Taiwan's tribes.

"Back then there was no TV, no electricity, no telephones, no roads – and you had to walk everywhere." The Father's tours of the faithful and administering of villagers' religious needs often meant days of hard walking that wasn't far short of mountaineering.

"It allowed me to get close to them. You need to develop love for your people if you are to work for them, and for all their faults they are a good people."

The mountain areas have changed beyond recognition since Father Weber first arrived.

"Now everyone has a TV and a phone, the pace is too fast, the family is gone, the social structure lost," he lamented with a pained expression and upraised hands that suggested a hopelessness.

"Young people leave the area, learn about the modern world. When they return to the village, they see the old people know nothing and so they no longer have authority. It's impossible when after just a couple of hours driving you are down in the cities of the lowlands."

"And they move away from the church?"

"Yes. I think Father Fisch was a little too quick in baptism. With the aborigines conversion is a community affair, and many follow because their neighbour did it. This is not the right way. You need faith to get into the blood and bones." He clenched his fists. "Otherwise it cannot stand and it falls away."

"And how much do you think the social breakdown is responsible for alcoholism," I asked.

"The old people say that in the past the rules were strict, that traditionally the young were not allowed to drink. A man only came of age at thirty, and in a, how do you say ... ceremony ... was beaten, and beaten quite hard. Given a headdress, a sword, and allowed to drink. But they could still not get drunk. Only those over seventy were allowed to get drunk, and that old it doesn't matter." He laughed and raised his hands.

While Father Weber thought drunkenness had come from contact with the outside world, he didn't sugarcoat the problem.

"Weddings always end in drunkenness – and they don't need to." He shook his head. "Some of the Seventh Day Adventists have come over to our church because of the ban on alcohol," he admitted with a laugh.

I brought up another controversial subject – the use of three hundred thousand foreign workers to make up for the labour shortage in factories and construction work. Aboriginal activists criticize the policy for taking jobs away from their people and depressing blue-collar wages.

"Our people are not organized and have very little business sense. They complain about the foreign workers – go on a march, protesting about losing their jobs. But they should also blame themselves. There are so many opportunities for construction jobs," he said shaking his head. He talked about the Tsou as a parent would about wayward children, "You find them a job. Some will think, 'Oh, I don't feel like going to work today.' He stays home, gets drunk and misses work the following day. No one can run a modern business like that!"

Since moving down from the mountains Father Weber has worked in Chiayi as director of a dormitory attached to a Catholic school that houses more than one hundred teenage aborigines. He teaches Tsou language classes, and was actually the first person to write down the language. And with a Hungarian linguist, Father Joseph Szakos, he compiled a Tsou-German dictionary, and helped the scholar complete a Ph.D. on the language.

"The Taiwan government recognizes the value of aboriginal culture. Before you weren't even allowed to write the language using the romanized alphabet – now they encourage it, and will pay you to do it," he explained with a characteristic laugh and flourish of hands at the fickleness of the secular world. It was either laugh or cry because there was a sadness to the Father's work – the likelihood that the Tsou will one day be nothing more than a historical footnote. He admitted as much himself, and without my prompting. "Sad, you know, the Tsou language will die out. A pity because it is such a beautiful language."

"The sound?"

"The sound and also its structure – very beautiful. We have three tribes in the dormitory and when they speak to each other they use Chinese, not their own languages." He paused for a moment. "And the Tsou tribe, it too, will die out."

# 21

# Searching For Paradise

DESPITE cultural similarities between Taiwan's tribes – headhunting, the high status of women, and strict monogamy rules – what stands out is the great diversity of languages. This suggests that the indigenous people came to Taiwan at different times and in different groups, both directly from what is now southern China and via islands further south. Aboriginal legends aren't much help, as many trace their origins not from the sea but from the mountains, the Atayal pinpointing theirs to a three-metre-high rock in Nantou County. Other tribal creation myths accredit human origins to snakes, the moon, pots, and bamboo. A sub-tribe of the Paiwan say that they sprang forth from a jug that when touched with sunlight split open, producing a man and woman.

Since the mid-1980s there has been a renaissance of aboriginal culture, with renewed interest and pride in arts and crafts, traditional ceremonies, and language. The yearning to discover their roots has sometimes seen the triumph of wishful thinking over evidence. All national and ethnic identities are, to a certain extent, based on invented mythology, but Lin Sheng-yi, the man who found the "pyramid" and "dinosaur sculptures" in Yangmingshan National Park, has taken tribal history into new realms. I met up with the fifty-eight-year-old maverick archaeologist in his shoe shop in the crowded central streets of Keelung. The shop was fitted out in imitation of a mine shaft, with undulating plastered walls, rail tracks, and mining equipment.

I spotted Mr. Lin, a white-haired and bespectacled man with a kindly glazed expression rather like a tipsy deer staring into oncoming headlights. He was talking on the telephone behind a counter, and seeing as I was a little early I took a seat and waited for him to finish. Five minutes later he was still talking and although I was in his field of view he apparently hadn't seen me. Another five minutes of droning telephone monologue dragged on, and then another, and despite my walking around faking an interest in shoes he still hadn't spotted me. I hoped that it was just the absent-mindedness of an eccentric. When he finally finished talking I introduced myself, and we went upstairs to a small office that looked like a low-tech version of the Bat Cave.

"I'm Ketagalan on my mother's side and Taiwanese on my father's. My father would've hated me for saying it, but my mother's blood is better," Lin explained with a typical exultation of tribal superiority over Han ancestry.

The Ketagalan were a lowland aboriginal group who lived along the northern coast from Hsinchu to Taipei and a little south of Keelung, but they have been assimilated into oblivion and are no longer a recognized group.

"When I was young my mother told me about tribal history and customs, and before she passed away when I was twelve, she told me to follow the culture. And at the same time I started to feel a closeness to nature – the land, sea, and sky."

I asked what had transformed his interest into an all-consuming crusade to investigate and promote Ketagalan culture.

"The nuclear power plant in Gongliao Township, Taipei County. I wanted to preserve the ancient relic site of the Ketagalan near the planned site."

It was the perfect choice of enemy – the nuclear power industry versus an ethnic minority, economic development versus culture. And perfect timing, too, because it coincided with the beginnings of an aboriginal renaissance and the rise of the fledgling democracy movement of the 1980s, which made stopping the nuclear power plant one of its prime missions.

"What was so important about the archaeological site?" I asked, recalling from something I'd read that it was just a shell midden – that is, a garbage heap of shells.

"It was a manufacturing and exporting area where the Ketagalan made pottery and forged iron."

"Pottery and metalworking?"

"Yes, and it was the best pottery and metalwork in the world, better than China's!"

"Ah ... sorry, what?" I double-checked that I'd heard him correctly and asked for an explanation. What followed was a wild disjointed ride through alternative history.

"The Ketagalan had a high culture – the highest in the world. They were great sailors, and traded with neighbouring countries, ... and they had gigantic rafts that could hold a hundred houses, and had vegetable plots on the rafts.

"You know Penghu?" he asked, referring to a cluster of islands in the Taiwan Strait. I nodded. "Well, Penghu is a Ketagalan name that means 'Transfer and Delivery.' And the Diaoyutai Islands towards Japan, the name means 'Midway Springboard.' The name 'Taiwan' also comes from my language, as does 'Keelung.'"

I picked up my tape recorder and checked that it was still working while he continued.

"In the Palaeolithic Age, there was a high civilization in Taiwan, and it is one of the cradles of world civilization. In the last ice age people lived in huge man-made caves in the mountains. Seashells were used as currency in China before the Xia dynasty [c. 2070 BC] and because the seashells came from Taiwan that meant the Chinese economy was controlled by Taiwan. After the Shang dynasty [c. 1046 BC] copper coins replaced shells, and Taiwan's economy and civilization weakened. And finally it was destroyed by the arrival of Chinese. Before the Chinese came Taiwan was a paradise, and the people lived noble lives like gods. Even the Chinese, in some ancient texts, refer to Taiwan as a paradise and the people living like gods. There was no fighting or headhunting – that only developed as a reaction to Chinese invasion."

Lin has spent more than a decade combing the mountains of Taiwan searching for archaeological evidence, both alone and with the help of hired research assistants. I admire his persistence and the fact that he has put his money where his mouth is. Lin's quest has cost him a small fortune and been financed by selling a clothing factory and two shops, leaving him with just the shoe shop where we were chatting; but that too was only a few months away from being sold.

A series of excavations by mainstream archaeologists in the 1990s, including one at Bali near Danshui, have provided evidence that there is, in fact, an element of truth to Lin's wild assertions. The origins of the people who lived at the Bali site are unknown but they stretch back 1,500 years, and the remains show that the inhabitants were manufacturing beautiful ceramics and forging iron. Coins from the Tang and Song dynasties indicate contact with the mainland. Houses were raised on stilts – a design still seen today in the South Pacific – and the inhabitants lived by fishing, hunting, and simple dry rice agriculture. On top of this, studies utilising genetic and linguistic evidence suggest that prehistoric Taiwan may have been the ancient homeland of the peoples who populated the South Pacific.

Lin showed me a glossy booklet that he had put together for a U.N. conference. It was a truly embarrassing publication full of bizarre interpretations of photographs of rocks, best described as a glorious history based on a sequence of psychiatrist's ink dots. The introduction asserts that the "'Keta Dynasty' Pyramid Relic area is a holy land for the world." There's a picture of a small triangular hillock. Lin explained that this "pyramid" functioned as a kind of navigational aid, and was part of an ancient route along the top of Taiwan because the rest was under water.

Other pictures show various "signs" of the gods (a child-king emblem that resembles some sort of extra-terrestrial), and stone sculpture after sculpture – none of which in any way come close to resembling their supposed shapes named in the captions: "two dinosaurs, turtle, dinosaur, gigantic animal, bird's head...." Amongst the strangest were a series of "stone sculptures" labelled "five-colour race." If you looked hard enough you could see some half-human features in a vague smiley-face fashion. Lin cleared up my confusion, "In ancient times there were five races of people: white, black, red, yellow, and green."

* * *

The idea of an island paradise has a long history in China. Ancient folklore told of three "blessed isles" where there were terraced mountains with caves, palaces made of gold and silver, all the animals were pure white, and, most enticing of all, there were miraculous plants that could extend life.

The Chinese took the existence of life-giving plants seriously and expeditions were sent forth to search for them, most famously under Qin Shihuang, the emperor responsible for uniting China for the first time in 216 BC. He was also one of the worst tyrants in history. His subjects were put to work building the Great Wall and an immense mausoleum for himself (complete with thousands of life-size terracotta soldiers). During his fifteen-year reign he executed hundreds of scholars, and ordered books – except for those on agriculture, medicine, and divination – to be burnt.

Qin Shihuang sent a Taoist alchemist called Xu Fu (also spelled Hsu Fu) to find the fabled islands in the Eastern Sea. On his return Xu Fu said he had found them but that he had failed to secure the plants because his offerings were too poor. He was convincing enough to get a second, larger trip financed, and an ancient Chinese historical text relates that Qin: "set three thousand young men and girls at Xu Fu's disposal, gave him seeds of the five grains, and artisans of every sort, after which he set sail. Xu Fu found some calm and fertile plain, with broad forests and rich marshes, where he made himself king – at least he never came back to China."

Xu Fu may have been a clever opportunist. Being from Shandong (a coastal province that had just been incorporated into the newly unified China), this trip provided him and his people with a chance to escape the tyrannical emperor. Japanese folklore has Xu Fu arriving in southern Japan and settling there; shrines in various locations commemorate his arrival and the blessings of Chinese civilization that he brought. It has also been suggested that he and his people settled in Taiwan and even America.

Sinologist Professor Joseph Needham of Cambridge University was a strong proponent of cultural contacts between America and Asia in ancient times. He was deeply impressed by the many similarities between the high Central American civilizations and Asia. The parallels include architecture, metallurgy, the sky dragon motif, worship of dragon rain-gods and ceremonies, musical instruments, and beliefs associated with jade. If this was not coincidence, then there was most likely some form of contact – either from the occasional boat blown off course, to trading, or perhaps even colonization, however small-scale and brief.

Tim Severin, an Irish historian and maritime adventurer, decided to put Needham's theory – that large bamboo sailing rafts could have made trans-Pacific journeys – to the test. Severin came to Taiwan to investigate these rafts but was too late. Bamboo rafts, still widely used until the 1950s, had been replaced by ones made out of plastic drainage pipes and were now powered by engines instead of sails. Nevertheless, he was encouraged that they had the same design with the characteristic upturned bow, and guessed that these fast and very low-slung craft were perfect for running contraband across the strait. Severin eventually found boat-builders using bamboo in Vietnam and had an 18.3 metre raft constructed.

The *Hsu Fu* departed from Hong Kong in May 1993 with a crew of seven and set sail for southern Taiwan. Severin's description of approaching the "Ilha Formosa" just out of sight of the beach resort of Kending is rather telling.

"We could tell we were approaching the coast of Taiwan by the amount of pollution floating in the water around us. The rubbish was everywhere – broken boxes, scraps of plastic sheet, lumps of Styrofoam packaging, old shoes, plastic bags, even metal boxes which should have sunk but somehow kept afloat and joined the rest of the trash circulating in a thin scum of dirty foam."

The raft rounded Eluanbi and was swept up the east coast and out to sea. On two separate occasions what Severin suspects were pirate ships approached the raft, checked it out, and, after apparently deciding that there was nothing worth stealing, left. Severin had wanted to stop in Taiwan for a break, but the raft was caught in a strong current known as the Kuroshio (the Black Stream), making landfall impossible. After passing Japan the craft rode the strong North Pacific Current across the Pacific. A terrible summer made for hard going, and the bamboo sailing raft started to break up. The *Hsu Fu* was abandoned without loss of life a thousand miles from the Californian coast after a journey of 5,500 miles and six months.

Despite failing to reach America, Severin believed his trip was a success in demonstrating the feasibility of trans-Pacific raft trips, and that with average weather, stopping over to repair the raft, making a few improvements in construction, or by leaving from farther north in China to shorten the distance, the *Hsu Fu* would have reached the New World.

# 22

# Harnessing Qi

MOST boys have watched action movie stars like Steven Seagal and Bruce Lee single-handedly destroying hordes of bad guys and daydreamed of emulating them. It usually goes no further than kicking your younger brother around, or perhaps a short spell of taekwondo or karate classes before giving up out of frustration at the endless drilling that produces less than spectacular results. For a hard-core minority, martial arts become a lifelong passion and a way of life. One of the Hollywood clichés in martial arts movies is to have the hero training under some wizened old oriental master. After some test to show his determination the apprentice learns lethal fighting techniques with a touch of Eastern mysticism thrown in and, if he's really lucky, gets the old man's beautiful granddaughter. Real life is often not too far removed from fiction.

American Bruce Frantzis arrived in Taiwan in the summer of 1968 as a confident nineteen-year-old karate champion looking to study under Wang Shujin. Wang had trained under the greats in China before joining the KMT exodus to Taiwan, and was the country's leading exponent of the internal martial arts of *xingyi* and *bagua*.

Internal martial arts don't rely on physical strength or muscular power, but the opening-up of energy channels through Taoist meditation and breathing techniques. Spiralling and twisting motions are generated deep inside the body – some too subtle and internal to be seen – and involve all parts of the body, including the abdominal cavity, the internal organs, even bone marrow and ligaments, as well as muscles. Sorry, it doesn't make much sense to me either but that's the way practitioners explain it. And it gets worse. Bagua is based on the changes in the eight trigrams and sixty-four hexagrams of the *I Ching*. Xingyi is based on the interactions of the five elements of wood, fire, earth, metal, water, and wood, which makes about as about much sense as saying a fighting system was based on the hand game of scissors, paper, and stone. Xingyi is more linear and aggressive than bagua and is best described as an internal-arts version of karate. The third internal art, *taiji*, works on the principle of *yin* and *yang*. Although best known as an early morning health routine for oldies, it can also be used as a martial art.

Frantzis learnt that Wang gave classes in a Taichung park at 5:30 in the morning, and was waiting there to meet him. Wang, an old man packing over 250 pounds on to a 5-foot 8-inch frame and dressed in what looked like pyjamas, came waddling down the street carrying two bird cages. Frantzis presented Wang with an expensive gift of ginseng and felt insulted when the master reciprocated with disparaging comments about karate being "only fit for fighting old women and children." The two sparred a little – or rather Wang toyed with the American, able to touch him at will and evade all his blows. Not that Wang needed to worry about getting hit, as he later demonstrated by allowing Frantzis to strike him anywhere on the body. He struck his hardest blows against Wang's exposed body, even vulnerable areas such as his knees, neck, and ribs, but all without effect. Wang seemed to have the ability to absorb blows without injury. The master tapped Frantzis lightly on the head and sent him to the ground with the sensation that he had been hit by a lightning bolt.

Before accepting Frantzis as a student there was a little test of resolve. Wang told him to assume the "Wild Goose Leaves the Flock" posture and hold it until told otherwise. Frantzis struck the position – one leg raised to waist height, arms extended, and the body leaning to one side – and every time he collapsed, he received a cold bucket of water, and the command to resume the posture. After two hours of this Wang announced he would take him on. The humbled karate champion's ordeal was still far from over. Next he got to fight Wang's students, who beat the hell out of him. It was a humiliating experience for a nineteen-year-old hotshot to be dealt with by old men and women, and he felt like calling it quits on that first day. He swallowed his pride and accepted the superiority of the "soft" internal arts over "hard" forms like karate.

In the words of another American martial artist, Robert W. Smith, "One simply could not practise with Wang and disbelieve in the Ch'i [qi]." Smith, who worked in Taiwan for the CIA from 1959 to 1962, had a similar experience of hitting Wang without effect, and also one of Wang's special moves in which he picked up an opponent and bounced him on and off his huge stomach. Hung I-Hsiang, one of Taiwan's most renowned martial artists, told Smith he had been knocked unconscious by it. Both Wang Shujin, who was still beating the toughest fighters into his eighties, and Hung I-Hsiang possessed incredible power and could send the strongest men flying many feet in any direction with an effortless touch. They also had a seemingly magical charge – a touch that didn't seem powerful but could inflict pain or injury.

\* \* \*

I had the good fortune to meet up with Chris Bates, a former student of Hung, and for breadth and depth of knowledge one of the greatest martial artists of his generation. He was on a business trip to Taiwan, and kindly took time out – after a long day of travel and negotiating plastic prices – to discuss his experience of studying martial arts in Taiwan. We talked over non-alcoholic drinks in a noisy cafeteria at a petro-chemical plant, a rather incongruous setting for the subject. Similarly, Chris, who was impeccably dressed in a suit and tie and wearing bookish glasses, looked more like an accountant than a lethal fighter. You would have to go a long way to find a nicer man, which made it all the stranger to think that he had spent so many years turning his body into a fighting machine, and that he could kill me with his bare hands in about 101 different ways without raising a sweat. And another 101 ways with weapons. In fact, Chris is an expert in the use of the *kukri* (a long curved knife from Nepal) and has trained the elite Singapore Gurkha Police Contingent. The Gurkhas are tough fighters from Nepal, and some of the most feared soldiers in the world, so when you are teaching them advanced combative techniques (and with their own traditional weapon) you obviously have to be pretty good.

Chris' interest in martial arts began early. "From about five, after seeing it on TV but it wasn't until I was seventeen, during my final year at high school that I had lessons. The first martial art I learnt was a Burmese form called *bando*, which is known as "the jeep" because it's not pretty to look at but very effective. It gave me a very good foundation."

"What was the attraction of the martial arts?"

"I wasn't an athletic boy, and the idea that skill could give me prowess rather than brawn appealed to me."

"And China?"

"Youthful rebellion! My parents collected Japanese art, and because they were interested in Japanese stuff then I had to do something different: Chinese. That was the extent of my rebelliousness! Also, when I was in school China was in the news, with a lot of good things happening: Nixon's trip and Ping-Pong diplomacy. I started playing Ping-Pong like a maniac, loved it! And of course I was interested in martial arts. I took my degree in Chinese Studies in Washington, D.C., and that's where I first met Robert Smith, who was working there, still with the National Security Agency. I wrote my thesis on the history of Chinese martial arts and Smith helped me."

Chris came to Taiwan in 1976 to spend his senior year studying Chinese at Tunghai University in Taichung. He was fortunate to be able to train under Kao Fang-hsien, a retired KMT general from Shandong Province, and perhaps the best Shaolin master in Taiwan. Shaolin takes its name from the famous monastery that is the legendary birthplace of the martial arts in China, and is an energetic and aggressive external form.

"Kao was a big tough guy but very accessible. In his youth he'd been a wrestling champion. He'd graduated from a martial arts academy in Qingdao, and held some teaching position there. When the Japanese overran Shandong he led a guerrilla band behind Japanese military lines. One of his eyes was clouded over from when he'd been captured and tortured by the Japanese. Kao was a wonderful guy and moved me through everything as fast as I could absorb it because he knew I only had a year, and he would teach me anything I wanted. And he never asked for a penny!

"Having come out of wrestling his applications were very practical. Northern Chinese martial arts have a reputation for kicking, and although he could kick very well, he said, 'You don't want to kick high because I'll dump you on your ass every time. I can see where it's coming from, I can take care of it.' So a lot of his applications in the forms and the systems that he taught me would move into a grappling mode, or a tripping, sweeping or throwing mode, combined with nerve striking and palming techniques. Just really nice stuff – no fluff. I learnt a lot of valuable things from him – not just martial arts but about generosity too."

"You were lucky," I said but thinking that it was actually me who was lucky, that I was, in a way, getting a return on the old fighter's generosity. Simply on the basis of a brief letter Chris had offered to change his travel plans and stay on an extra day just so I could speak to him.

"Yes. Everything fitted into place; studying in Washington, which was the centre of Burmese bando in America, then coming to Taiwan to study the language, culture and history, and to train in martial arts under a top teacher."

"Meet a girl."

"That was the icing on the cake."

Chris was set up on a blind date with a Taiwanese girl by a class-mate and it was love at first sight. Well, for him at least.

"She had no time for me but I was smitten," he recalled breaking into deep laughter. "I persisted and by the time my year was up I seriously thought about staying on to get to know her better and continue train-ing. My father pushed me to return home and I did a master's in inter-national management. Before I left Taiwan I promised Ling-li I'd come back in a year. She said, 'Yeah, yeah, sure, sure, I'll believe it when I see it.' We wrote to each other and a year later I returned to Taiwan for ten days. We got married, did all the paperwork, and she followed me back to America a month later."

Work took them to Singapore and then to Taipei from 1982 to 1989, and once again to Singapore. Chris used his experiences in Taiwan to write, with the help of his wife, the funny and informative, *Taiwan – Culture Shock*. He has also written a novel, *The Wave Man*, which is about a Western businessman learning martial arts in Asia (that sounds familiar).

"When I came back in 1982 I did stick fighting for a while under another Shandong fighter, but I didn't enter his school because he taught praying mantis, which I wasn't interested in learning."

"Sorry, praying mantis?" I queried, expecting an explanation.

"Yes, praying mantis," he repeated a little louder as if I hadn't heard him, apparently not considering the possibility that I was too ignorant about Chinese boxing to know even the most basic terminology. My books from Amazon.com hadn't arrived yet and I hadn't been able to read up on the subject. I felt embarrassed and just nodded my under-standing to Chris, who continued.

"I just practised what Kao had taught me, and was looking around for something to do."

"So you went to train with Hung I-Hsiang?"

"Actually, I didn't go looking for him. I'd read about Hung in Robert Smith's *Chinese Boxing – Masters and Methods* and been put off. Smith described him as a gruff chain-smoking tough guy who would turn up to class drunk. Although Smith did tell me that those were actually the classes when he taught you the really good stuff. Only problem was that he was likely to demonstrate punches with a little too much power, and when I saw Smith in Washington he said his shoulder was still painful from one of Hung's punches. Anyway, an American friend from Tokyo came down to Taiwan to visit and asked me to help find Hung. Clearly, in the twenty-some years since Smith had trained with him he had mellowed out a lot; he had cut down on his drinking, and he wasn't smoking.

"Hung was a really impressive person to talk to. When we asked him a question he would get up and demonstrate. The internal arts have a different way of generating power and when he moved I could see the linkage in his body, his power chain, and this was something which not been made evident to me before."

"And how did you get accepted as a student?"

"His eldest son handled it. Rather like his father he has mellowed with age but back then he had quite a temper, and was very demanding, perhaps protecting his father. He told me 'If you train with us you have to commit for two years, you only train with us, and you have to study xingyi first,' even though I wanted to study bagua."

Among the exodus of mainlanders who came to Taiwan with Chiang Kai-shek in 1949 were many martial arts masters. Several destitute masters were taken in and looked after by Hung's father. In return they taught his five sons. Hung proved to have exceptional ability, what the Chinese call a "sleeping dragon," and under the training of over a dozen masters was able to fulfil his potential. He eventually developed his own system of martial arts called *tangshoudao* (the Way of the Hands of Tang).

Hung I-Hsiang had a reputation for enforcing the law and putting down street fights. In those days, fights were fairly common, especially in red-light areas. Sometimes the fighting was just for fun – at other times it was deadly and could involve swords. Robert Smith mentions in *Chinese Boxing* that two young boxers he knew and practised with were killed in such fights.

Hung destroyed all his challengers. He was built like a tank but combined subtlety with his awesome power. Loose and flexible, his body moved as if he had no bones, and his hands were so sensitive that he could feel minute shifts in body energy and counterattack instantly. His specialty was the use of very small angles but unlike others could work in tiny spaces.

"Did you ever see Hung do anything that seemed to be," I grimaced but it had to be asked, "outside the realms of physics?"

Chris laughed. "Well, I think everything can ultimately be explained by physics. There's a picture of Hung breaking bricks in Smith's book.

Normally when people break blocks they have spaces in between the blocks and under the last one. Hung broke the bricks lying flush on a table without spaces between them. He told me the secret of how to do that. It's not a trick, it's a skill. He said that the picture showed the hair on his arm standing up, which was the 'qi' travelling down it. First you have to relax your body, bring the hand down with a twist, hitting sideways instead of straight on, which sends an extremely subtle shock wave through the bricks. This level of skill is extraordinary," he explained whilst demonstrating on the cafeteria table with a lack of self-consciousness that comes with living in Asia. I scanned around the room to see if Chris' mock blows were drawing stares but typically there were no more, no fewer, than before.

"And what did you train with Hung?"

"Xingyi. When I joined his school I didn't know that he hadn't taught bagua to anyone. He hadn't even taught his sons. I was unaware at the time that a lot of the senior students had fallen out with him because he wouldn't teach it to them. I didn't realize the impossibility of what I was asking for, and after four, five, six years I was still waiting. With the end of my seven years approaching bagua was nowhere in sight! I told him 'I'm leaving, sir. You know I came here originally to train bagua. At least let me study the taiji form.' So I learnt that from him. It's quite unique, created in the late 1930s as an amalgam of different taiji systems, but I never got to bagua, and bagua is a lot of what Hung used.

"Fortunately one student persevered, and managed to piece it together from Hung and various others, a guy who teaches up in Taipei called Eric Luo. He's about my age, a very powerful fighter, very strong but a nice guy. No bullshit – ask him a question, he'll give you an answer. He's pretty much carrying the mantle, unofficially at least."

One of the strange things about Hung was that he made a big deal about health and longevity being the true goals of martial arts but he didn't even make seventy. I put the question to Chris.

"Hung had a tough early life, was conscripted into the Japanese navy, underwent hard training before and after the war, and of course there was a level of self-abuse – drinking, smoking...."

"Living in Taipei!" I added.

"Yeah. Living in Taipei. But at least he died well – let's put it that way. He was at a meeting of the martial arts federation. Hung lost his temper with some pedantic couch potato who was talking, hit the table with a massive blow, and then grabbed his chest, and collapsed. He was sent to MacKay Hospital. And, as my relatives say, if somebody checks into MacKay then you should start looking for a burial plot! I came back to Taiwan for his funeral and went up to the mountains with his sons to find a plot."

Since Hung's death Chris has focussed on taiji. "I was training with an eighty-four-year-old Chinese woman who studied under some of the great masters in China and graduated from the Nanking Martial Arts Academy in the 1930s, but she's getting a bit old, so I train alone now."

I thought Chris was a walking advertisement for martial arts – relaxed through hours of talking in a hellishly noisy place after a long hard day, and despite his receding hairline and greying hair, he looked a very young forty-four.

"Are there any health benefits from martial arts that other exercise doesn't give you?"

"Yes. Immediately after starting xingyi it made changes within me. I mean I'm not trying to say that I'm a big guy now, but I used to be thinner. My chest and arms got thicker, and allowed me to put on bulk even though the Shaolin training I had done before was actually much more physical."

"Anything else?"

"Well, for fear of offending delicate sensibilities, I'll just say it improved my sex life."

# 23

# The Miracle

TAIWAN has more to teach than ancient Chinese arts – its economic and democratic successes are a lesson to the world. To call the country's rapid economic progress a "miracle" is no exaggeration. Living in Taiwan today it is difficult to imagine just how poor it once was. Actually, in the 1950s the country was not just poor but destitute, written off by many as a basket-case, and there were few prospects for improvement. Even places like Burma, Vietnam, and Laos were richer. The fundamentals were not good: an already crowded island of six million newly swollen with 1.5 million arrivals from the mainland, almost no natural resources, a penniless and discredited government, the traditional markets of Japan and China gone, runaway inflation, and hanging over everything the threat of invasion and the consequent need for high military spending. In the 1950s per-capita income was only marginally higher than China's.

After three decades of rapid growth it had climbed to twenty times higher. Importantly, the quick economic growth wasn't accompanied by some of the perils of inflation, social upheaval, political instability, and income disparity.

The foundations for the economic miracle were laid by the Japanese, who built an excellent infrastructure, including railways, roads, and electrification. They also cultivated a trained and educated workforce, and created an export-oriented economy.

Taiwan was saved from ruin in the post-war decades by a huge injection of American aid. This enabled a model land-reform programme to be implemented; rents were reduced and landlords were forced to sell most of their unused land, and this capital was then invested in the industrial sector. After an initial period of import substitution in the fifties the government opened up the economy, and when American aid stopped in 1964 the country was strong enough to stand on its own two feet. More than that, in the next two decades Taiwan had the fastest-growing economy in the world. Rising labour costs in the 1970s saw a move away from labour-intensive industries like textiles to capital-intensive ones such as electrical and electronic products, chemicals, and machinery.

In the 1980s the high-tech computer sector got into full swing while traditional industries moved offshore. The 1990s were notable for a flood of investment into China, and the increasing importance of the information technology industry. Once ridiculed for poorly made goods – cheap plastic toys and unreliable appliances – Taiwan has become synonymous with high-tech electronics.

What has always given Taiwan its competitive advantage is the workforce: well-educated, hardworking, and cheap relative to skill and education. Another important factor has been the contribution of small and medium-sized enterprises (SMEs). These have been the backbone of Taiwan's economic miracle, in sharp contrast to the huge corporations that have built Japan and Korea. People prefer to be their own boss rather than work for someone, and perhaps as an offshoot of the national passion for gambling they are ready to invest in new businesses. Taiwan has a culture of entrepreneurship, and the environment of chaos, capitalism and democracy gives ample room for business creativity.

Despite the successes of the high-tech sector, there are concerns about the ability of the industry to move up the manufacturing food chain. Can Taiwan develop its own world-class brands? Can it keep developing sufficiently innovative products to compete?

\* \* \*

THE bursting of the dot.com bubble at the start of the millennium signalled an end to the years of high growth and ever-increasing prosperity. Yet, as Taiwan's economic progress stalled, the success story of the country's democratization took centre stage. In 2000 President Lee Teng-hui became the first leader in Chinese history to willingly hand over power to an elected political opponent. During his twelve years at the top President Lee had struggled against the old power faction in the KMT to carry out reforms to take the country from authoritarian rule to democracy, and to bridge the gulf between Taiwanese and mainlanders. The transformation was remarkable for its speed and the lack of violence, and the wholehearted way democracy has been embraced. The assertions from Asian politicians such as Singapore's Lee Kuan Yew and China's Jiang Zemin that Western-style political and human rights are incompatible with Asian values and Confucian society are never heard in Taiwan.

Lee Teng-hui was born in a small rural community outside Taipei in 1923 and grew up as part of the Japanese-speaking intelligentsia. After graduating from high school he attended a university in Japan and later gained a doctoral degree in the United States. A year after becoming president he pushed through major changes to the constitution: geriatric mainland-elected politicians, who had been representing their provinces in China in absentia since the long-gone days of the civil war with the Communists, were stripped of their mandate, and the parliament and office of president were opened up to full democratic election.

In Lee's struggle against the mainland faction in the KMT he often relied on support from corrupt local politicians. He failed to stem corruption and to tackle reform of the KMT party itself. It's doubtful whether corruption was actually worse than before, but it was certainly more visible thanks to new press freedoms. It was now common knowledge that parliament was infiltrated with gangsters or those connected to gangsters. The galling thing was that once elected to positions, these crooks were able to claim legal immunity and escape justice.

When I first came to Dounan my boss told me that most people usually didn't know where Dounan was, but that a recent murder had put the place on the map. A politician had ordered the assassination of one of his rivals but the attempt had been bungled. The favour was returned, this time with no mistake.

Yunlin County, in which Dounan lies, is a poor rural backwater where "black gold" politics – criminal influence and money – hold sway. Gangs distort local elections by threatening grassroots leaders and buying votes, and some local politicians are actually gangsters.

Toward the end of 1999 a by-election in Yunlin put the county under the national spotlight. This was the first election after the earthquake and was to be the last real gauge of public opinion before the 2000 presidential election. Votes were being bought for NT$500–1,000 (US$16–32) per person, but in certain areas, such as the opponents' hometown, payments were said to be going for as high as NT$3,000. Vote-buying is an integral part of Taiwanese politics, especially in rural areas like Yunlin. A candidate's team enlists the help of influential local players – such as heads of townships, temples, and farmers' or fishermen's associations – who in turn enlist neighbourhood leaders to actually buy the votes. In the end an independent candidate with very deep pockets and ties to the KMT won the by-election.

Of course, if a candidate has spent heavily to get into office he is certainly going to try and recoup his expenses once in power, and the vicious cycle of corruption continues. Large construction projects such as freeways offer some of the easiest money, which has lead to an over-abundance of concrete around the island: what has been called Taiwan's "Construction-Industrial Complex."

\* \* \*

The March 2000 presidential election was a tight three-way race between the Democratic Progressive Party's Chen Shui-bian, the KMT's Lien Chan, and populist James Soong, who had broken away from the KMT to run as an independent. Voters ignored the Chinese premier's warnings not to elect the "wrong candidate," and the KMT's television advertisements claiming that electing Chen would mean war. The Democratic Progressive Party has dropped its hard-line approach for the more pragmatic one of not declaring independence because Taiwan already enjoys *de facto* independence. The party has also moved away from drawing on ethnic divisions between Chinese Taiwanese and "real" Taiwanese and become more mainstream, preferring to focus on more productive local issues like government efficiency and corruption.

The electorate chose hope over fear, deciding that cleaning up the government was more important than the threat of war, and Chen Shui-bian won. However, it wasn't quite that simple – the independent candidate, Soong, came within 3 percent of winning despite being mired in a corruption scandal. Taiwan's great milestone of democratic change only came about because of the personal political ambitions of Soong (who broke with the KMT because he was angry he hadn't been chosen as his party's candidate). Soong's splitting of the KMT vote gave Chen the presidency with 39 percent of the ballots. The KMT's candidate, Lien Chan, came in an embarrassing third.

Chen Shui-bian was born in 1951 in Tainan County. The son of a poor agricultural labourer, Chen overcame his impoverished childhood to make his way to the prestigious National Taiwan University. He trained as a lawyer and joined a firm specializing in maritime law. The turning point in his life was acting as a defence lawyer in the high-profile trial for a group of pro-independence leaders known as the "Kaohsiung Eight." Following the trial he became involved in politics; he served on the Taipei City Council, spent eight months in prison for libel of a KMT politician, and was mayor of Taipei from 1994 to 1998.

\* \* \*

Five weeks after the historic presidential election I visited Chen's old family house. It was drawing over twenty-five thousand visitors a day, and more than a hundred thousand on weekends. The traffic was turning the whole area into a giant traffic jam, causing mayhem for locals and visitors alike, and plans were being drawn up for a new road.

I managed to arrive at a relatively quiet time. The narrow village streets, which had been blocked off to vehicular traffic, were lined with vendors selling Chen Shui-bian souvenirs. Finding Chen's house was simply a matter of following the Chen Shui-bian watches and dolls, the bottles of Chen Shui-bian water and other tacky merchandise around the streets and alleyways, whilst dodging umbrellas that women tourists were using to shield their skin from the sun. At the edge of the crowd massed in front of Chen's old-fashioned three-sided farmhouse was a "doctor." He was sitting on a stool between a table full of miracle cure-all potions and a billboard plastered with hideous photos of skin disease, genital and bottom rashes, and gangrene.

*Visitors outside President Chen Shui-bian's boyhood home, NT$100 for a photo with a cardboard cutout of President Chen*

I moved through the crowd to a low fence separating Chen's house from the street where two life-size cardboard cut-outs of the newly-elected president Chen stood guard. "Take your picture with President Chen," a tout shouted. "Just one hundred dollars." Although the area resembled a crowded street market as people cashed in on Taiwan's hottest new tourist attraction, there was a good-natured atmosphere. The fact that Chen's family house wasn't much to look at and that the inside was closed to visitors didn't really matter because the main point of curiosity was the feng shui of the surrounding area.

"Look at that!" a woman shouted at her friends as she pointed at a three-storied building. The house was directly in front of Chen's home, which is one of the big no-no's of feng shui. "It's impossible for him to become president!" she declared. Others agreed in more reverential tones, no doubt feeling added admiration for Chen – he hadn't just overcome a humble upbringing but bad feng shui. "It shows he really deserves to be our president," a man summed up. An elderly woman with an air of authority offered her interpretation, "If someone's fate is to be president it is his fate – feng shui can't change that."

\* \* \*

The presidential inauguration took place on May 20, 2000, amid speculation that China might try to shake things up with a missile "test." Instead they responded with a temper tantrum directed at the aboriginal pop star A-Mei, denouncing her as a "Taiwanese independence supporter" for singing the ROC national anthem at the inauguration. China banned state-owned television and radio stations from playing her songs, and stopped the broadcasting of her commercials for Sprite. The irony is that the national anthem is an old KMT song that faithfully toes the "One China" line. The reaction against A-Mei shows the extent of the Communist leadership's obsession with the Taiwan issue.

It is time the world told China's leaders to grow up. Having this would-be superpower bullying a small peaceful democracy is unacceptable. China's energies would be better employed on making itself into a place Taiwan can admire as the fount of Chinese culture, and leave the retaking of the island to economic forces. Despite the political chasm between the two countries, economic interaction continues to bind the two together. It's hoped that growing prosperity and Taiwan's example will be the catalyst for democratic change.

This is mostly wishful thinking. The best bet is that the Chinese Communist Party will die a slow death as it clings to power for another generation. Its leaders believe that without a single-party state (and a strong and centralized one) the country will break up, bringing chaos and war. More personally, the leaders fear being held accountable for their misuse of power and ending up behind bars. China will not see a rerun of Taiwan's rapid and relatively smooth transition to democracy.

For so many centuries caught up in the currents of greater political events beyond its shores, this island of twenty-three million industrious and friendly people seems likely to have its future, once again, determined by external forces: this time the country's fate resting on domestic Chinese developments and the question of whether the world will sacrifice it for the promise of the fabled China market.

# Afterword
# The Retirement Home

WRITING this update is not a pleasant task. The twelve years since the first edition of *Formosan Odyssey* have been difficult ones for Taiwan.

The historic presidential election in 2000 was the perfect ending to an epic story. From the lifting of martial law in 1987, the country had risen to new heights – exploded with long-pent-up energy and prospered in so many ways: from a renaissance of local languages and aboriginal cultures to an unprecedented dynamism of music and film; from environmental awareness to women's rights; from the emergence of a free, vibrant media to the growth of civil society with citizens coming together in political parties, social movements, and NGOs, as well as in leisure-time associations such as dance groups and bird-watching clubs; from the first mass wave of Taiwanese traveling overseas to a new interest and pride in Taiwan itself; from a reputation as a giant factory for cheap consumer junk to a producer of world-class high-tech electronics. And above everything was the democratic success story par excellence: the transition to democracy made without political violence or an economic downturn, and in such a short span of time it seemed as if a half-century of progress had been crammed into little more than a decade. The crowning glory of this transition was an end to fifty years of one-party rule with the election of the son of a poor Taiwanese labourer from the rural south.

As I write this, however, former president Chen Shui-bian is serving a seventeen-year prison sentence for corruption, sovereignty is steadily slipping away to China, the economy is anaemic (real average incomes have not risen since 2000), and there is an air of pessimism about the future. All in all, it's enough to drive a man to drink.

Things started to go wrong soon after the historic transfer of power. The bursting of the dot-com bubble and global downturn of the first years of the 2000s hit Taiwan hard because of its reliance on exports of computer components and consumer electronics. The stock market plummeted and still hasn't recovered to its year-2000 levels, and the steady flow of investment from Taiwan to China became a deluge. Economic problems were accompanied by gridlock in parliament. Chen and his Democratic Progressive Party did have their victories, but these were often symbolic and rather trivial. For example, the English word "Taiwan" was added to the cover of passports (previously the cover had only "Republic of China" in both Mandarin and English).

Chen won re-election in 2004 in controversial circumstances. On the day before voting there was an assassination attempt that left Chen and his vice president slightly injured. The lone gunman, who had fired on their passing vehicle from a roadside crowd, escaped and later committed suicide. The election went ahead the following day, with Chen winning by fewer than 29,500 votes. Polls before the shooting incident had had the electoral race as too close to call, and it's generally believed that sympathy for Chen pushed him over the finish line. Many opposition supporters – whether or not they bought into conspiracy theories claiming the assassination attempt was staged – felt cheated. Things weren't helped by KMT candidate Lien Chan's refusal to accept defeat. He demanded a recount. After getting this – and once more coming up short – he tried and failed to get the courts to call a new election.

Chen Shui-bian's second term was from the very beginning dogged by political partisanship, and, not long after, by corruption charges against his wife, son-in-law, and, in turn, himself. Chen was arrested on numerous corruption charges as soon as his immunity expired upon his leaving office.

Promising better relations with China and renewed prosperity, the KMT candidate, Ma Ying-jeou, won the 2008 presidential election (and was re-elected in 2012). Disillusioned with Chen and politics in general, the public were willing to trade some long-term security by binding itself more tightly to China for the prospect of economic growth. Closer ties with China included direct flights, opening the floodgates to Chinese tourists, freer trade, and the easing of restrictions on Chinese investment.

But still the economy stagnated, and it was more than just fallout from the global downturn. Taiwan is suffering from a long-term lack of investment. Since the late 1980s Taiwanese industry's response to higher labour costs has been to move their factories to China rather than invest more aggressively in research and development or in building their own brands. The country has haemorrhaged about US$200 billion in investment across the strait. The result is a hollowed-out local manufacturing industry, and a failure to create high value-added products and value-added jobs. People have followed the money too. Today more than a million Taiwanese are living and working in China. Taiwan's greatest threat is also its most important trading partner, the largest source of tourists, and the largest recipient (approximately 80%) of Taiwan's foreign investment.

The last dozen years have seen some visible achievements obvious to even the short-term visitor: the world's tallest building (2004–2010), the continuing expansion of Taipei's superb metro system, and a 245-kilometre high-speed railway between Taipei and Kaohsiung. And yet these were all projects conceived and started in the last century; they're accomplishments that bring pride but are more like echoes of the glory days than symbols of present-day success.

Overall, I feel the Taiwan of 2013 is a better place to be than it was back in 2001 when I wrote the first edition. The situation reminds me of how Japan is often described as having suffered two lost decades of economic stagnation; but when you visit the country you're surprised by the enviable prosperity. Similarly, Taiwan still strikes visitors as dynamic, wealthy, and developed.

Taiwan is cleaner, greener, and more civilized than it used to be. Sure, it's less vibrant in terms of raw energy, less frenetic, and less crazy; but it's only natural that the country's rapid growth should tail off. What happened before was a unique, often-chaotic burst of freedom and wealth after so many years without; and much of the resulting excitement was the tasteless exuberance of the nouveau riche. Taiwan has matured and sobered up. Exit the naked pole-dancing girls at weddings, and make way for flower-arranging classes at the local community centre. Good-bye pet orangutans and hello cycling craze.

I've also mellowed, grown older with Taiwan, though I've managed to skip the sobering-up part. I'm married to a local lass and living in the sticks of Chiayi County. Otherwise not much has changed. Here I am writing this second edition, with my faithful companion Taiwan Beer by my side, just as it was when the original was written. I'm looking out from my study through large, south-facing windows, the warm light of late afternoon streaming in and turning my glass to liquid gold. It's a perfect early December day – blue sky overhead and 25 °C. Life is good.

In such glorious weather I like to get some exercise working on the neglected family farm or go for a scooter jaunt through the neighbouring countryside. A typical ride at this time of year takes me past golden green fields of sugarcane, winter crops of corn and cabbage, and the last of the rice harvest. Cruising the many small back roads is one of the simple pleasures of life here. There's a touch of sadness too though. The farmers – sun-shy women covered from head to toe, and men, wiry and bronzed – are old, really old. (Government statistics put the average farmer's age at sixty-three.)

Taiwan is in the first stage of a devastating demographic shift. In the 1960s having four or five children was the norm. The fertility rate (the average number of children per woman) fell below the replacement level of 2.1 in the mid-1980s, and for the past decade has, at a shade under 1.1, been among the world's very lowest. Put simply, there are a lot of old people and few young ones.

I can see the early effects of the population crisis during a weekly 20-minute scooter commute. The ride takes me past kindergartens closed from a lack of students, a university expected to soon shut its doors for the same reason, and past the Chiayi high speed train station. The station is surrounded by empty roads and overgrown plots built in the expectation of development that never came. The largest building along the route – and in my entire district – is a massive new hospital and nursing home. It sometimes feels like the country is turning into a retirement village.

What happens to Taiwan from here? Unfortunately, the conversation turns inevitably to the cross-strait question. It's true that Taiwanese self-identity is stronger: when I first arrived, most people identified themselves as both Chinese and Taiwanese, whereas now the majority say they are simply Taiwanese. But the will and means to resist China's pressure is weaker. The people – especially the wealthy – have voted with their feet and money, with their indifference, and at the ballot box. Slowly but surely I see Taiwan falling under Beijing's influence, a creeping de facto annexation that ends with full Chinese control.

This seemingly inevitable slide doesn't mean that military action against Taiwan is unlikely. Impatient PLA generals and hawkish leaders must be chafing at the long wait as they watch the weakening of Taiwan's resolve to fight. Conscription (now down from two years to four months) will end in 2017, and the professional army is struggling to get recruits.

Optimists see the possibility of a less strident China content to wield its influence with a light touch, a China that allows quasi-independence in exchange for a few token kowtows like in the old imperial days when tributary nations paid periodic respects to the capital. This is only a possibility if you believe in fairy tales.

Some Taiwanese shrug off the prospect of unification with China as a mere change of boss that would make little difference to their lives. This is wishful thinking; coming under direct PRC rule would cause an exodus of talent and money, and it would be a huge step backward for a vast array of freedoms – whether political, religious, economic, or cultural – and for the growing demand for the rule of law.

Unification would not usher in a *Pax Sinica* that sweeps away national political squabbles and military tensions on the island, because the question of Taiwan's sovereignty is not some anachronistic legacy of the struggle between Mao Zedong and Chiang Kai-shek or a relic of Cold War geopolitics. Instead, it is an important part of China's rise to superpower status. Unification would be the start of a dangerous new chapter.

Have a look at a map of the region – a good map of the Chinese seaboard showing not only the main landmasses of Japan, Taiwan, and the Philippines but also the many islands linking them. These islands (some of which are, like Taiwan, claimed by the PRC) form an unbroken chain thousands of kilometres long that ring China – a great maritime wall preventing it from projecting power into what it believes is its rightful sphere of influence. China wants Taiwan as an unsinkable aircraft carrier, a stepping-stone to the return of other disputed islands and to supremacy in the western Pacific.

As I've tried to chronicle in *Formosan Odyssey*, Taiwan's prime location has seen it conquered and coveted by numerous powers through the centuries. Becoming a PRC territory would put it centre stage in the most important strategic competition of our times – the power struggle between China and the United States.

# Bibliography

NOTE: Some of the books listed below have new editions. I give the dates for the editions I read while writing the first edition of *Formosan Odyssey*.

Bates, Chris and Bates, Ling-li. *Culture Shock! Taiwan.* Times Books International, 1995.
Campbell, William B. *Formosa under the Dutch.* 1903 (reprinted by SMC Publishing, Taipei, 1997).
———. *Sketches from Formosa.* 1915 (reprinted by SMC Publishing, 1996).
Copper, John F. *Taiwan, Nation-State or Province?* Westview Press, 1996.
Davidson, James W. *The Island of Formosa, Past and Present.* 1903 (reprinted by SMC Publishing, 1992).
Frantzis, Bruce Kumar. *The Power of Internal Martial Arts.* North Atlantic Books, 1998.
Hartzell, Richard W. *Harmony in Conflict.* Caves Books, 1988.
Jordan, David K. *Gods, Ghosts, and Ancestors.* Caves Books, 1995.
Knapp, Ronald G. *China's Island Frontier.* University of Hawaii Press, 1980.
Lintner, Bertil. *Burma in Revolt, Opium and Insurgency Since 1948.* Westview Press, 1994..
MacKay, George. *From Far Formosa.* 1896 (reprinted by SMC Publishing, 1991).
McGovern, Janet B. Montgomery. *Among the Headhunters of Formosa.* 1922 (reprinted by SMC Publishing, 1997).
Meyer, Mahlon. *Taiwan Personalities.* Bookman Books, 1998.
Pickering, W.A. *Pioneering in Formosa.* 1898 (reprinted by SMC Publishing, 1993).
Reid, Daniel P. *The Tao of Health, Sex, and Longevity.* Simon & Schuster, 1989.
Rutter, Owen. *Through Formosa, an Account of Japan's Island Colony.* 1923 (reprinted by SMC Publishing, 1995).
Seagrave, Sterling. *The Soong Dynasty.* Harper and Row, 1986.
———. *Lords of the Rim.* Corgi Books, 1996.
Severin, Tim. *The China Voyage.* Little, Brown and Company, 1994.

Smith, Robert W. *Chinese Boxing, Masters and Methods.* North Atlantic Books, 1990.

Spence, Jonathon D. *The Search for Modern China.* W.W. Norton & Company, 1990.

Storey, Robert. *Taiwan.* Lonely Planet Publications, 1998.

Takekoshi, Yosaburo. *Japanese Rule in Formosa.* 1907 (reprinted by SMC Publishing, 1996).

Taylor, George and Dudbridge, Glen. *Aborigines of South Taiwan in the 1880s.* Shung Ye Museum of Formosan Aborigines, 1998.

Van Gulik, R.H. *Sexual Life in Ancient China.* E.J. Brill, 1974.

Zheng Yi. *Scarlet Memorial, Tales of Cannibalism in Modern China.* Translated and edited by T.P. Sym. Westview Press, 1996.

# Further Reading

Caltonhill, Mark. *Private Prayers and Public Parades.* Taipei City Government Department of Information, 2002.

Crook, Steven. *Keeping Up with the War God.* Yushan Publications, 2001 (new e-book version 2011).

———. *Taiwan: The Bradt Travel Guide.* Bradt Travel Guides, 2014.

Keating, Jerome F. *The Mapping of Taiwan: Desired Economies, Coveted Geographies.* SMC Publishing Inc., 2012.

Kelly, Robert and Chow, Chung Wah. *Taiwan.* Lonely Planet Publications, 2014.

Parfitt, Troy. *Why China Will Never Rule the World: Travels in the Two Chinas.* Western Hemisphere Press, 2011.

# Also by the Author

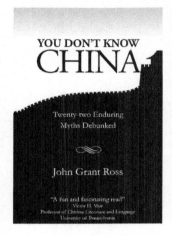

## You Don't Know China
### Twenty-two Enduring Myths Debunked

Published 2014

| Format | ISBN |
| --- | --- |
| Paperback | 978-1-910736-21-0 |
| epub | 978-1-910736-18-0 |
| Kindle | 978-1-910736-19-7 |

*You Don't Know China* takes a wrecking ball to misconceptions old and new. Each of the twenty-two chapters debunks a particular myth on topics ranging from history and economics to language and food. Learn the truth about feng shui and Chinese medicine. Find out whether Marco Polo really went to China. Does the Great Wall actually deserve its name? Is studying Mandarin worth the effort? Should smartphone owners lose sleep over suicides at Chinese factories?

Informative, entertaining, and sometimes controversial, *You Don't Know China* is a welcome antidote to the schizophrenic hyperbole surrounding China's supposed rise to global supremacy or, conversely, its imminent collapse. John Grant Ross, author of *Formosan Odyssey*, gives the general reader access to information from specialist sources and insider knowledge from long experience on the ground. The format of self-contained chapters allows for both breadth and depth, helping to make sense of a complex subject.

*You Don't Know China* is an amusing, eye-opening, and ultimately uplifting shortcut to understanding this complicated country. Recommended reading for anyone with an interest in China, it's especially invaluable for businessmen not wanting to lose their shirts, or journalists looking to avoid embarrassing themselves.